FAMILY
ROYAL

FAMILY ROYAL

Audrey Whiting

W. H. ALLEN · LONDON
A Howard & Wyndham Company
1982

Copyright © Audrey Whiting 1982

Phototypeset by Tradespools Ltd, Frome, Somerset
Printed and bound in Great Britain by
Mackays of Chatham Ltd, Kent
for the Publishers, W. H. Allen & Co. Ltd,
44 Hill Street, London W1X 8LB

ISBN 0 491 03040 1

For Jack Nener

Contents

Introduction: *A Family Off Duty*   9
1   *The New Head of the Family*   27
2   *Early Years and a Family Crisis*   49
3   *The Children at School*   69
4   *A Family Holiday*   87
5   *The Swinging Sixties*   109
6   *The 'Second Eleven'*   127
7   *Uncle Dickie*   149
8   *More Babies*   162
9   *Charles at University*   173
10   *Hurdles for Anne*   190
11   *A Love-Match*   209
12   *A Family United*   228
13   *A View to the Future*   243
Epiloque: *Prince William of Wales*   248
Index   259

Introduction

A Family Off Duty

IT IS SOMEWHERE around eleven o'clock on the morning of Christmas Eve and the Royal standard flies high above the great medieval Round Tower at Windsor Castle, signalling that the Queen is in residence. Busily packing her own last-minute parcels, she is preparing for the happiest time in her annual calendar – the splendid and very private Royal Christmas. Although on Christmas Day and Boxing Day mornings her red, black, blue or green leather State 'boxes' arrive as usual by special GPO van accompanied by a police escort – unless some national or international crisis explodes – the official papers are, for once, very few. This is the one short period when the Queen can put aside all official duties.

Like other families throughout the country the Royal Family gather to celebrate Christmas together as they have done for generations past. In a fabulous Royal residence that has been a home for Royalty since the days of William the Conqueror, some thirty members of the House of Windsor meet to enjoy every sort of fun and relaxation imaginable. In the present reign, no outsiders are ever present and because the circle is so closely knit all the Royals can relax in an exclusively family atmosphere – from the youngest member, Prince William of Wales, son of the Prince and Princess of Wales, to the beloved and oldest member, the Queen

9

Mother, now in her eighties.

Long before the festive season, the Queen begins to make her Christmas arrangements and plan menus, which vary little from year to year. They are discussed early in November with the Queen's Housekeeper at Buckingham Palace who works in close liaison with her counterpart, the Housekeeper at Windsor Castle. For many years the women who have held these key jobs have been single but have always had the courtesy title of 'Mrs'. Both of them know the Queen intimately and are well aware that she enjoys what she calls simple food but which is nevertheless always of the very best quality. She does not like rich sauces or heavy dishes and, apart from a good traditional English breakfast, when she and Prince Philip enjoy egg and bacon, a kipper or smoked haddock, she is a dedicated weight-watcher and a relatively spartan eater. The Queen only uses eye-level scales and even during the holiday period she always knows exactly how many ounces she has gained.

One of her special personal tasks before Christmas is to go into the strong rooms of Windsor Castle to choose pieces of silver, including four sets of three-feet high candlesticks, for the oblong family dinner table. She delights in selecting the dinner service to be used over the holiday. When she is not entertaining guests the Queen uses ordinary china but for special occasions like Christmas she can choose from a fabulous collection which includes Dresden, Coleport and Furstenburg china. Special pieces made for Queen Victoria and George III are often chosen for display on sideboards in the dining room.

As she wanders in the strong rooms, accompanied by the Yeoman of the Pantry, the Queen is in a modern Aladdin's cave. There are hundreds of priceless pieces of gold and silver which include great fire dogs of the Charles II period, trophies of every kind, a huge silver gilt punch bowl which can hold forty gallons, and even gold and silver spades used at one time or other by members of the family or visiting statesmen to plant trees in Windsor Great Park. Everything in the vaults is in perfect order, and heirlooms of the past are displayed on baize-lined shelves in glass cabinets.

It is usual for the Queen to arrive at the Castle two or three days before Christmas. There are eight main entrances to the Castle and she uses the Sovereign's Entrance which is reserved for members of her immediate family. Before her arrival the staff make sure that everything is gleaming. Some of the great chandeliers, which can have as many as 8,000 pieces of crystal, are taken down and each crystal is washed and shined. All the furniture is highly polished with a special non-commercial product made by two French polishers, men who use a preparation which has been kept secret for generations and which costs a fraction of the price of commercial polish. Knowing the Queen's eagle eye for detail, the Housekeeper who controls the cleaning staff, including a team of bright and chirpy daily women who all live locally, makes sure that there is not a speck of dust anywhere.

It was only early in 1954, when the Queen decided to use the Castle as a weekend retreat from Buckingham Palace in London, that it first began to acquire a relaxed and lived-in atmosphere. It has no less that 684 rooms – many of them only very large closets – and until the Queen took it in hand it was a bleak, cold and comfortless place, only used by the family for great State occasions, like the Order of the Garter Ceremony at Easter time, or for Ascot in June.

Over the years gradual improvements were made to the lighting and heating, and apart from making life much easier for the family, the castle was made far more comfortable for visitors. Before the Queen moved to Windsor for weekends, life was decidedly uncomfortable for guests. Some had to sleep on hard mattresses on very old-fashioned beds with huge head- and foot-boards, many of which were five feet in height and, with dim lights, the occupants were quite obscured once they had climbed into bed!

In the old days, except for five wartime years, it was always Sandringham House not far from The Wash in Norfolk that was the Christmas haven for the family. But in 1964, a year when four Royal babies were born – Prince Edward, Lady Sarah Armstrong-Jones, Lady Helen Windsor and James Ogilvy – the Royal population was so great that the Queen decided to change the Christmas venue to Windsor. There simply were not suitable or sufficient facilities at Sandringham to cope with all the young babies, young children and their nannies, plus all the nursery paraphernalia that had to be housed. The switch to Windsor pleased everyone, especially as the Castle is only twenty-three miles from London, thus cutting down travelling time at a very busy period.

The family Christmas celebrations take place in the Private Apartments which occupy about a quarter of the entire Castle where semi-State rooms like the Crimson, Green and White Drawing Rooms, never open to the public, are used for music, dancing and games. It is the East and South Terraces which house the family over the holiday. Windsor Castle is essentially a series of towers and the Private Apartments embrace four of these – the Queen's Tower, which includes the private suite of four rooms, York Tower, Chester Tower and Brunswick Tower. Each Tower is as big as a large family house and all the flower-filled rooms are large and spacious with high ceilings. All have lovely terraces with magnificent views over the great lawns and wide expanses of woodland and forest. On warm days in the summer months the Queen often has her breakfast on her own terrace as she reads the newspapers.

Although so much modernisation has been carried out, everyone gets plenty of enforced exercise just by staying in the Castle: many rooms are on different levels and holiday guests are constantly having to walk up and down steps, some of them quite steep. Even the wood-panelled Great Corridor lined with marble statues on pedestals which leads to the Private Apartments is a fair journey – it is 550ft long! Adult members of the family, who each have a private suite which consists of a sitting room, bedroom and bathroom, are careful not to leave anything in a drawing room when it is time to go to bed since to retrieve an object would often take at least eight minutes of brisk walking. For this reason nothing is left lying around – certainly nothing connected with Christmas presents like wrapping paper or fancy ribbons.

The family vie with one another to see who can make up the most spectacular parcel. Buying presents is not all that easy for the Royals since each of the unmarried members and each family group has to give more than thirty gifts, at least one for each relative. The Queen does some of her own shopping in Harrods, the famous store in Knightsbridge, always going there at a pre-arranged time shortly after nine o'clock in the morning and well before the Christmas rush has started. She is received by the manager of Harrods who, with two of his senior assistants, accompanies the Queen throughout the visit. With the party are two ladies-in-waiting, both old and close friends of the sovereign, and the shopping spree usually lasts about two hours, although members of the public seldom realise the Queen is standing near them. Those who do recognise her always instinctively understand her need for privacy and never gather round and stare. No money is ever exchanged, but the Queen will make a careful note of prices and put an object down if she considers it to be expensive. Accounts are sent to Buckingham Palace in January and are first checked by a lady-in-waiting before being passed on to the Master of the Household, Admiral Sir Peter Ashmore, for settlement.

During the course of the year, say when she was on holiday at Balmoral in Scotland, the Queen used to pick up odd presents in local shops or at fetes in Ballater and other nearby villages, but crowds now make this once pleasant habit impossible. In the main it is the ladies-in-waiting who, on the Queen's instructions, buy the majority of the presents she wants to give. A long time ago the Queen solved part of her present-buying problem in a most sensible way. She became a devotee of mail-order catalogues which are now supplied not only by famous firms like Fortnum & Masons, Aspreys, Harrods and big publishing houses but also by mail-order-only companies all over the country. Some even arrive from big department stores in the United States. The Queen spends happy hours pouring over the endless pages and, being the highly efficient person she is, makes sure that her orders sent in by a lady-in-waiting are posted early in October.

What is unusual about the Queen's present-giving is that she has a minutely detailed index which records the individual measurements of all her relatives so that if she is ordering any item of clothing, the size is always right. She also carefully lists presents given in previous years so there is never any risk of duplication. The Queen does not go in for lavish presents, nor does she expect to receive them either. One of her most treasured personal possessions was given to her by an observant friend who realised that wherever the Queen went she nearly always carried a handbag and often never remembered exactly where she had put it down. After official dinners she would look down to her left and then to her right searching for her bag. The inexpensive but novel and useful present the friend gave her was a small gadget with a metal hook that could be attached to any table so that the Queen could always keep her handbag in front of her. This gadget is in daily use both when the Queen is on duty or at home. She once said, 'I don't know what I'd do without it.'

Present-buying is much easier for Prince Philip who, like other members of the Family, acquires many of his gifts during solo travels abroad and on private holidays with his German relatives. Some of the younger members, and this has included Prince Charles in the past, make last-minute purchases from the 'Token House', a high-class china shop immediately opposite the Castle's Henry VIII door. The firm still has a horse and wagon in which Royal purchases are taken up Castle Hill and delivered to the Sovereign's Entrance. Some interesting personal gifts are exchanged and great emphasis is made on objects, often quite small ones, which are associated with individual hobbies. Prince Philip and two of his sons, Charles and Andrew, are good amateur artists and they sometimes give water colours as presents. Nearly every member of the family is an enthusiastic photographer and some, like Princess Margaret and the Duke of Gloucester – a photographer of professional standard – have been known to give framed pictures. Princess Margaret's son, David Linley, who trained at the School for Craftsmen in Wood at Parnham House near Beaminster, Dorset, is now a skilled craftsman in his own right and makes many of his own presents. His first major effort was a table he designed and made himself and presented to the Prince and Princess of Wales as a wedding present.

The Queen not only receives pretty sensible presents but like everyone else also receives her fair share of joke gifts.

No one, however, receives cigarettes or cigars as a gift. All the Royals are non-smokers with the exception of Princess Margaret whose every attempt to cut down has failed.

The late Lord Mountbatten, like so many of the family, used to do his Christmas shopping over the year in order to avoid any last-minute rush. He would often be found wrapping up his presents at Broadlands, his Hampshire home, in the middle of summer. He spent a great deal of time pondering over the problem of a gift for the Queen and often ended up by giving her a very expensive, leather-bound copy of a book he knew she wanted. It was not at all unusual for him to give her a volume about himself or the Mountbatten family. When he was on trips abroad he used to love wandering around open-air markets and bazaars buying hand-carved objects in Africa or India in readiness for Christmas. He would inevitably purchase a variety of trinkets or baubles that caught his eye, only to dismiss them later because he did not feel that they looked expensive enough. Mountbatten always spent Christmas with his two daughters and their families at Broadlands but he would telephone the Queen early in the morning to exchange Christmas greetings, always staying on the line long enough to have a breezy festive chat with Philip and Charles as well.

To his chagrin Mountbatten's own family commitments always caused him to miss out on the traditional ball given by the staff of Windsor Castle for the Royal Family. This is held early in Christmas week in the great Waterloo Chamber, one of the largest rooms in Europe which has the biggest one-piece carpet in the world – made for Queen Victoria and always rolled up for the ball. There are no seams and it is so closely woven that the underneath is almost as good as the top. A special stage, with a huge Christmas tree at either side is erected at one end for a variety show in which the artists are always top stars drawn from the world of theatre and television. The ball is always tremendous fun for everyone and is paid for by the Castle staff who raise funds throughout the year from social events organised by a staff committee. Preparations begin in October and formal written permission to use the Waterloo Chamber is sought by the staff from the Queen – and always granted. Personal invitations are sent to the Queen, Prince Philip, the Prince and Princess of Wales, the Queen Mother, Princess Anne and Mark Phillips, Prince Andrew and Prince Edward, who all arrive in time for the cabaret which begins around 9.30pm. After this, a splendid banquet is held in St George's Hall. The 150ft-long table is laden with smoked salmon, fresh salmon, turkey, roast beef, pheasant pie, fruit salad and mouth-watering sweets. Guests and staff serve themselves and to drink there are wines, beer and lager.

The feast is followed by dancing which continues until the early hours of the morning when members of the staff, not only from the Castle but from Royal Lodge, Frogmore House and the Dean of Windsor's establishment, all take the floor, taking it in turns to dance with the Royal Family. Among the men and women who partner the family are highly skilled craftsmen from the Windsor workshops, seamstresses, upholsterers, cabinet-makers, gold-smiths, metal-smiths, footmen, coal porters, cleaners and their wives and husbands. Every member of the staff receives a present from the Queen which she presents personally. It is usual for each individual to choose from a previously drawn up list the present she or he would like. These are often quite expensive items such as shooting sticks, travelling clocks, cutlery, bed-linen, tobacco pipes or eiderdowns.

Looking down on the ballroom scene are great portraits by Sir Thomas Lawrence of sovereigns, statesmen and generals who contributed in some way to the downfall of Napoleon. During the Second World War these masterpieces were taken down and housed in a place of safety and only the empty frames remained. Someone – no one knows the culprit – decorated these frames with pictures of nursery-rhyme subjects including Puss in Boots, Red Riding Hood, Cinderella and Jack and the Beanstalk. These nursery-rhyme pictures still remain today behind Lawrence's portraits.

Like any large family group, the Royals are a mixed bag, both in temperament and in life-style, who do not always see eye-to-eye with one another but at Christmas minor hatchets tend to be buried. A change has been coming over the Royal scene in that a very strong teenage group has developed and has increasing influence on its activities, especially at holiday times. These young people are urged and encouraged to voice their own opinions and those in any sort of quandary find guidance from senior members of the family who are always ready to present the pros and cons on any argument.

Some of the older members of the family, like the Queen Mother and Princess Alice, Duchess of Gloucester, can recall the days when their father-in-law, King George V was monarch, and Christmas Days, then spent

17

at Sandringham, were run on far more formal lines. His relatives, while they were glad to relax from official responsibilities, were nevertheless frequently quite relieved when the time came for them to return to their own homes. George V always brought his personal unease to the Christmas morning gathering because he was so pre-occupied and anxious about his afternoon radio broadcast to the nation. In his reign the broadcast was live and he became gradually more and more agitated as the time approached for him to sit before a microphone in his study at three o'clock in the afternoon.

Life at Windsor is very different in the 1980s, although even on a holiday like this some protocol will be observed by the family – in a way like any family's 'house rules'. As they gather together for Christmas, one by one, on Christmas Eve, the first act by the Royals is one of fealty to the Queen – a bow or curtsey, followed by a kiss on her cheek. Even the very young children are involved: Lord Frederick Windsor, three-year-old son of Prince Michael of Kent, has been trained by his mother, the six-foot Austrian-born extrovert, Princess Michael of Kent, to make as good a bow as he possibly can. During the rest of their stay every member of the family, with the exception of her husband, Prince Philip, will always either curtsey or incline the head in what is known as the 'Coburg bow' when meeting the Sovereign for the first time in the day. From that point on, it is the Queen herself who sets the tone for festivity and merriment.

Any relative can pick up the telephone and speak to the Queen in her private suite. At other times in the year when there are many house-guests, say during Royal Ascot, the normal procedure is for the individual to ask the Windsor switchboard for the Queen's personal page to find out whether the Queen is free to talk.

One person who sometimes rings up early in the morning is the Queen Mother, who does not spend the night at the Castle. She and Princess Margaret stay at Royal Lodge, on the edge of Windsor Forest in Windsor

Great Park, a charming Georgian-cum-Regency pink-washed country house with about thirty rooms almost four miles down the Long Walk from the Castle. This lovely home, originally built as a summer house for George III, was dilapidated and utterly neglected until the early 1930s when the late King George VI and the Queen Mother, then the Duke and Duchess of York, realised its potential and enthusiastically set about restoring the building. The grounds were then a complete wilderness and the Queen's parents embarked on a remarkable gardening feat transforming this into glorious woodlands, glades, lawns, and flower beds planted with shrubs and blooms for all seasons. The Queen's parents roped in their two daughters, and all their friends and members of their staff to help in the mammoth task of clearing the overgrown grounds. At weekends the King worked in overalls and his wife and children were either pushing wheelbarrows, or raking leaves to dump on a bonfire, always ending up grimily and happily tired. The Queen Mother and the late King loved Royal Lodge so much that they never stayed in the Castle when they went to Windsor and, after her husband's death, the Queen Mother continued to enjoy her Windsor retreat and still does so, even at Christmas.

The Queen's Christmas guests tend to turn up in family groups, driving themselves in saloons or estate cars, piled high with luggage which is taken into the Castle by Windsor porters wearing battledress uniforms in navy blue, handed on to footmen and then taken to the private suites. First family guests tend to arrive, parcel laden, at some time during the early afternoon of Christmas Eve, always making sure that they allow themselves enough time to unpack and change in time for afternoon tea. This is always splendidly old-fashioned with thinly cut sandwiches of ham, and cucumber pâté, hot toast, cakes, biscuits and chocolate wafers. It is the Queen who pours out the tea.

Among the early arrivals are the Prince and Princess of Wales, the Queen Mother and Princess Margaret with her two children, David, Viscount Linley and Lady Sarah Armstrong-Jones. Their father, Lord Snowdon, who has remarried and has a second daughter, Lady Frances Armstrong-Jones, from this marriage, is never present although he remains on close terms with the Queen and his former Royal in-laws. At intervals come the Duke and Duchess of Gloucester with their three children, Alexander, Earl of Ulster, Lady Davina Windsor and Lady Rose Windsor and with them is always the Duke's mother and the Queen's aunt, Princess Alice, Duchess of Gloucester. There will be the Duke and Duchess of Kent and their three children, George, Earl of St Andrews, Lady Helen Windsor and Lord Nicholas Windsor; Princess Anne and Captain Mark Phillips, their son Peter and daughter Zara; Prince Andrew and Prince Edward; Prince and Princess Michael of Kent and their two children, Lord Frederick Windsor and Lady Gabriela Windsor; Princess Alexandra and the Hon. Mr Angus Ogilvy and their son and daughter, James and Marina Ogilvy.

What is most important about Christmas for the Queen is that, freed from her normal pressing duties, it gives her ample opportunity to have long and easy conversations with this large family. Although they see her at fairly regular intervals in the year, they never have as much time to relax in her company without interruptions as they can over the festive season. It also gives members of the family plenty of time to discuss freely with one another what is on their mind. As they travel a great deal as part of their work and are always meeting an extraordinary cross-section of people from all parts of the world and in all walks of life, they are never at a loss for conversation.

They have a vast fund of experiences to exchange and no-one holds back when it comes to recounting difficult, embarrassing or amusing moments encountered on tours. The range of topics aired is almost limitless and can range from the particular foibles of a certain Head of State to the passion shared by the Queen Mother and the

Princess of Wales for flying in helicopters. The Duke of Edinburgh may expound on some aspect of new technology that has impressed him while Princess Anne may debate the particular merits of a new nanny. Teenage girls have their legs pulled about boy friends and similarly boys in the same age group are teased about current girl friends – none of whom ever receive an invitation to the Windsor Christmas.

On the whole, it is the broad spectrum of Royal engagements that is at the forefront of conversation when individual anecdotes and ideas for future tours are swapped. This is particularly therapeutic for working members of the family since the peculiar nature of their work – and their own attitude towards it – is never fully understood by outsiders. The only exceptions are private secretaries, equerries, ladies-in-waiting and other close senior aides who are employed in an official capacity. As a group the family are quite merciless when it comes to taking the mickey out of one another; there are many excellent mimics among them and well known public figures, politicians included, are often victims pf their talent.

The entire family is always in a rush on Christmas morning in order to be ready on time to attend early morning service in St George's Chapel in the Castle grounds, so the Queen decided a long time ago to continue the tradition begun by Queen Victoria and exchange Christmas presents on Christmas Eve. During the afternoon of Christmas Eve there is an excited tooing and fro-ing as gifts are placed on individual tables – each bearing the name of a member of the family – that stand beneath the twinkling lights of a magnificently decorated tree. This is always selected from the finest of hundreds of conifers cultivated on the estate.

No one ever appears at Windsor Castle wearing a Father Christmas costume. Prince Philip is master of ceremonies and it is he who begins the handing-out of presents shortly after six o'clock, two and a half hours before the Queen leads everyone into the huge dining room for dinner. Special Christmas stockings are prepared for the very young children, most of them under three years of age, and they are the only Royals to wake up with presents on Christmas morning, excluded as they are from the church service. As with all children, they will believe in the magic of Father Christmas until, as the years go by, the dream gradually wears off. No one however, certainly not the Queen, would ever break the spell as long as it lasted.

When the Queen was a young child and her grandfather King George V was on the Throne, the Royal Family always left their presents out on display. In those days writer Osbert Sitwell, whose company the King enjoyed and who was once invited to Sandringham as a guest for Christmas, was solemnly reproved for taking his presents up to bed with him. He wrote later, 'Members of the Royal Family were very fond of coming down in any spare moments to gloat over the presents, other people's as much as their own.' No such display happens these days.

On Christmas morning, except for the toddlers, everyone goes down to breakfast in the Oak Room, the family common room, and helps themselves to food from hot silver dishes on huge sideboards – eggs and bacon, kedgeree, kippers, sausages. Only the Queen has breakfast alone in her suite. They are all early risers and several, including Princess Anne and Mark Phillips, manage an early morning ride before breakfast. No matter what the weather and with cheeks aglow, many of the group are on horseback at some point on Christmas Day, including the Queen and Princess Margaret, just as the Royal Family were hundreds of years ago when another Elizabeth was on the Throne.

In twos and threes the family walk from the Private Apartments the short distance to St George's Chapel for morning service at ten o'clock which is attended by local dignitaries from the town of Windsor, the Constable and Governor, the Deputy Constable and Military Knights of Windsor Castle, officers and troops who are not on duty and the families of men and women who work on the estate. After this is over, the Queen and her relatives assemble in the great Crimson Drawing Room for champagne served by footmen bearing gleaming silver trays. This is one of the few occasions when the Queen has an aperitif during the day – but she seldom has more than one glass.

At one o'clock precisely comes the high-spot of the Royal Christmas, the four-course lunch when, seated around a huge table which can accommodate fifty people – two hundred if the leaves are used – the Royals tuck into traditional English fare. There is a table plan near the door so that everyone knows where they are seated: the Queen and Prince Philip always face each other across the middle of the table, something they always do in every Royal home when they have guests. Philip has a fine palate and well before Christmas selects the white and red wines from the richly stocked Castle cellars. No toasts are ever made and the Queen is always served first.

The starter, very often fresh asparagus or melon, is followed by a fish dish, usually fresh salmon. The great moment arrives when the Royal chef, complete with white apron and white linen hat, brings in the splendid Norfolk turkey, on a huge silver dish, which is carved by the Royal Steward. The Queen only eats fresh vegetables and at Christmas they are Windsor grown and served by Windsor footmen in their black tail coats with scarlet waistcoats. The grand finale to the lunch is an enormous Christmas pudding made in the kitchens of Buckingham Palace and served with brandy sauce.

Once this is eaten and fruit is served, come the novelty crackers which are always provided by the same Norfolk firm and filled with the usual mottoes, funny hats, plus a novelty gift – often something quite sensible like a dog whistle or a clever puzzle. Only Royal babies and tiny toddlers, all left in the care of nannies, are excluded from this happy luncheon. For two people Christmas Day is a double celebration since it brings with it their birthdays:

23

Princess Alice, Duchess of Gloucester in her eighties, and Princess Alexandra, who is in her mid-forties.

A must for every member of the family, including the Queen herself, is her Christmas Day radio and television broadcast to Britain and the Commonwealth which is televised in this country at three o'clock in the afternoon. This is filmed long before the holiday and the Queen and Prince Philip spend long hours with television advisers considering and preparing it, knowing that it will be seen by an estimated 27 million people throughout the world. The family watch the programme, which usually lasts about fifteen to eighteen minutes, in a drawing room with four large sofas, a dozen or so easy chairs and where, by the side of the two fireplaces at each end, is a large colour television set. When it is over the Queen always tends to be critical of her performance.

One of the great joys about the holiday is that everyone can do their own thing; at Windsor the family can spend hours in the Mews with the horses, walk for miles with dogs at their heels, play golf on a course often used as a landing strip for a Royal helicopter, enjoy badminton or swim in a heated pool. Anyone who is polo minded can use a fully saddled model pony to swipe polo balls at a tightly stretched netting, the brainchild of Prince Philip some years ago. There is also a small private cinema and at Christmas there is a great choice of films to be seen, old favourites as well as pre-releases. The most popular sport for the younger members of the family is badminton: there is a court near the swimming pool where they play in white shirts and shorts – and now even jeans – watched by the eagle eye of a bust of Queen Victoria. The Queen never plays but is content to cheer from the sidelines.

Although not a lover of badminton, since childhood the Queen has been a devotee of a whole host of classic parlour games ranging from musical chairs to hunt the slipper. But the art of dressing up, once so popular a generation or two ago, no longer has the same appeal. During the war years when the Princesses Elizabeth and

24

Margaret lived at Windsor the great joy of the Christmas holiday was a pantomime in which they appeared in the male roles, while the rest of the cast included children whose parents worked on the Windsor estate. The first panto, *Cinderella*, was in 1941, with Princess Elizabeth as a dashing Prince Charming and her sister a very lively Cinderella. As they grew older the fun of dressing up began to wane and modern young Royals have shown little interest in pantos. Some of the family do their own special turns and this is where Princess Margaret always comes into her own, singing and playing the piano and doing stunningly professional impressions of famous stars. The Queen Mother is also a good pianist and often leads singsongs. But the favourite game at Christmas is charades, played in a highly skilled and almost professional way, which all the Royals adore. This is known by the family as 'The Game' and it has been played for years. Everyone has to mime, very much in the mould of the television game *Give Us a Clue*. The family is divided into teams and without using words have to indicate by gestures the clue they are given. These happy games are played after a cold buffet supper and later, while some members of the family dance, older relatives, like the Queen Mother, play cards.

I always remember the words of one person who subsequently became a member of the Royal Family describing a first Christmas at Windsor:

Honestly, it was fantastic! I never had so much fun in all my life. I never believed it was possible to enjoy oneself so much. I laughed and laughed until my sides ached and tears poured down my cheeks. We played the most wonderful games like hide-and-seek and you know all the adults entered into the whole spirit of the party just like the children. Once, when we were playing a game of hide-and-seek I decided to hide under a big table covered with a heavy table cloth, and imagine my astonishment when I discovered the Queen already there on her hands and knees. We could hardly contain our laughter and held our breaths hoping not to be discovered. The Queen constantly had me in stitches and when it came to finding good hiding places, she always knew the best ones.

No one ever retires before the Queen who, on this special night in the year, never goes to bed until oneo'clock in the morning or even later.

For five full days, until the morning of 31 December, the family continue a similar pattern, all following their individual pursuits, enjoying their presents until it is time to go their separate ways. After leaving the Castle the Queen, Prince Philip, Prince Edward, the Queen Mother, the Prince and Princess of Wales and Princess Margaret spend two weeks at Sandringham while the others return to their own homes and responsibilities ready to start work again in mid-January.

As the festive season draws to a close, the family gather together in the Queen's beautiful white and gold drawing room, with glorious blooms everywhere, and magnificent panoramic views stretching across lawns and woodlands to Windsor Great Park beyond. Here, one by one, the Royals bid farewell to the Queen, ready to face a new year with all its formality and protocol and with all the domestic and personal problems that, like everyone else, beset each of them in one way or another.

In a less impressive setting, they would simply appear to be just another family group, breaking up at the end of the holiday, soon to go back to work. But as they make their farewells, each looks ahead to a new year that differs in almost every respect from that which you and I experience. Even in this modern day and age the British Royal Family are forever set apart from the rest of us. Closely knit and loyal to one another, what are they really like as a family? The aim of this book, while describing the ups and downs of the world's most photographed and talked about group, their hopes and fears, loves and hates, is an attempt to answer that question.

1

The New Head of the Family

THE QUEEN SPENT some of the happiest times of her early married life in Malta. She was then Her Royal Highness Princess Elizabeth, Duchess of Edinburgh, and sought every possible opportunity to escape from London in order to join Prince Philip when his ship docked for refitting at the George Cross island in the Mediterranean. Sometimes she was away for two weeks, sometimes for a month and once for an unforgettable protocol-free period of two long months.

In the early spring of 1951 eyebrows had been raised in court circles when Princess Elizabeth said firmly that she was going back to Malta for the fourth time in just over a year. There had been certain unkind mutterings that she had not been fair in leaving her two young children behind in London in the care of her parents. But all the time she was comforted in the knowledge that her understanding father was all in favour of her getting away from it all. Although he was King George VI and as his elder daughter she was Heir to the Throne, in Malta she was living the happy carefree life of the wife of a young naval officer.

In fact, for the second time during her three years of marriage, the King had urged her to forget family traditions, to spend Christmas away and have fun in Malta; she had taken him at his word and her happiness was such that instead of being away for five weeks she remained on the island for just over two months. As the wife of a young naval officer who was then in command of the 1,430 ton frigate *Magpie* attached to the Mediterranean Fleet, she had always seized every opportunity to be with him whenever his ship was in dock for refitting. He had no special leave privileges and when he was on duty on board his ship berthed in Valetta, she sometimes did not see him at all during the day, but like most of the crew he lived ashore and there were always the lovely evenings to look forward to.

As she dozed in the peace and quiet, the telephone seldom, if ever, disturbed her afternoon siestas. She adored the informality of the small but charming Villa Guardamangia standing high on Guardamangia Hill in Pieta which could only be reached by a narrow road with just enough room for one car to go up or down. She was a good driver and unlike many other people, she never scraped the sides of her two-year-old Daimler. The creamand pale green villa had first been rented some years before by her husband's uncle and from the upstairs windows she could look out over the main harbours of the island and see his ship in the distance.

She made many new friends among the thousand or so officers' wives and if she had no engagements during the day she always had the company of an old friend, who was also acting as her Lady-in-Waiting, Lady Alice Egerton. They were both heading for their twenty-fifth birthday. Quite a lot of the time, however, she got behind the wheel of her Daimler and drove alone wherever the whim took her. Parties on the island were mostly informal; she wore simple cotton dresses and compared with some of the women she went in for very little jewellery. What she always wore above her wedding ring, made of Welsh gold, was her diamond-studded engagement ring which had been designed by her husband from one of the few old family heirlooms he possessed. Occasionally she wore a beautiful brooch and, without fail, copying her mother, three strings of real pearls around her throat.

The evening social life, such as it was, began to stir on the island somewhere around seven o'clock. Often the most important event of the week was a dance at the island's only 'posh' hotel, the Phoenicia, or at the Queen's Hall in Sliema, when some of the men who could not really dance very well endeavoured not to step on her toes. Sometimes she went to a performance given by one of the local amateur dramatic companies. She particularly enjoyed a version of Edgar Wallace's thriller *The Ringer*. The villain had almost lost his false moustache when he was in the centre of the stage, and she had clutched her young husband's sleeve and along with all the other young naval couples hooted with laughter until tears came to her eyes.

Every evening, somewhere around six o'clock, she would receive a breezy call from the husband she had grown to love so much, cheerfully warning her to be ready because he would soon be on his way from the naval dockyards to pick her up in his open jeep. Often they went for evening drives, just the two of them, bumping over pot-holed roads that in the early fifties were never meant for tourists. Hedgerows and gardens were already ablaze with wild red poppies and marguerites, and old women and young girls, sitting on stools in their doorways crocheting Maltese lace, waved as the carefree couple sped by. He was tieless and she was hatless and their life in England, with its rigid schedules and inescapable formality, seemed far away.

When her light brown hair was ready for a shampoo there was twenty-one-year-old Gladys Conti at her small salon in Sliema's Prince of Wales Road, who was always more than ready to oblige. Gladys was amusing, efficient and very chatty and only charged six shillings for a shampoo and set. There was seldom any need to make an appointment since somehow or other Gladys never failed to fit in all her clients, even when there was a sudden rush because of an evening dance arranged on one of the naval ships in the harbour.

Elizabeth and her husband enjoyed simple things such as going with their friends to the tiny Lido Cinema in Birzebugia, where the manager charged 2s 6d for seats with cushions and 1s 6d for seats without. They often went there alone and held hands in the back row. But perhaps the best part of the holiday was when in the late afternoon they raced across the beach and splashed together in the already warm waters of the blue Mediterranean and then breathlessly towelled themselves dry, one or other of them bubbling over with news of the happenings of the day.

She would tell him about her adventures such as when she drove the Daimler, stopping here and there to wander idly in and out of tiny shops and stroll around market stalls searching for souvenirs to take home for their children. Occasionally she bought an odd item of food which caught her eye, and it was in this way that she and Philip developed a taste for swordfish, one of the staple dishes of the island. On her previous visits to Malta Elizabeth had always insisted on going down to Valetta harbour along with the other naval wives who, like her, were bent on seeing their husbands off as the fleet left on exercises. She was always there on the quayside, in a tightly belted coat or mac with scarf over her head and knotted under her chin, waving madly and calling out words of farewell which he could not hear.

All too swiftly this last holiday came to an end. There were twelve days of official duties for them both to perform in Rome before Philip returned to his ship and she flew back to London. Before she left the Villa Guardamangia she found time to wander into the orange grove and pluck fresh oranges to take home to her children. Each was wrapped in tissue paper and placed in a raffia basket. She then made her last farewells and promised everyone that she would be back again soon. To Miss Mabel Strickland, a remarkable woman who owned the island's newspaper *The Times of Malta* and had entertained at her magnificent home many world-famous politicians, admirals and generals, she confessed,

'I shall miss everyone terribly. It won't be easy settling down at home again.'

That April holiday she left behind spelled the end of the only time in her life when Princess Elizabeth, Heir Presumptive to the throne of Great Britain, was ever to enjoy an ordinary everyday existence. Within a month of her return to London, doctors diagnosed that her father, King George VI, had a terminal illness. Although the word cancer was never mentioned to him, his closest family understood that it would not be very long before his eldest child would have to follow him as monarch.

For Elizabeth, his eldest daughter, those carefree days of spring were replaced by what must have been the most appalling and distressing time in her life. It is grim enough for any daughter to accept that her father has not got long to live, but this father was the sovereign, and she was his heir and every moment of her painful ordeal was a very public one. It also meant that for the next nine months Elizabeth had to live with the knowledge that a draft accession declaration with a message both to the House of Commons and the House of Lords had already been drawn up – and was ready for her immediate signature the moment the worst happened. Only two other members of the Royal Family at first shared her secret: her mother, Queen Elizabeth, for whom the prospect of widowhood was the same sad experience it would be for any other woman with grown-up daughters and in the prime of life; and her husband Philip, an ambitious young Lieutenant Commander with his professional sights already set on a career in the Navy. He was suddenly given indefinite leave of absence from the Service. Elizabeth's younger sister, Margaret, already a heady and flirtatious twenty-one-year-old, did not at first realise the gravity of the situation – but once she did Margaret did not fully recover for many years from the tragedy which was to strike the family.

But the business of State had to continue. It was touch and go as to whether Elizabeth and Philip would be able to carry out an already planned State visit to Canada and the United States in October. The King underwent a major operation for the removal of his left lung but he recovered for the couple to fly across the Atlantic on their first major overseas tour together which was to prove, despite their growing anxiety, an outstanding success. It was an exacting tour and they criss-crossed North America twice, capturing Canadian hearts. There was one memorable occasion when, pushing to the back of their minds the tragedy which news from home could bring them any minute, they entered into the spirit of a square dance in Government House, Ottawa. Philip, for the first and last time, appeared in jeans worn with a black and white check shirt and Elizabeth was in a gay dirndl skirt.

It is interesting to look back upon these four people – Elizabeth, Philip, the Queen and Margaret – and consider the manner in which they coped with those trying and long-drawn-out months, their hopes occasionally being falsely raised – because they willed themselves to hope against hope – only to be dashed again by the obvious and relentless progress of the disease. More than anything, the thirty-five-day tour of Canada, when they covered more than ten thousand miles and were rapturously acclaimed everywhere, was of greater consequence for Elizabeth and Philip than people outside the Royal Family ever realised. This, they knew, would soon represent the future pattern of their lives and it was then that Philip gradually and reluctantly began to accept that his hopes of a Naval career might have to be jettisoned. When they were off duty and away from the public gaze, the Royal entourage noted that Elizabeth did not smile as often as usual and Philip seemed unduly pre-occupied.

In London, where nurses from Westminster Hospital were tending the King in Buckingham Palace, Elizabeth's mother, the Queen, was constantly at the side of a man who, although still frail and weak, nevertheless had State papers placed before him for signature within three days of the operation. Before a month was out she made up her mind that the wisest course for everyone (and especially to ease the King's anxiety about his state of health) was to carry on as usual. She resumed her public engagements and with her heart almost breaking, and although she was often quite exhausted, she always brought back bright and cheerful news to the sick room. She would gently go over arrangements for their postponed Australian tour – one which she knew would never take place.

Believing that her father's health was improving, Margaret celebrated her twenty-first birthday in August of that year and continued her inconsequential socialising style of life mixed with official engagements. Her independent spirit was already manifesting itself and various eligible young aristocrats were being tipped as possible suitors for her hand. The hot favourite at the time was Billy Wallace, a man who did not love the Princess and yet was later to render her an unselfish and consolatory service at a time when she was emotionally distressed and distraught by the break up of a dramatic love affair.

Despite the hidden strain felt by all of them, Elizabeth, Philip, the Queen and Margaret remained outwardly self-controlled and if there were breakdowns, as indeed there must have been, then this only happened in the privacy of their own homes. That these senior members of the Royal Family were able to exercise such discipline is quite incredible. In January 1952 Elizabeth and Philip, representing the sick King, set off on their next overseas tour, this time to East Africa, Australia and New Zealand expecting to be away for five months.

Princess Elizabeth became Queen without knowing it while she was up a giant fig tree watching wild animals drinking at a water-hole in the famous Aberdare Game Reserve in Kenya, Africa, during the night of 5/6 February 1952. When the tragic news came from England Elizabeth and Philip were staying at the Sagana Hunting Lodge and had arranged to spend the night at the Tree Tops Hotel, a wooden structure built in a giant fig tree. They encountered a herd of wild elephants on their approach to Tree Tops and were having supper at the hotel when they were told that there was a rhino at the watering hole below and they left their table to look at it. Princess Elizabeth, in brown slacks and a bush jacket, and Philip were so thrilled by the scene that they sat up all night watching elephants, rhino and their young coming to the hole for a drink. Indeed, so fascinated were they that they did not use the camp beds which had been made up for them.

It was some time during the night when the Princess was watching the entertainment laid on for her by nature, that she became, unbeknownst to her, Queen of Great Britain, Ireland and of the Dominions Beyond the Seas. Her father in far off England had died in his sleep. The party were due to leave Tree Tops for Sagana Lodge soon after 8.00am but the Princess who was now a Queen was so amused by the antics of a party of baboons, who climbed through the windows of Tree Tops to grab slices of sweet potato, that she insisted on staying for another hour.

There are many conflicting versions of the exact processes by which the news of the King's death finally reached the new Queen at Sagana Lodge. As was to be expected a scene of great chaos developed with telephones and wires buzzing all over Africa in government and newspaper offices. Meanwhile Elizabeth, still unaware of the destiny which had befallen her, was looking forward to an easy day at the Lodge. While servants were shutting doors and windows against a sudden tropical downpour a call came through from the Outspan Hotel seventeen miles away. Lt. Commander Michael Parker, Philip's close naval friend and Equerry, picked up the phone to find himself talking to a reporter on the *East Africa Standard*, Granville Roberts. News of the King's death had been flashed around the world by news agencies before Buckingham Palace could contact the new Queen and Roberts said, 'There is terrible news about the King. I have just had a call from my office in Nairobi . . .'

Colonel Martin Charteris, Elizabeth's Private Secretary, then took the phone from the reporter and broke the news to Michael Parker. He said, 'The King is dead. Don't tell the Lady until I have confirmation.'

Confirmation was unhappily soon forthcoming and Parker had to break the news to Philip. Philip was with Elizabeth in the sitting room at Sagana Lodge when Parker managed to signal to him that he needed to see him privately. Wondering what could be the matter Philip excused himself to his wife and went outside to see Parker. He returned white faced to break the news to Elizabeth that she was now Queen of Great Britain.

So well trained had she been throughout her life that even at this most traumatic moment Elizabeth remained quite composed when she faced the waiting Royal entourage. Many of them she had known for a long time and all of them would have understood if she had openly failed to stand the stress. Yet she gave no outward sign of her bereavement. It was indeed an iron will which made it possible for the Queen to remain so in command of herself. The Queen has always had extraordinary reserves and can, when the occasion demands it, be a very tough person indeed. That she could cope in public at the age of twenty-five with the death of her beloved father and reveal nothing of the terrible emotion which tortured her mind, gives some idea of the increased degree of self-control she possesses today, nearly three decades later.

Some twenty-four hours after her experiences in Kenya, Elizabeth, a black coat over her greyish blue dress, her face a pale wan oval beneath a tight black hat, stood at the door of a BOAC Argonaut aeroplane which had just taxied into London's airport thirty-two seconds ahead of time. She stood looking down at the bared heads of the men who had come to meet their new Queen.

Standing with tears in his eyes was the Prime Minister, Winston Churchill. Followed by Philip she walked gravely along the line of Privy Councillors, shaking hands and murmuring words to each. Then she drove to her home, Clarence House; as she stepped from the car a guardsman tugged on a halyard and sent the Royal Standard fluttering up the flagstaff. Minutes later her grandmother, Queen Mary, drove out of the gates of nearby Marlborough House to do homage to her Sovereign: 'Her old Grannie and subject,' she said, 'must be the first to kiss Her hand.' At Clarence House she was received by Elizabeth while outside the white walls, the lamplighter of St James's came round as usual to set the old-fashioned lamps aglow. Neither grandmother nor granddaughter realised that that elderly lady only had less than a year to live and would never see the Coronation.

The King had died at Sandringham where a Royal servant, bringing him his morning cup of tea, found him dead with the book still open at the page he had been reading. Some necessary official business was hurriedly done before the new Queen made the hundred mile journey to Sandringham where she became an ordinary daughter again, bringing the solace of an eldest child to her bereaved mother. The new Queen and the Queen Mother – as she was to be styled – embraced and Princess Margaret curtseyed to her elder sister for the first time. A few minutes later Elizabeth and Philip were reunited with their two children, three-year-old Prince Charles and one-year-old Princess Anne.

State life does not stand still when a British sovereign dies and the Queen Mother knew that she had no choice but to move out of Buckingham Palace, which had been her home for more than seventeen years, as soon as this could be practically arranged, and her daughter, as Queen, would move back to this old childhood home. The Palace, a Royal home through seven reigns, with its vast rooms and high ceilings, was in sharp contrast to Clarence House, one of the most charming of all the Royal residences in London. It had been the Queen's first home when she married. Almost at once it was decided that Clarence House should now become the official residence of the Queen Mother to be shared by Princess Margaret. It was impossible for the changeover to take place overnight and it ultimately took three months before the Queen Mother's personal standard finally flew over Clarence House.

Despite its impressive façade, Buckingham Palace has never been liked or regarded as a real home by generations of Royalty. The prospect of returning there dismayed Elizabeth and Philip and, to add to the general strain and not inconsiderable confusion, for a time four Royal Households, those of the Queen, the Queen Mother, Princess Margaret and the embryo Household of Philip all overlapped, with everyone doing their best not to trip over one another or upset one another.

During the early days of the move Philip, depressed by the impersonal atmosphere of the Palace, had to make do with a ground-floor room as his bedroom and for a while was separated at night from the Queen. A bed was taken over from Clarence House along with a television set; he found himself, however, sleeping in a room surrounded by ornate and heavy furniture. The walls were of red silk and lined with solemn portraits of former Spanish kings. Tired and strained, he was taken ill with jaundice and had to stay in these depressing quarters for three weeks.

The Queen Mother, grieving and lost, remained in the Sovereign's Private Apartments which she had shared with the late King for so long and seemed disinclined to move, all the time desperately trying to calm a sometimes nearly hysterical younger daughter. Added to this Buckingham Palace was simply not geared to function as a massive modern communications centre, dealing not only with complicated domestic matters, keeping a new monarch constantly informed but also coping with an impending Coronation.

Courtiers had to adjust to changing Royal patterns. They had long since been accustomed to picking up a telephone receiver and hearing a familiar and often tetchy voice on the other end of the line saying 'King here . . .' King George VI had never hesitated to rebuke anyone responsible for a job that had not been done well in his eyes. The new monarch's style was different. Her gentler and higher pitched voice came over, 'This is the Queen speaking . . .' But even though her words often seemed mild, her general approach, even in those early days, was firm and courtiers soon found that she possessed much the same sort of steely will as her father.

Wisely, the Queen and Philip decided that in order to withstand all the pressures they were facing, they badly needed some form of escape and relaxation. So they planned, whenever possible, to weekend at Windsor Castle where they could spend more time with their young children for whom, since no monarch had needed a nursery at Buckingham Palace for more than a hundred years, temporary accommodation had had to be found in the Palace. Windsor Castle however was a decidedly uncomfortable residence and the Queen and Philip were appalled by the blasts of icy air which penetrated all the great rooms and which even huge log fires did little to counteract. The Queen immediately ordered electric fires to be bought – as a stop-gap until she and her husband could find more time to consider ways and means of modernising the historic Castle.

The staffs at both Royal homes soon discovered that the Queen had an eagle eye about many things, especially where furniture was concerned. She noticed any new burn or ink stain. On her express orders, plenty of ash-trays were always left about. Like her father before her, she would not hesitate to warn a visitor, 'Please be careful of your ash . . .' A changeover always brings problems and the staffs had to adapt to new foibles. In the past they had grown used to the King's strange dislikes. For instance he loathed mirrors and never liked anyone to move an ornament. He once complained to a guest who had slightly changed the position of a vase, 'Why do you keep moving my home about?' This was a curious trait inherited by his daughter who also noticed any similar attempts to move favourite objects.

King George VI often took a long time to reach quite minor decisions and would hesitate over small matters. His wife often speeded things up by saying, 'Oh Bertie, I don't think it's worth making so much fuss . . .' The new Queen, however, was quite different: she never dawdled about making up her mind. She also made it clear that she favoured strict economy and when it was occasionally pointed out to her that a particular carpet was showing signs of wear and tear and ought, perhaps, to be replaced she would say, 'We do not need a new carpet. We will have the old one repaired.' The Queen had other thrifty habits, she saved string and always made sure that a used piece of soap was stuck on to a new tablet.

The Queen worked long hours without any sign of strain or fatigue and some of the late King's older and experienced aides wondered how long they could keep up the new pace. She seemed to take to this side of the monarchy quite naturally, although prior to this her work load had, by comprison, been relatively light. It was in those hectic days before the Coronation, in which the sovereign was to be 'hallowed' – a ceremony dating back to Anglo-Saxon times – that many people both in government and court circles slowly began to realise that the influence of Prince Philip was likely to prove more disturbing than they had been led to believe.

'An independent and interfering so and so . . .' was how he was frequently described. The Queen shrewdly appointed Philip Chairman of the Coronation Commission and it was then that the closely knit establishment surrounding the monarch soon discovered that while Philip possessed many of the strong characteristics of his uncle, Lord Mountbatten, he totally lacked his tactful and subtle approach. From the start, Philip often felt frustrated and was blunt and forthright and did not always trouble to mince some of his more nautical words. Many people would have gladly ignored him completely. But, of course, Philip always had the upper hand. He could, as he sometimes chose to point out, always refer any matter to the Queen who, after all, was his wife. It is hardly surprising that living under such new and extraordinary circumstances, with his wife spending long hours behind closed doors dealing with State affairs, he began to show early signs of irritation. Also he felt a certain lack of identity. His actual role of Consort was not even defined in the British constitution: no doubt he recalled the words of Queen Victoria when she realised the nebulous position of her own husband, Prince Albert, and commented: 'It is a strange omission in the Constitution that while the wife of a King has the highest rank and dignity in the Realm assigned to her by law, the husband of a Queen regnant is entirely ignored.'

Little wonder that at this time in his life, Philip felt isolated and cut off: the move to Buckingham Palace brought with it a dramatic role reversal for Philip and the strain on him showed. The men and women who had once served his late father-in-law and were now closeted for long hours on end with his wife, were not the sort of people towards whom he naturally gravitated; he found them uncommunicative, and on what he considered to be important matters he was politely ignored. Irritation on Philip's part sometimes flared into outright anger which did nothing to improve the situation. For a time, at least, he had to come to terms with the fact that he had no real role to play in the business of British monarchy.

Prince Philip's acceptance of this difficult situation was largely due to a man who over the years has had more influence on the Royal Family than anyone else. It was his wisdom coupled with great understanding and patience that helped Philip over those irksome months. That man was Lord Mountbatten, Philip's uncle, who apart from emerging as one of the great heroes of the Second World War, knew the business of monarchy inside out. He had been connected with the Royal Family too long not to know that unless Philip acquired a new and positive approach to his as-yet-undefined role, everyone close to him would suffer in some way, including Philip himself. His nephew's days were often free and unplanned and for the most part no matter what important aspect of the Queen's new life he wished to enter and understand, he constantly came up against a brick wall. Mountbatten was well aware that Philip would have to fashion out a life-style of his own, but for the moment he cautioned him and urged patience. Mountbatten had played no small part in smoothing the way for his nephew to be accepted as a suitor for the hand of the future Queen of England and, for his own sake at least, he wanted Philip to win through during this testing time.

First hand, he had watched the personal quirks and foibles of his near relatives close to the Throne. His best friend had been the man who had abdicated in 1936 – his cousin, the uncrowned Edward VIII. He had known Edward when they were both young men years before the former King went into exile as the Duke of Windsor. Mountbatten had recognised in Edward the personality traits that could well lead him one day into dangerous waters. But Mountbatten was also a man who, when it became necessary, found he could switch allegiancies from one cousin to another without too much difficulty and so he had soon come to share the same intimacy with George VI as he had had with Edward. With this background he recognised, even more than Philip, the strong and stubborn Hanoverian characteristics the new Queen had inherited from her father. He also knew that like it or not, Philip would have to play his cards carefully if he was not going to upset the Royal applecart in any way.

This young, headstrong man was far less equipped to face the traumas of the new reign than either his mother-in-law, the Queen Mother, or even his starry-eyed young sister-in-law, Princess Margaret. Unlike them he had never really witnessed the pressures, strain and complex workings of monarchy from within. The Queen Mother, especially, knew it all by heart. She too had been a consort but with her inbuilt shrewdness and basic commonsense, she had established a partnership which became so strong that the words 'the King and Queen' became synonymous. Born a commoner, she became a Queen in the regal sense and as to the manner born. Her gracious carriage, her winning smile, her obvious devotion both to her husband and children, rapidly gave her the perfect image. Frankly, it was a difficult accomplishment to follow, and it is true to say that Philip has never really achieved it, but that he was of enormous support to his wife during those early days of the reign is without doubt.

Elizabeth possessed far greater resilience and patience than Philip. She had inner strengths developed in her by her father since childhood and was not only mature for her years, but extremely self-reliant. Immersed in the pressures of her new life, the Queen was intent upon continuing the same positive family pattern of monarchy that had been so carefully established by both her parents. How Philip would fit into the future pattern neither she nor her husband knew, but it became very clear that duty to the Crown now, as always, came first in all their lives.

It is interesting to consider the Queen's basic make-up at that time. She required no special stimuli, she had no interest in alcohol except for a social gin and tonic and she certainly never needed sleeping pills. Unlike her father who was almost a chain smoker, she had on interest in cigarettes. In fact she appeared to need next to no external encouragement. She had always relaxed easily with a relatively small circle of friends, most of whom she had known since childhood, and her only other intimates, apart from her husband, were members of her own family. Considering her very unusual background, she had an extremely well integrated personality.

Although her early life was one that has often been described as lonely and isolated behind Palace walls, she actually actively enjoyed herself most of the time and never expressed any regrets. She certainly did not grow up with any feeling that she had seriously missed out in some way. Equally important, there is no suggestion that at any time in her more formative years had she harboured any deep-seated doubts about her own ability to take over her pre-destined job. What she had never envisaged was taking over as head of the Royal Family at such an early age. Both she and Philip had automatically assumed that their married life would remain relatively tranquil for many years to come – her great-grandfather, Edward VII, and her grandfather, George V, both died in their seventies. Her father only lived to be fifty-six.

Even before the St Edward's Crown was placed on her head at the Coronation in Westminster Abbey the Queen had already begun to assert her authority and show signs that she was not prepared to be thwarted over matters about which she felt strongly. When Winston Churchill heard that the BBC wanted to televise the ceremony, he was appalled: he argued that not only the essential dignity of the ceremony would be lost if an audience of millions was watching every minute of it but also that the very circumstances in which people would be watching it, at home over cups of tea, in pubs with pints of beer, were not in any way compatible with the event.

At that time Elizabeth and Philip were one of the lucky 1,500,000 licence holders in Britain who were able to watch the BBC's black-and-white single channel on their fourteen-inch screen in the sitting room of their Private Apartments in Buckingham Palace. Intrigued by the sedate programmes which went out from Alexandra Palace Elizabeth was both irritated and worried when she discovered that not only Churchill but also the Archbishop of Canterbury, Geoffrey Fisher, and the Earl Marshal, the Duke of Norfolk, were against televising the Coronation. What could she do to make the three dogmatic men change their minds without creating discord?

BBC experts played their part: they submitted a 'suitable' shooting script for consideration plus a detailed explanation of proposed techniques to be used in the Abbey. All their efforts came to nothing. Pontificated Churchill, 'Just imagine if there were the slightest slip or mishap . . . it would be witnessed by half the nation.' So far as the Prime Minister was concerned, that was that.

What he had not counted on was the personal intervention of Elizabeth, at that time still very inexperienced in the awesome world of State affairs and often both hesitant and nervous in the presence of the ageing elder statesman. Only fifteen months earlier, on learning that King George VI had died in his sleep at Sandringham, Churchill had been openly disconcerted at the prospect of having to deal with Elizabeth because of her youth and inexperience. She was only twenty-six and Churchill bemoaned to Cabinet colleagues, 'She's only a child . . .' So when he rejected and ruled out any possibility of televising the Coronation, he was convinced that was the end of the matter.

But Churchill totally misjudged Elizabeth. She felt very strongly about the issue and Philip fully supported her view that coverage by radio was simply not good enough. In private Elizabeth expressed her conviction that the Coronation, with all its ritual and splendour, was a State occasion that should be shared and enjoyed by as many people as possible – and this could only be achieved by television. This was indeed bold thinking on the part of Elizabeth, coming as she did from a very conservative family. Both her father and grandfather had always assiduously avoided anything but the most formal photographic sessions. The Queen and Philip tried to decide ways and means by which they might win over the antagonists to their point of view without causing the eminent trio to lose face.

In the end it was Elizabeth who found a solution: she gave a private luncheon party at Buckingham Palace and her really brilliant stroke was to include Richard Dimbleby, a leading BBC commentator who had covered many Royal events and whom she knew, like herself, to be strongly in favour of televising the Coronation. Invitations were also extended to other senior BBC executives – and the Archbishop of Canterbury himself, the man who would actually perform the crowning ceremony and whose views had to be changed if cameras were ever to be installed in the Abbey.

Elizabeth faced the luncheon party with some trepidation and with Philip sitting opposite her at an oblong table, she encouraged first one and then another BBC expert to explain to the Archbishop just how inconspicuous television cameras would be and how the use of new telephoto lenses would allow close-up shots to be taken with the utmost discretion. In his characteristic urbane and distinguished manner, Dimbleby, carefully and in his resonant voice, presented the case for television. At regular intervals the Archbishop nodded his head in approval.

Three short weeks later it was officially announced by the Earl Marshal that live television would be allowed in the Abbey. Elizabeth had won the day. And yet at the same time, whether she fully realised it or not, she had laid down a pattern that was destined to take the Royal Family along a strange new road: it was to flush her relatives out of the privacy they had enjoyed all their lives and ultimately subject them to the sort of scrutiny no other family in the world has ever had to experience.

The great day of the Coronation eventually came. When Elizabeth and Philip left Buckingham Palace on the morning of 2 June 1953 they were watched from an upper room by Charles and Anne and fifty other children invited to see the start of the procession. Princess Anne, aged two, was considered too young to go to the Abbey and was little placated by the prospect of watching the events of the day on a new fangled television set. She was crying and very cross indeed. Prince Charles, however, aged four, was later driven in a car by a back-street route to the Abbey and then through back corridors to join his grandmother and Margaret in the Royal Gallery in time to witness the actual Crowning ceremony. It was his nurse, Miss Helen Lightbody, who escorted him to the Gallery. Dressed in a

cream silk blouse and trousers he stood between the
Queen Mother and Margaret on a stool so that he could
have a proper view of the majestic ceremony. He behaved
impeccably, occasionally whispering to his grandmother.

As the ceremony with all its pomp, splendour and
pageantry unfolded in the Abbey that day there was great
hope for the future and a definite sense of a break with the
wartime past: the evocative words 'The Birth of a New
Elizabethan Era' were heard everywhere. Within the Royal
Family too there was also hope and a certain speculation as
to how Elizabeth would fulfil her role as head of the family
group. Relatives watched from the great stalls of Westminster Abbey as the fabulous St Edward's Crown, with its
gold circlet and arched frame encrusted with pearls,
rubies, diamonds, sapphires and emeralds, was raised
high in the air by the Archbishop of Canterbury and placed
solemnly upon the young Queen's head.

It was an unforgettable scene – the heads of State
resplendent in their Orders; everywhere there were
glittering uniforms; peers and peeresses in their robes of
ermine, church dignitaries in their robes of gold and silver,
banners of chivalry hanging above them. I was one of six
commoners invited after the crowning into the great
Annexe of Westminster Abbey reserved for the Queen,
members of the Royal Family and the Royal Procession. I
saw there the Royal Dukes and princes and princesses of
the blood royal in their magnificent robes, Pursuivants
with their brilliant mantles of pink, grey, blue, red and
crimson, men and women of the Royal Household in
glittering uniforms, the Heralds, the King of Arms, the
Lord Great Chamberlain, the Lord High Chancellor in wigs
and damask and gold robes, young page boys in the white
and red livery of the Earl Marshal.

Outside the vast and cheering crowd was waiting for its
first glimpse of the newly crowned Queen with her
Coronation cavalcade of 13,000 troops, twenty-nine bands
and twenty-seven carriages. Inside the Annexe, during the
Coronation 'break' which lasted almost an hour, we were
all drinking coffee and champagne, eating wafer thin

sandwiches of smoked salmon, cucumber and ham, sausage rolls and cheese and biscuits. I could see the Queen, who only drank water, quietly talking to the Duke of Edinburgh; the Queen Mother chatting to Princess Marina, then Duchess of Kent; and the Duke of Gloucester was in earnest conversation with Lord Mountbatten.

I then saw Princess Margaret appear from one of the retiring rooms, anxiously looking for someone, her eyes intently scanning the richly robed company where everyone was absorbed in conversation. For several minutes Princess Margaret's eyes continued to rove the Annexe, then she found what she was looking for – a young Group Captain, immaculate in his RAF uniform with the gold epaulettes of a Royal Equerry. His eyes caught those of the Princess and quickly they moved towards one another.

As they came together I saw the Princess reach up and pluck an offending piece of thread, the kind of gesture which could only occur between two people who knew each other intimately. Intuitively I said to myself, 'Those two are in love . . .' As Princess Margaret raised her hands, the officer caught hold of her wrists, and they looked at one another, oblivious of everyone in this splendid setting. I was with a group of peers and asked them if they knew the identity of the young Air Force officer. One of them replied, 'That's Peter Townsend, don't you know? Nice fellow. The King always spoke well of him . . .'

The great bells of the Abbey were peeling outside and music from the splendid organ enveloped us. At 2.50pm the splendid State Procession began through the streets of London with rapturous cheers from the excited crowds. Then, finally, came the long awaited moment, just after five o'clock when the Queen, wearing the Imperial State Crown for the last time that day and surrounded by her family, appeared on the Balcony of Buckingham Palace before a vast, happy and cheering throng. On either side of her, only just tall enough to see over the edge of the famous Balcony, were her two children. Elizabeth was the sovereign – but she was also a mother. Both Anne and Charles enjoyed themselves hugely, chattering away ten

47

to the dozen to their parents and occasionally copying them and waving their small hands to the crowds. Neither of them seemed to find it at all unusual that their mother was wearing a crown on her head.

2

Early Years and a Family Crisis

DURING THE FIRST four years of his life with Elizabeth it was essentially Philip, still an officer in the Royal Navy, who was the dominant partner in the marrige and made most of the important domestic decisions. He was like many other husbands of his age in the Services and in civil life, who had to spend periods away from their wives. The wife necessarily had to make minor decisions affecting her day-to-day life but it was the husband who usually had the last word in major decisions.

After their Scottish honeymoon Philip and Elizabeth, to their intense chagrin, had to spend more than a year living in the ornate Belgian Suite of Buckingham Palace waiting impatiently for the completion of renovations to their new home, Clarence House. It was the former home of the Duke of Clarence before his accession as William IV in 1830. It was used during the Second World War as offices by the British Red Cross but unfortunately had suffered from war damage. Philip spent hours pouring over Ministry of Works plans, constantly suggesting improvements and revealing a flair for detail that was to become his hallmark in later years when he turned his attention to streamlining and modernising great Royal residences like Sandringham House in Norfolk, Balmoral on Deeside in Scotland, Windsor Castle and Buckingham Palace itself.

It was in these early days that the terrific differences in background and experience between Philip and Elizabeth became most apparent: like all sailors, Philip had been trained to be self-reliant, he could sew on buttons with dexterity and knew how to use an iron, but Elizabeth had never been engaged in any of the ordinary activities involved in running a house. So it was left to Philip to take the lead in designing their labour-saving home with its ultra-modern kitchen and full central heating, explaining his ideas to his wife as they went along. An entirely new world of domesticity opened up for Elizabeth and among other things she soon became adept at mixing paint to get the exact shades she wanted; for example, she mixed a delicate apple green for the walls of their dining room.

Clarence House became a relaxed Royal home and in the autumn of 1948 finishing touches were made to a second-floor nursery overlooking St James's Park in readiness for the birth of their first child, a son who arrived late in the afternoon of Sunday, 14 November 1948, and who was christened Charles Philip Arthur George. His sister Anne, conceived when Elizabeth and Philip were in Malta, was born on 15 August 1950 and a simple nursery routine was established for both children. It was the custom in the Royal Family that as their charges grew too old to need their care, nannies were handed down from one member of the Royal Family to another. In this way, the Elizabeth and Philip household were joined by Scottish born Miss Helen Lightbody who had brought up the two sons of the Duchess of Gloucester, Prince William and Prince Richard.

As there was no other nanny available within the ranks of the family, it was necessary to find somebody from outside. She was therefore a newcomer to the Royal world, Miss Mabel Anderson, who had put an advertisement in the 'Situations Wanted' column of a nursing magazine and was astonished to find herself being interviewed for a job by the Heir Presumptive. She is still in the family service today, looking after Princess Anne's two young children at their home, Gatcombe Park in Gloucestershire.

After her Accession the daily routine for the children continued in much the same pattern and their new nursery in Buckingham Palace looked almost exactly like the old one at Clarence House, the same pale yellow curtains at the windows, the same round table for meal times and the same chests and cabinets for familiar toys. Nana Lightbody was essentially a no-nonsense sort of person who, although kindly, did not believe in over-spoiling the children. She had always dealt firmly with the two Gloucester boys, William and Richard, never mollycoddling them and always urging them to do things for themselves – simple things like putting on their own clothes just as soon as she felt they were able to do so.

In 1944 when the menace of U-boats was still very great, she sailed to Australia with her charges and their parents when the Duke had been appointed Governor General of Australia. For much of the trip the weather was very rough and in terrific gales she placated William and Richard, both regularly seasick, as the ship lurched its way towards the southern hemisphere and as every-thing in the cabins crashed to the floor and spilled out from cupboards and drawers. When U-boats were known to be in the area and depth charges went off, she was told that conditions were so bad that no baby could survive if it had to be transferred to a lifeboat. Nana Lightbody said that if the ship should go down, she would go down with it and never leave the children.

Some of this tough spirit came over in the Buckingham Palace nursery and when an artist went to draw a picture of three-year-old Princess Anne she recalled that the little girl had a heavy cold at one sitting. The Princess asked Nana Lightbody for a sweet biscuit with her morning hot milk only to have this request turned down. Plain biscuits only were allowed in the mornings.

'Mrs' Lightbody was a stickler for punctuality, meals were always served on the dot of time, breakfast at eight o'clock, lunch at noon, tea at 4.00pm and a light supper of milk and biscuits at 6.00pm. Whenever she was free, the Queen was always in the nursery at teatime, playing games with her son and daughter – but this was not often. For the Queen, the twin roles of monarch and mother were daunting; her heavy work schedule often left her tired and exhausted and she found it impossible to enjoy the company of Charles and Anne as often as she wanted. Under these difficult circumstances and when she became immersed in matters of State, how did she fulfil her role as a mother?

If you put this question today to each of her four children, Prince Charles, Princess Anne, Prince Andrew and Prince Edward, they would all come up with a loving but quite different picture of her during childhood years. Because she was so often away from home on official engagements both in this country and abroad, Charles and Anne saw far less of her during their young and formative years than did their two younger brothers who arrived on the scene nearly a decade later. Whenever possible there was fun in the nursery but it was not every evening that the Queen had the opportunity to put on a plastic apron over her dress, bathe them, put them into pyjamas and tuck them up in bed. She saw them every morning but usually only for a very little while before she began her work in earnest at 10.00am. After that her official schedule was so tight that she seldom had time to play with the children during the day.

Of necessity, there was a great difference between the upbringing of Charles and Anne on the one hand and Andrew and Edward on the other. The first two were born during the early years of the marriage before the Queen and Philip had the slightest notion that they were going to be plunged into the heavy burdens of State. Thus it was while their mother was learning to take over the great responsibilities which were her fate, Charles and Anne, to a great extent, suffered the frequent absences of their mother who so often had to put the needs of the nation before her maternal instincts. This caused the Queen great unhappiness and great heart-searching but she could see no alternative. The toddlers accepted their mother's enforced absences and learned not to protest when Mrs Lightbody told them, 'Mummy is very busy, but she will come and see you as soon as she can.'

Philip, still trying to come to terms with the gloomy grandeur of Buckingham Palace, made his own special contributions to his children's upbringing and saw to it that they made their own beds every morning and were always punctual for mealtimes. He was much firmer with them than the Queen and while strongly against physical punishment of any sort he always reproved a child for any display of bad manners or uppity behaviour. When he once heard Charles address a Palace servant by his surname he rebuked his son saying, '*Mister* Watson, if you please', and sent the boy to apologise. Servants who became very close to the two children were the gardeners working in the magnificent eleven acre grounds of Buckingham Palace, with its lakes, lawns and trees of every kind, where the children had their own swings and sand-pit. Here in the middle of London they spent hours riding tricycles and playing to their hearts content, sometimes with one or both parents, blissfully unaware of the crowds and traffic on the other side of the Palace walls.

In the winter of 1953/54 the Queen and Philip were away for six months on a gruelling 50,000 miles tour of the Commonwealth which was to take them through fourteen countries. On the very last lap of this long journey and desperately longing to see her children again, the Queen arranged for Charles and Anne to make their first trip abroad and join her when she arrived in Malta. In the care of Nana Lightbody, the two children sailed from Portsmouth to the George Cross island to be reunited with their parents. Charles could hardly contain himself at this first glimpse of his mother and it was only with some difficulty that Lord Mountbatten managed to prevent him from rushing up to her. Mountbatten explained to the little boy that he must first wait until the Queen finished shaking hands with a long line of officials. Solemnly the little boy nodded his head and remained standing to attention like his great uncle.

These were especially trying times for Elizabeth, still new to her job, and there were always distressing Royal tears before each departure. It was to Philip that the Queen turned for comfort knowing, so often, that she would not see the children again for many weeks. The partings were softened for the children by the fact that they were always left in the loving and often indulgent care of their maternal grandmother, the Queen Mother, who was not only delighted to have them for company but also entered into all their activities with great enthusiasm. She spent hours playing cricket with Charles who complimented her once on becoming an excellent overarm bowler!

Because the Queen Mother had always been such an integral part of their lives, the children did not miss their parents as much as one might have suspected, and were well satisfied by the occasional telephone calls and masses of postcards which reached them from all parts of the globe. On all her tours the Queen was inundated with gifts for her children ... dolls, prams, an electric train set, and games of every sort, but the vast majority were quietly handed over to children's charities, the recipients seldom, if ever, being aware of the identity of the donor. Nevertheless some of the novel treasures were kept for the Buckingham Palace nursery, always being fairly shared out in order to avoid any question of squabbles or jealousy.

Even at this early age the difference in temperament in Charles and Anne was already apparent and the boy, whose nose was first put quite out of joint by her birth, was more reserved and far less outgoing than his sister. In the early days he showed signs of bewilderment at finding himself no longer the sole focus of his parents' attention and there were times when sibling jealousy manifested itself in no uncertain way. Yet by the time they had moved from the nursery to the schoolroom, it was Anne who showed the greatest streak of envy – for her older brother; she was already aware in some way of his senior position. When Prince Philip brought the children boxing gloves he had to take them away again because Anne almost knocked her brother out 'in temper'.

It is difficult to know at exactly what age the Queen's children had any real awareness that they were 'Royal' and 'different' but it is generally conceded that it began around the age of three. It was at this time in his life that Charles and later Anne, in her turn, began to ask questions like, 'Why does everyone wave to us?' The answers they were given were deliberately vague. When a visitor once met Charles in a Palace corridor and in answer to a question said he was going to see the Queen, the little boy looked puzzled and asked, 'Who's she?' At no time were the children ever allowed to interrupt their mother's work schedule. Passing her study one day Charles had urged his mother, 'Please come out and play with me.' 'If only I could,' she replied wistfully, gently closing the door.

She was much more relaxed a decade later when Charles was twelve and Anne was ten, and she and Philip, their official lives better organised, embarked upon what was tantamount to a second family. Prince Andrew was born in February 1960 and Prince Edward, their fourth and last child, in March 1964. By this time the Queen had not only matured as a person but was far more experienced as a mother and had positive ideas about the way in which she wanted to relate to the children. Above all, she was determined to make more time to enjoy them and be with them, even if it meant packing more into her work load in a shorter space of time.

Unlike their elder brother and sister, these two boys were allowed to use their mother's private study on a floor below the nursery and unless she had important appointments had almost free access to go in and out as they pleased, provided they promised to behave and were not over-boisterous. Certainly Andrew and Edward were far more easy to handle as children and there were less tantrums both in the nursery and the schoolroom than there had been with Charles and Anne. They replaced sulky squabbles with healthy fights.

This happier and relaxed atmosphere delighted Elizabeth who had always harboured regrets about the earlier restrictions which were inevitable when she was still mastering the intricacies of the art of queenship. For generations all Royal Children had to bow or curtsey before the sovereign and even the Queen and her sister Princess Margaret had to perform this act of fealty before their own father. This tradition was abandoned by Elizabeth when she came to the Throne and became the first monarch to be greeted by happy children rushing up to her and crying, 'Hello, Mummy!'

When they became parents both Elizabeth and Philip really believed it would be possible to bring up their family very much on similar lines to other children from wealthy families. They accepted that there would be some sticky problems to overcome but had enough self-confidence to think that with the right amount of common-sense applied, these could be surmounted without too much difficulty. To begin with, they were bringing up Charles, a Prince and Heir Apparent, in what they wanted to be a modern way but they had no guidelines to help them, there was no recent precedent. The last Prince of Wales had been the Duke of Windsor who was born at the end of the nineteenth century and had looked back upon his days of childhood under the martinet George V with horror.

Philip and Elizabeth decided to keep their children out of the public eye as much as possible and in the years that followed her Coronation, Charles and Anne were only occasionally glimpsed sitting at the back of a Royal car, sometimes copying their parents and waving, or tightly gripping the hand of a nanny as they walked across a red carpet laid down over a railway station platform to join a Royal train bound for Balmoral or Sandringham. At that time Elizabeth was satisfied with the progress her children were making and the pattern of her own working life was settling into a daily routine that she basically still follows to this day.

In Buckingham Palace she and Philip shared adjoining bedrooms separated by a large connecting double door but at Windsor Castle they shared the same bedroom. It was always Mrs Margaret 'Bobo' MacDonald, Elizabeth's great confidante who probably knows her as well as anyone else in the world, who brought her morning cup of tea at 7.45am. Bobo – she has always been known by this nickname since the days when Elizabeth used to hide behind curtains as a little girl and spring out and cry 'Bo-bo' to surprise Miss MacDonald – is the daughter of an Inverness farmer; at the age of eighteen she first nursed Elizabeth in her arms when the Princess was only six weeks old. Throughout childhood years they shared the same bedroom.

As Elizabeth grew older, Bobo became her personal maid and dresser and her direct and frank attitude, not only to her mistress but to senior members of the Royal Households became legendary. She was given the traditional title of 'Mrs' and developed a formidable personality, always being a stickler for protocol. When she was recounting the happenings of the day with other members of the rank-conscious staff she would always use the Royal 'we', commenting 'We found this very enjoyable' or 'We didn't like this at all'. Although she was subject to moods and could be waspish at times, Bobo had a good sense of humour which endeared her to Elizabeth. She always had a strong influence over her mistress in the choice of clothes and she sometimes cramped Elizabeth's style.

Now in her seventies and after more than half a century of personal service, she lives a quiet life in her suite of rooms at Buckingham Palace, stubbornly refusing to regard herself as being retired. Many times she has been urged by Elizabeth to move into one of the lovely cottages on one of the Royal estates where she would be well cared for, but Bobo always refuses to leave. Bobo no longer takes Elizabeth her morning tea – a page does the job. A pipe major of the Argyll and Sutherland Highlanders still plays bagpipes beneath Elizabeth's bedroom window, much to the chagrin of Philip who still does not enjoy this Royal tradition dating back to the days of Queen Victoria.

Elizabeth always baths and dresses before eight o'clock in time to breakfast with Philip in their private dining room, where they listen to the BBC news and read the morning papers. Her official day begins at ten o'clock and invariably continues, with a ninety-minute break for a light lunch, until six or seven o'clock. She has the stamina to stand on her feet for hours but her habit at the end of any day is to sit back in an easy chair and kick off her shoes. Faced with two engagements in the same day Elizabeth is often involved in at least two changes of clothes but she is not the fastest person in the Royal circle to get in and out of clothes. This record was held by Lady Mountbatten who in the space of nine minutes could change from her St John Ambulance Brigade uniform into a dazzling evening gown complete with a tiara on her head, a diamond necklace round her throat and diamond bracelets on both wrists. She always fitted in time for a bath and her hair remained impeccably in place because she fastened it in pipe cleaners the moment she took off her uniform hat.

Elizabeth has never used a great deal of make-up and has kept to the same moisturiser to keep her skin supple and the same night cream to combat age lines. She uses a light, slightly peachy foundation cream plus a little rouge and light eye make up. Her hair is thick and shiny and has a texture that usually only goes grey late in life so that it is only in recent years that she has used a light chestnut rinse. Elizabeth has always been weight conscious and now weighs just over eight stone, having put on less than ten pounds since she became sovereign.

Elizabeth and Philip have their offices side by side in Buckingham Palace with their individual secretariats working together on a floor below. Early in her reign the Queen discovered that she positively disliked dictating letters and so began the habit of writing many important personal communications by hand, a practice still maintained today. At first a number of people in the Royal Household found this disconcerting but recipients were always delighted.

The pattern of the Queen's working life when she is in London has varied little over the years and her only relaxations before she begins the day – when her private secretary takes in her mail shortly before ten o'clock – are two telephone calls, one to her mother and the other to her sister, and a start on the crossword puzzle in either the *Daily Telegraph* or *The Times*.

While the Queen's working days were often over crammed with official business, it was very different for Philip who, after the abrupt termination of his naval career on the death of George VI, had to cast around for new ways in which to exercise his talents and expand his interests. There were humdrum routine engagements which did not make enough demands upon him. Bored by formal words presented to him by officials, he began to write his own speeches and developed his own witty and to-the-point style of delivery which was in sharp contrast to traditional and formal Royal speeches of the past. He felt strongly about many worth-while causes, some of which he started himself, and for them he worked tirelessly.

In his early efforts to streamline Royal homes Philip often came up against experts who tried to dazzle him with words. He was presented with long-winded statements about repairs and would listen patiently before saying, 'I just don't believe that . . .' or 'I'm sure you've got your facts wrong . . .'. Philip was essentially a practical man and when he inspected old bathrooms at Windsor Castle he spent hours studying ventilation and lighting problems. He discovered that some bathrooms used by guests were not soundproof and that people could overhear bathroom conversations because double bathrooms had been divided by thin partitions. He ordered new walls to be built to remedy the embarrassing situation.

Philip made great use of Windsor Castle workshops and instructed that where the light was too strong in some of the 20ft high rooms with great floor-to-ceiling windows, they should be reduced by false panelling which concealed a third of the light. Thus no windows were taken out and money was saved. He ordered notices to be placed near all light switches which read, 'Please turn off the lights when you leave the room' and when guests left the Green Drawing Room to go into the Principal Dining Room he gave instructions that stewards must turn off the lights at once. No light is ever left burning in a Royal residence today if it is not in use.

Like Elizabeth, economy was always his watchword and he saved hundreds of pounds by 'making do'; when he wanted a cocktail cabinet fixing in his study, instead of ordering something new – as he could well have done – he searched the Royal stores and came across an old walnut desk with a drop front. No alteration was needed for the cocktail cabinet but Philip had it lined with birdseye maplewood and inside shelves fixed and holders placed for bottles. Again like Elizabeth, he would never buy something new if something old would do. His passion for a long time was making model aeroplanes and as in everything else he was scrupulously tidy and meticulous about putting his papers and tools away in their proper place.

He often liked to do some jobs himself and one weekend at Windsor Castle he persuaded Elizabeth to help him to change around some heavy furniture in a drawing room in order to make a central space. They shifted several sofas and heavy chairs which were so heavy that normally strong porters would have been required to do the job. Ironically, the next day the housekeeper was appalled to find that 'some idiot had completely disarranged the room' and promptly ordered everything to be put back in its proper place.

While seemingly all was set fair on the Royal scene, there was nevertheless a stormy passage ahead unsuspected by all, which was going to cause Elizabeth much heartache and the Royal Family grave concern. The reign was only two years old and the great hope of all, Royalty, Government and people, was that it should prove stable, unclouded and successful. The Throne seemed really to have settled down after the period of turmoil which ended in the Abdication of the uncrowned Edward VIII. That was almost twenty years before in 1936. But this terrible blow to the stability of Royalty had not been forgotten and the prayer of everyone was that there should never be another upset like that again. Unhappily there was a cloud on the horizon.

The storm broke with the revelation of a love affair involving Princess Margaret whose frivolous life-style was in such contrast with that of Elizabeth. Spoiled by her father and indulged by her mother, she had hardly endeared herself to her future brother-in-law during their early encounters when she often deliberately played gooseberry, joining the couple when they wanted to be alone. As a child she had never come to terms with the role of being a younger sister and looking back it seems unfortunate that such talents as she had, and they were not inconsiderable, were never harnessed.

She was sophisticated, attractive, temperamental and vivacious but her attitude to work was basically light-hearted: she utterly lacked Elizabeth's sense of dedication. If anyone was really to blame for her almost wilful refusal to take her role seriously, it was George VI: he was aware that Princess Margaret would find it difficult to play second fiddle to her elder sister all her life and as though to compensate in some way he indulged her every whim. When she was thwarted she became petulant and it was not only her father but also her mother and sister who found it easier to give in to her demands, small as they sometimes were, rather than face temperamental outbursts and scenes.

Her pleasure-seeking life-style was headline material
and her name was constantly romantically linked with
young men from rich and aristocratic family backgrounds. She thrived on late nights when, as the focus of
all eyes, she quickstepped and tangoed the hours away.
She revelled in elegant house parties where her presence
always added an exciting and dazzling element. But
unknown, even to her parents, there had really only
been one man in the life of the Queen's sister since she
was sixteen.

He was Group Captain Peter Townsend, a wartime
RAF ace who, like other men with distinguished records,
was appointed by George VI as a temporary Royal
Equerry. His talents were such and he fitted in so well
with the Royal Family that this good looking man with
charming manners rapidly climbed the Royal Household
ladder to become Deputy Master at thirty-six. He was at
hand at all the most intimate and informal Royal Family
gatherings and it seemed the most natural thing in the
world that he should accompany Princess Margaret
alone riding and be at her side in a Royal Family group at
the Horse Riding Trials at Badminton. Sixteen years
older than Margaret, he was a married man with two
children and had an impeccable background. What was
there to worry about?

When George VI died and Margaret went into a black
depression her relatives felt only gratitude for the
Deputy Master of the Household who seemed to one
and all to be fulfilling the role of surrogate father in a way
that no one else could. Yet only a short time before the
Coronation Princess Margaret, then twenty-three, confessed to a blissfully unaware mother and sister that
Townsend, who six months before had divorced his wife
on grounds of her adultery, was the man she wanted to
marry. What is extraordinary is that although Townsend
had been part and parcel of the Royal scene for so many
years and was tantamount to being the closest intimate
of them all, neither the Queen, her mother nor Philip

recognised the growing intensity of the relationship between Margaret and the Deputy Master. It seemed perfectly normal to the trio that the couple should ride for hours together in the grounds of Windsor Great Park and disappear on picnics in the hills around Balmoral. On the other hand, some senior members of the Royal Household were only too well aware of what was going on, frequently encountering them hand in hand and giving all the signs of two people deeply in love.

In looking back on an emotional situation that was to be of such unhappy and lasting consequence to so many people in the family, it must be realised that at that time, a decade before the swinging sixties, divorce remained a stigma for anyone in public life: the prospect of Elizabeth's sister marrying a divorced Royal servant, albeit the innocent party, presented not only constitutional problems but in addition it was felt in government and Court circles that the resulting outcry would do nothing but harm to the start of Elizabeth's new reign. At first the Queen and her mother urged patience and pleaded for time so that further thought could be given to the possible outcome of such a union. They loved Margaret and wanted her to be happy and both of them admired and respected Townsend. Philip, however, took a much harder line from the start and made no bones about the fact that he was a hundred per cent against the marriage.

This was one of the occasions when his better judgment was overruled by his emotions. While he had always been critical of Margaret he had been, to say the least, antagonistic towards Townsend. Except for the love they both had for two sisters who were daughters of a sovereign, they had little else in common. Townsend had an unusual and secure place in the heart of the Royal Family long before Philip appeared on the scene as a serious suitor for the hand of Elizabeth. He had not only earned the confidence and respect of the late King but had also become an intimate of the often taciturn and difficult man in a way that Philip, a breezy latecomer, never was. Townsend also held down a highly responsible and powerful job within the Court at a time when Philip was still struggling to find a positive role for himself. There was no open clash of personalities but Philip, a forthright man accustomed to naval discipline and giving sharp orders, had no personal rapport with the less thrusting and gentler Townsend. Philip made it clear that he felt that not only was Margaret – and so Townsend – letting the Royal side down but that they were also putting an unprecedented extra burden on the already hard-pressed Elizabeth.

It is curious that while the early stages of the drama were being played out in Buckingham Palace, Fleet Street newspapers were quite unaware that something was amiss. When I returned to the *Daily Mirror* office after representing the newspaper at the Coronation, I immediately reported to senior executives and expressed my certain conviction that after what I had observed in the Annexe of the Abbey, I was certain that Margaret and Townsend were in love. In any other circumstances this would have caused an editorial sensation but on this day of the great celebration all attention was concentrated on the Queen and the publication of a Coronation issue. The debate that ensued was short and it was decided not to publish any report that might detract from the Queen's great personal triumph. And the Margaret story was never followed up until a few short weeks later when an American newspaper report, linking the names of the Queen's sister and Townsend, burst on the world like a bombshell.

When the scandal broke it was handled from start to finish in a glare of publicity, so badly mismanaged that there was very real fear in Government circles that unless drastic action was taken there was serious danger that the image of the Queen would be damaged. With undignified haste Townsend was banished to Belgium to the relatively obscure job of air attaché at the British Embassy in Brussels, where he behaved impeccably and remained for just over two years.

In the months that followed the separation a bitter schism developed in the Royal Family and the person who undoubtedly suffered most was the Queen, torn by the knowledge that her mother and sister living in Clarence House were strongly opposed to what they considered to be Philip's unsympathetic and dogmatic approach to the problem. Margaret and Townsend, who had two brief meetings, when they were hounded by reporters, remained in constant touch by telephone and exchanged scores of letters. But while she continued with her official round of engagements, so often poker faced and unsmiling, behind the scenes the moods of the Queen's sister ranged from deep bitterness to serious depression. This soon became one of the most stressful periods that the Queen and Philip had ever encountered together and the only place where no sign of friction was ever manifested was in the Buckingham Palace nursery where life continued in its usual peaceful and rhythmic pattern.

At first, the Queen Mother, who was gradually beginning to overcome the shock of her husband's death by immersing herself in work – making it clear to everyone that she had no intention of retiring – now found herself in the position of being the main support for Margaret. As a distraction she urged her younger daughter to spend a holiday in the north of Scotland where in the early days of her widowhood she had been shown the isolated and dilapidated sixteenth-century Barrogill Castle, just north of John o'Groats in the bleak but lovely county of Caithness. She was told the castle was soon to be pulled down. 'Pull it down? Never!' she said and bought it for an almost knock-down price with her own personal money, reverting back to its ancient name, the Castle of Mey. She had hoped that Margaret would share the Castle with her but her daughter showed little enthusiasm for restoring the new retreat with its great slate turrets looking out over a magnificent and rugged coastline.

The Queen Mother had accepted an invitation to open

the Rhodes Centenary Exhibition at Bulawayo in Southern Rhodesia before the crisis broke and it had been arranged that they should carry out the engagement together. It was hoped that the change of climate and scenery would relieve some of the tension. Instead Margaret went down with a chill and spent most of the time counting the days to her last opportunity to meet Townsend before his departure to Brussels, planned for the day after their return to London. But Townsend was ordered to the Belgian capital the day before her return and Margaret, infuriated by what she regarded as a deliberate manoeuvre against herself, vented her fury on those who were closest to her in the family. Margaret continued to carry out her engagements, including a tour of the Caribbean but the family situation remained strained. She found solace in a small Georgian house in London's South Street, the home of a man who had been a close friend since childhood; he knew the secret of her love for Townsend long before it ever leaked out and agreed to act as cover for them.

He was Billy Wallace, the son of Captain Euan Wallace, a former Minister of Transport who died in 1941 and whose four elder sons had died in the war. Plagued by liver trouble, Billy was a kind, considerate and unassuming person and someone to whom Margaret was devoted. He kept her secret so well that even his mother, who later married American-born Commander Herbert Agar, a writer and Pulitzer Prize winner, was convinced like so many other people that she would one day become Margaret's mother-in-law. It was Billy who was sure that Margaret and Townsend were ideally suited to one another and urged her to go ahead and marry the Group Captain no matter what the consequences. But Margaret, while she had sympathetic listeners within her own family, people who wanted her to be happy, knew that at the bottom of their hearts all wished Townsend in Timbuctoo. The Queen sought advice from all quarters. Constantly at the back of her mind were the traumatic events of 1936 when her Uncle

David had abdicated for love – of a divorced woman.

When she celebrated her twenty-fifth birthday in August 1955 Margaret, under the terms of the Royal Marriage Act of 1772 which stipulated that members of the Royal Family required the sovereign's permission to marry before the age of twenty-five, was technically free to marry. By then, however, the Royal love affair had become a national issue reaching near-hysterical proportions and there were openly expressed divisions of opinion within both Government and Church ranks. Elizabeth felt helpless and, unable to make up her mind and reach a positive decision, endured agonies of heart-searching in the quietude of her study in Buckingham Palace. The alternatives facing her were to forbid or permit the marriage. Her decision was a compromise: for Margaret and Townsend who had been separated for over two years to see each other again and for her sister to make up her own mind.

It was from Clarence House, in October 1955 and after a ninety minute meeting that Margaret issued a statement that said:

> I would like it to be known that I have decided not to marry Group Captain Townsend. I have been aware that, subject to my renouncing my rights of sucession, it might have been possible for me to contract a civil marriage. But mindful of the Church's teaching that Christian marriage is indissoluble, and conscious of my duty to the Commonwealth, I have resolved to put these considerations before all others ...

And so Margaret remained a fully integrated member of the Royal establishment. Happily for her the crisis had ended without any material loss. Her Royal life-style remained secure. As for Townsend, he returned alone to Brussels, his once brilliant career dashed to pieces.

The Royal Family carried out its duties as usual but it was many months before deep rifts which the affair had created showed any signs of healing. The strain told on the Queen and Margaret and this was the only time in their lives when the love and great warmth that existed between them was tested to the utmost. As it turned out, it was to her elder sister that Margaret finally turned for comfort and consolation and both wept for the other. The rift between Philip and his sister-in-law was so great that it was not until she married Lord Snowdon five years later in 1960 that their relationship gradually began to improve.

Two people who were totally oblivious of the drama that was going on around them were Charles and Anne who celebrated the following Christmas (1955) with a party for forty children at the Palace. They were seven and five years old respectively and for Elizabeth the time had come for her to consider their education; she knew also the wrench it would be for her when they went away to school.

3

The Children at School

DESPITE ALL THEIR well-meaning intentions, their express
desire and determination that their four children,
Charles, Anne, Andrew and Edward should grow up as
far as possible like other children from affluent homes,
the high hopes of Elizabeth and Philip were never to be
fully realised. The quartet were better integrated into a
broader spectrum of society than any previous Royal
generation but despite every effort that was made to
make their schooldays ordinary, it proved impossible for
any of them to even temporarily put their birthright to
one side. Their unfortunate handicap was that everyone
they encountered knew their mother was the Queen and
accordingly reacted in their different ways, often upset-
ting the children or rousing them to anger. Elizabeth and
Philip unwittingly made several elementary mistakes –
Charles, for instance, was acutely embarrassed at school
when he was created Prince of Wales – but they learned
by experience and each child who went away to school
was happier than his (or her) predecessor. The boy who
suffered most during school years was Charles and the
one who actually enjoyed himself most was Edward –
and in between and fitting in with school life far better
than Charles were Anne and Andrew.

As the time came for each child to go away to school,
Elizabeth and Philip could only cross their fingers and

hope for the best, knowing that they were unable to help any of them once they had left the secure and over-protected world of Buckingham Palace. They could only stand by in the wings, hoping that the basic temperament of each child, combined with such training as they had been given at home, would help them to withstand the strange new pressures of boarding school life. Undoubtedly the Royal child who fared worst was Charles. He was often faced with schoolboys – and schoolboys can be merciless in any strata in society – who either studiously ignored him or ragged him to the point of tears. Perhaps because previous male heirs to the throne had experienced such unhappy and difficult childhoods and consequent chequered careers in adulthood, Elizabeth and Philip often seemed over-anxious in their attitude towards their eldest son. Indeed, Elizabeth tended to be over-protective.

Charles's education began when he was five years old and he was put in the hands of a Scottish-born governess, Miss Catherine Peebles, known in the Royal Family as Mispy. She had previously been in charge of Elizabeth's younger cousins, Princess Alexandra and Prince Michael, children of Elizabeth's widowed Greek-born aunt, the Duchess of Kent. Although she had no kindergarten training behind her and had never been to university, Miss Peebles attracted Elizabeth because she was known to be both kind and patient, qualities that needed to be amply demonstrated by anybody coping with Charles: he was not only acutely shy and nervous but was a slow developer and, although no one put it into these precise words, did not seem to be particularly bright. He was slow to learn the basics, learning to write did not come easily and arithmetic baffled him. One of his few schoolroom enthusiasms was to follow the overseas tours his parents made on a large globe installed by Miss Peebles, who thereby showed a real stroke of imagination. For Philip the task of bringing up a son so opposite to him in almost every basic characteristic was a formidable one. In those early days when

Elizabeth and Philip only had two children the forceful and outgoing child of the marriage was Anne, who had all the qualities Philip longed for in a son. Then, as now, Charles relates much more closely to his mother than his father while Anne, although remaining close to her mother, enjoys a powerful bond with her father.

Shortly before his eighth birthday and while continuing his morning lessons with Miss Peebles, Charles became an afternoon-only pupil at Hill House in Knightsbridge, a fashionable London day-school for boys not far from Buckingham Palace. To Elizabeth and Philip this seemed to be a gentle way of easing Charles into the company of other boys of his own age but even when he walked into the main hall of the school in his short grey trousers and grey jacket, his maroon school cap clutched nervously in his right hand, he was ill-at-ease and glanced uncertainly from face to face. For a little boy who had led such a sheltered existence and who had been brought up almost entirely in an adult world, had never gone out alone, never bought a packet of sweets in a shop, never walked along a seaside promenade eating icecream and never, for that matter, handled money, even this minor break from home was traumatic. During his two terms at Hill House and through no fault of his own, he remained too much of an object of curiosity ever to become fully integrated into the school, let alone be accepted as 'just another little boy'.

His behaviour in the classroom was unusual for an eight year old boy: he was desperately anxious to please and except on very rare occasions, always did as he was told. He seldom got into scrapes and never returned home with a black eye, bruises, an ink-spotted jumper or scuffed shoes. Both parents, especially Philip, longed for Charles to show signs of a fighting spirit but as each end of term report was received, they were disappointed. Their son always got top marks for good behaviour. As Philip was frequently away on solo tours in this country and abroad, the people to whom Charles turned to recount his school activities at the end of the day were always women – his mother, his grandmother, his Aunt Margaret and Miss Peebles—all of whom spoiled him to a greater or lesser degree. It was hard for either the Queen or the Queen Mother to hide from Charles their innate sadness that he was in an environment he did not enjoy at all.

Mercifully there was one man who really understood Charles at that time and whom the little boy adored. That person was his great uncle, Lord Mountbatten, born at the turn of the century, who was to have a far greater influence on Charles than probably anyone else. An extraordinary side to Mountbatten was that while with his tough quarter-deck manner he was always impatient for results, he nevertheless had qualities which endeared him to children. He had a remarkable rapport not only with Charles but also with his own grandchildren. He talked to the children as though they were adults and listened to them with infinite patience, playing and chatting with them so easily that the age gap dwindled into nothingness.

Mountbatten, who always described himself as a 'sub Royal' had had a very democratic upbringing himself with his own parents, Prince and Princess Louis of Battenburg. Although they were born in the Victorian age, the Prince and Princess actively encouraged their children to be both seen and heard. Mountbatten grew up in a cultivated home where he and his elder brother George participated in stimulating conversation which ranged over all manner of subjects, from the arts to science; they were treated as equals even when distinguished visitors were present at the dinner table. This same free and easy tradition was continued by Mountbatten when he grew up and had a family and two daughters of his own – Patricia, who married film director Lord Brabourne and had five children; and Pamela who married internationally famous interior decorator David Hicks and had three children. As far as his naval career would allow it, Mountbatten saw as much of his daughters as possible and when he and Lady Mountbatten went on world tours Patricia or

Pamela – often both of them – were with their parents.

Charles's father, Philip, entered Mountbatten's life as an eight-year-old exiled Greek Prince who was handed over by his parents, Prince and Princess Andrew of Greece, then living in Monte-Carlo in the south of France, to be brought up as an English boy. Philip was jointly adopted by Mountbatten and his brother George Milford-Haven, who died from cancer in 1938. The boy divided his time between them when he was not with their remarkable mother Princess Battenburg.

From the beginning there was a great understanding between uncle and nephew and many people believe that among the outstanding achievements of Mountbatten's life was his moulding of Philip. Mountbatten, to his deep regret, had never had a son of his own and in many ways Philip filled the gap in his life. As I have mentioned, Mountbatten was of tremendous aid to Philip in helping him to cope both with the responsibilities which followed upon his entry into the British Royal Family and the problems of creating a place for himself in the totally new and different world he had entered. This was to be followed by an even more remarkable relationship – that which grew up between Mountbatten and his great-nephew Charles.

Staying with his great-uncle on his five-thousand-acre estate at Broadlands, in the heart of the Hampshire countryside, or visiting him at his London home in Wilton Crescent were the great highlights of Charles's childhood. There had never been any sense of age gap between Mountbatten and Charles and as the boy grew older so their respect and love for one another increased, so much so that with the passage of years Philip came to resent their powerful bond which at times seemed to exclude him.

It was Mountbatten who recognised that compared with his father at the same age, Charles was far more vulnerable and it was Mountbatten who, more than anyone else, bolstered his often flagging self-confidence. Few people realised then or now how wide was Mountbatten's appreciation and knowledge of life. He combined a thorough acquaintance with the life of ordinary people under ordinary and extraordinary circumstances with a deep understanding of the importance of Royalty and of the problems it faced. He could be hail-fellow-well-met with Hollywood film stars, trade-union officials or government ministers and at the same time could be depended upon to settle the most abstruse point of court etiquette which, at times, could even baffle members of the Royal Family and their advisers. When Mountbatten was looking after Philip he was dealing with an unknown quantity. Nobody, Mountbatten least of all, knew what Philip would develop into or what his rank in society would be. With Charles it was an entirely different matter.

Mountbatten knew that in helping to shape and encourage Charles, he was dealing with someone who must inevitably one day be King of Great Britain. His great depth of knowledge was always available to Charles who was not slow to seek the help and guidance of a man who meant so much to him then and was to mean even more to him in the future. With all his undoubted devotion to the Throne, Mountbatten could look at the Royal scene with an unclouded vision. He had known Charles's parents since infancy and if there were any parental failings, he knew them and could advise his protégé accordingly. As Charles was continually to find himself running up against problems in his life, the telephone bell often rang in the Mountbatten home and a voice on the other end of the line would say, 'Charles here. Can I come and see you. . . ?'

When he was almost nine years old Elizabeth and Philip after considerable debate and heart-searching decided that it was time for Charles to make a complete break from home. They chose his father's old prep school, Cheam, near Newbury in Berkshire, which had a hundred boys between the ages of eight and fourteen. The family made a private reconnaisance of Cheam before Charles was finally committed to boarding-school life; outwardly Elizabeth, Philip, Charles and Anne appeared to be relaxed but in fact Charles was appalled at the prospect of being left alone among strangers and Anne was in a furious temper because she had been told that the time had not yet come for her to go away to school and she must continue her lessons in Buckingham Palace. There, unlike Charles, she had the benefit of two other children to share her lessons, Susan Babington Smith and Caroline Hamilton, daughters of friends of Elizabeth.

Charles was taken to Cheam on his first day by his parents, and although Elizabeth managed a tight smile she was nevertheless just as distressed as her son at the moment of parting. Headmaster Peter Beck had been asked to treat Charles like any other boy and to his credit, he did so. He doled out punishment when necessary and Charles was caned at least twice on the bottom for ragging and fighting with another boy. Charles was to spend four-and-a-half years at Cheam but despite all the efforts that were made to make him feel at home, he loathed boarding-school life, especially its lack of privacy which meant so much to him. He longed for the holidays but protestations that he did not want to go back to Cheam fell on deaf ears. His parents really had no alternative. Both felt it would be a retrograde step if they weakened and gave way and allowed him to be tutored at Buckingham Palace. Somehow or other Charles had to learn to stick it out and try and win through on his own.

Unwittingly and at a time when he was desperately trying to assert himself, Elizabeth and Philip did little to help him overcome shyness by their timing of his creation as Prince of Wales. The announcement was made at the closing of the Empire and Commonwealth Games at Cardiff Arms Park and because Elizabeth had sinusitis, Philip took her place and her tape-recorded message, 'I intend to create my son Charles Prince of Wales today', was played. At Cheam, Charles and a small group of boys were invited into the headmaster's study to watch the ceremony on television. Only Charles and the headmaster knew what was to come and when the schoolboys heard the announcement they all cheered a red faced and embarrassed schoolfellow. Nothing did more to emphasise the gulf that separated Charles from the rest of the school.

As Charles headed towards his fourteenth birthday Elizabeth and Philip paid private visits to various public schools trying to make up their minds which establishment might help in the task of bringing out their son and giving him a chance of greater happiness. Elizabeth was in favour of Eton and went to considerable lengths to point out that it had the special advantage of being on the doorstep – when the sun is in the west, the Round Tower of Windsor Castle casts a shadow over the college. More than anything, the closeness to home appealed to Charles but his father made his own views quite clear: Gordonstoun, his old school in the north of Scotland, would be the right toughening-up place for his somewhat dreamy son.

All the pros and cons were put to Charles about the various choices open to him and he was allowed to make up his own mind about the next major move in his life. The very obvious preference of his father swayed his final decision: hesitant as always, Charles settled for Gordonstoun. Some of his early tutors and teachers are convinced that the spartan school, with its cult of physical fitness and its intensive spirit of competition, was the last school in the world to which he should have been sent. Eton, where Charles would have been among his peers and so more at home, would have allowed him to develop at a pace that was more leisurely and suited to his reserved and sensitive nature.

Other Royal children have been to Eton with excellent results – Prince William of Gloucester loved his years there. The Earl of Harewood, now director of the Royal Opera Company; his brother, the Hon. Gerald Lascelles; the Duke of Gloucester; the Duke of Kent and his two sons, George, Earl of St Andrews and Lord Nicholas Windsor; and Princess Alexandra's son, James Ogilvy;

all attended the school and other Etonians did not regard them as oddities and all did well and established firm and lasting friendships there.

Charles was not a namby-pamby boy. Although rather plump, he was energetic in his own way and not at all a bad swimmer. He learned to shoot the hard way – out on the moors and at the clay pigeon pits at Balmoral and Sandringham and he had a mind of his own. Philip desperately tried to get his son to learn to box but Charles refused point blank, saying that he had no interest in pugilism. No one can say that he was frightened of Philip but he deferred to him. He had been unhappy when he went to Cheam but no one had prepared him for Gordonstoun, which was to prove even worse when he went there in the summer (May) of 1962. His day began at seven o'clock with a four hundred yard run in all weathers followed by a cold shower, making his bed and tidying his locker by 7.30. In order to get everything done in thirty minutes it meant that every boy had to run the four hundred yards like fury.

One of his shared chores was to take turns waiting at table and he had to gulp his food down very fast in order to be ready to clear away the dishes for the next course. The tough Gordonstoun daily schedule, which placed great emphasis on open-air activities such as sailing, rock climbing, mountain-rescue practice and other back-breaking expeditions, including going out once a term with a rucksack on his back and covering fifty miles in a day, developed his muscles and body but did little to bring him closer to other boys. Once again because of his unique position he often found himself the odd man out. Coming up against taunts and general unpleasantness from boys who were his senior, all increased his loneliness and sense of isolation.

Regulation school clothes did not particularly appeal to him: he had a hooded duffle coat: one set of dungarees, bibbed and pocketed, striped pyjamas and a striped dressing gown; pocketless navy blue flannel shorts; two navy blue sweaters; four blue grey shirts worn with an open neck. At Gordonstoun there was no badge, no blazer, no scarf – and no old school tie. Boys at this spartan school in the chilly isolation of North Scotland slept in huts with unpainted walls, bare floorboards, and iron bedsteads; Windmill Lodge where the heir to the throne was put was no exception.

Several times Charles pleaded to be moved to another school but again his pleas fell on deaf ears; he would have to steel himself and remain at Gordonstoun. There was a conflict of parental opinion but in the end Philip's view that Gordonstoun would 'make a man' of Charles was accepted by Elizabeth. Charles was allowed no special privileges and much of his time was spent counting the years ahead to the time when this so-called character-building part of his education would come to an end. Some boys did not possess enough stamina to stick the course at Gordonstoun and some of them, like the Marquis of Tavistock, heir to the Duke of Bedford, ran away. Tavistock did this twice and later when he recalled his life at Gordonstoun observed, 'I hated my two years there.'

Gordonstoun accepted boys from very different backgrounds and sons of farmers and fishermen mixed with sons of the famous. If any reprimand was to be given, it was given by the head boy, Dugal Mackenzie, whose father had a joiner-contractor's business in Ross-shire. At school Charles was never more than a very average scholar. He never mastered mathematics but he showed a strong interest in the arts. He became an adept potter and his early efforts, which included making a white and blue marmalade pot, a dark brown jug and a small green mug, were very good.

The one area in which he was well ahead of his fellow pupils was in his general knowledge and wider appreciation of the facets of the world outside the school. Those long talks and play with Mountbatten were bearing their fruit then as they were to bear fruit in extraordinary profusion later in his life. Charles, the schoolboy, was introverted and withdrawn and soon tagged a loner – terrible handicaps to anyone in his position; that they have been so magnificently overcome is not only a tribute to Charles's courage and will-power but also to the untiring devotion of Mountbatten.

While there were doubts about the progress Charles was making, there were none about his sister Anne, who at thirteen and much to her relief, was sent to the famous girls school, Benenden, 380 feet above sea level on one of the highest points on the Kentish Weald. When she arrived on her first day, driving with Elizabeth to the great Victorian house with its stone inglenook fireplaces, oak panelling and wistaria-covered red brickwork, the entire staff and all the pupils were gathered in groups under oak trees to welcome them. In sharp contrast to her brother, she did not find this experience either embarrassing or unnerving.

Elizabeth was greeted by the easy mannered headmistress, forty-eight-year-old Miss E. B. Clarke, MA, a local Justice of the Peace, who took Elizabeth to the first floor of the school to see the Magnolia dormitory where her daughter was to sleep – named Magnolia after a great tree which climbed the walls beneath. The dormitory looked out across the school terrace over six hundred acres of parkland and a three-acre lake full of carp. There was a blaze of azaleas and rhododendrons and several rare trees like the *Eucryfia Cordifolia* which bloomed with white flowers only in August.

Elizabeth was impressed. Like Charles, Anne never came to terms with the lack of privacy in a world she shared with three hundred other girls but she adapted far better to school life and made lasting friendships with several girls drawn from well-to-do parents. One of them, Miss Victoria Legge-Bourke, is now one of her four ladies-in-waiting. Some of the other girls she met at school have remained friends throughout the years and still see her from time to time.

From the beginning of her life at Benenden, Anne, who was made of much sterner stuff than her brother, occasionally came up against sycophants and the manner in which she rejected these approaches often made her appear to be a more aggressive child than she really was. The way was made easier for Anne because girls in the school had previously been accustomed to Royalty joining them in their studies. Girls had previously accepted Princess Benedikte of Denmark and joining the school with Anne were Princess Mariasina, thirteen, and her sister, Princess Sihin, from Ethiopia and Princess Masma, sister of Harrow-educated King Hussein of Jordan. Benenden had a strong academic tradition and was one of the few schools in the country which ran a special course for girls who wanted to take up medicine as a career.

From the beginning Anne was prepared to make a stand if she came up against problems; not for her were there lonely nights filled with a longing for home and things known, understood and familiar. She adopted an 'anything you can do I can do better' attitude and regarded school life as a challenge, determined that unlike her brother, no one was going to hurt her or take the mickey out of her – and no one ever did. For a girl with her unusual background she settled down well and soon adapted to the school routine. She did not take the common entrance examination but 'evidence was furnished of her academic standard'.

Like the other girls, she wore a navy blue tunic, a white blouse and an orange tie and belt. For Church on Sunday she wore a dark blue Harris tweed suit. Benenden followed much the same daily pattern as other girls boarding schools of similar standing. Anne got up every morning at seven o'clock and breakfasted in the communal dining room forty minutes later. She made her own bed and attended morning prayers shortly before nine o'clock. Basically her school record was undistinguished but happy. Benenden allowed girls to develop at their own academic pace and it became clear very early in her school career that Anne, inclined to laziness, would have to stretch herself to the maximum if she was going to get to the necessary academic standard to qualify for a University.

Anne was fortunate that she found her all-absorbing passion early in life. It was horses. With her brother she learned to ride at a very early age by sitting in a cradle saddle with a groom leading the horse. Charles never took to horseriding willingly as a little boy and had to be accompanied by both a groom and his nanny. Anne had no problems and when she was very young received great encouragement from her Aunt Margaret, who in the 1950s was regarded as the best horsewoman in the Royal Family, having a decided edge even on Elizabeth. Anne had her early lessons from her mother and later went to a riding school near Windsor run by Sybil Smith. At Benenden she had regular riding lessons at Moat House from Mrs Cherie Hatton-Hall, who soon recognised her potential as a possible future horsewoman of distinction. It was in her first year at Benenden that Anne won the Garth Pony Club silver cup as the best rider under thirteen.

Charles and Anne were well established in their school careers when Elizabeth's 'second family', Andrew, born in February 1960 to be followed by Edward in March 1964, were beginning to find their feet. And life in the second nursery generation was to prove far more relaxed than it had been a decade earlier for Charles and Anne. For one thing both parents had matured, even if it was in different ways, and it has also to be borne in mind that Elizabeth and Philip felt that a far greater responsibility rested on them and on their first two children because in Charles and Anne they were dealing with an heir to the throne and a girl who, if anything happened to Charles and no further children arrived, would herself become heir. That was a burden which weighed heavily on the parents and reflected itself to some extent in their attitude to their two elder children.

Over the years there had been a tremendous change in the behaviour and personality of Philip. In the beginning he had not found it easy to fill the role of a man whose function in life had seemed to be to walk, hands behind his back, a few steps behind his wife. The rough edges had shown themselves all too obviously and that they were eventually toned down with the emergence of a new Philip, we owe to the unswerving work and dedication of Elizabeth who was very much aware of the problems her consort was facing. If she had been his guide and mentor in the early stages he, in his turn, when he had found a role which took him all over the world and acquainted him with the problems of many people, was able to guide and advise his wife in her dealings with these problems. Philip still retains naval characteristics. He has no patience with fools and has always sought the quickest way to the heart of a problem.

It was with the arrival of her two youngest children that Elizabeth became engrossed in family life in a way that had never been possible before. The burden on her had grown no less with the passage of the years – in many ways it had increased – but Elizabeth was now far more experienced and much better fitted to cope with affairs of State. In her early days on the throne everything was new to her, including the terrific responsibility which she felt rested on her shoulders and her entourage could almost feel the tenseness with which she went about her business. There was a time, indeed, when those close to her grew very worried about the demands that were being made on her health. She began to look tired and drawn and was sometimes confined to bed with sinusitis. When first Andrew and then Edward arrived on the Royal scene, Elizabeth, still in her thirties, had learned to relax more and this relaxation was reflected in the children.

From early days Andrew's basic make-up was quite different to that of Charles: he had a happy nature and was not handicapped by shyness. On the contrary, he had a strong streak of independence which caused ructions in the Buckingham Palace nursery. The schoolroom was reopened when he was five and this time governess Catherine Peebles found herself in charge of a real Royal handful. Andrew was brimful of excitement when it was decided to send him to Heatherdown, a prep school near Windsor where he was a lively, cheerful and outgoing boy and soon had the reputation for being one of the rowdier pupils. There was nothing introspective about Andrew and the way in which he accepted his role as a member of the Royal Family proved to Elizabeth and Philip that it was possible for a child with a Palace background to integrate into a mixed society – provided the child had the right make-up.

In turn, his younger brother Edward was sent as a day boy to Gibbs, a preparatory school in Kensington. He was a much quieter boy but also settled in easily with the other boys. By the time Andrew went to Gordonstoun, it was no longer the grim spartan school that Charles had known. With the arrival of a new headmaster, Mr John Kempe, cold showers were no longer obligatory and the school boasted central heating and a swimming pool. Other old disciplines were relaxed and there was a much closer relationship between master and pupil

The school authorities decided that Gordonstoun should become co-educational and before Andrew went there thirty girls had already been accepted and by the time he left there were more than ninety pupils of the opposite sex. This dramatic change in school policy meant that from his early teens Andrew developed an easy relationship with girls: with his fair hair, deep blue eyes and all the charm inherited from his father, his conquests became legion. The girls he met at Gordonstoun sometimes invited him home to meet their parents and whenever he made such a visit he made quite an impact on parents.

One middle-class mother who recalled Andrew's visits to her Sussex home was convinced that he had brought her daughter 'out of her shell'. The way she put it to me was like this:

She used to get terribly anxious about exam results and her father and I got quite worried about her. She went around with Andrew for quite a time and somehow he seemed to jolly her out of the doldrums. He did her the world of good. He was always useful and helpful when he was about the house and we got so used to him being with us that his special connections never troubled any of us. He was just another nice boy with a huge appetite and good manners.

It was this break-away from the closely-knit circle of courtiers and their families, which Andrew achieved totally on his own, that pleased Elizabeth and Philip so much. They could never close their eyes to the fact that if anything ever happened to Charles, then Andrew would step into his shoes. For this reason they had to encourage to only a slightly lesser degree in Andrew those qualities which were needed by Charles. It was almost like a trainer running two horses for the Derby knowing that only one could win.

Fortunately they were greatly helped in this by Andrew's own bright personality. He seemed to think that it was a huge joke that he was, as it were, second starter for the Throne and ribbed Charles openly about this when other more serious people would only talk about the dread possibility in whispers. Andrew would openly rag his elder brother about their respective roles and warn him to watch out and not break his neck. In later years when Charles was taking considerable risks, this wasn't to prove very funny. There was an occasion when a ball grazed his chin when he was playing polo – a ball that might easily have killed him. Twice Charles was to be involved in forced helicopter landings and there were minor incidents when he was on an Army Commando course. Through no fault of his own Charles had three near misses when he was driving his own car. He had serious falls from horses when he was steeplechasing but fortunately he got off lightly and only once had to have six stitches on his cheek.

Andrew certainly experienced a broader education than Charles ever had at Gordonstoun. At fourteen he spent three weeks as an exchange pupil to a Jesuit College near Toulouse, in the south-east of France, and stayed with a doctor and his family in one of the suburbs of Toulouse. Here again he fitted in very well and was able to share in all the French family's normal activities without ever being recognised. He used the name 'Andrew Edwards' and when asked about his background he duly informed the questioner, 'My father is a gentleman farmer and my mother doesn't work.'

Academically Andrew was always more ahead than Charles had been at the same age and in the field of sports and athletics he had an edge on his brother. But there was another side to Andrew that was not at all like his brother: he was impulsive and had a tendency to arrogance. Being the son of Elizabeth was no handicap to this son: he revelled in it. He liked showing off and this was one of the reasons why he was happy to join in amateur dramatics. When he was seventeen he did a good job when he took on the title role in *Macbeth* which meant working hard at memorising the long part. This was something else that pleased Elizabeth since so far as the Royal Family are concerned amateur dramatics are not just an idle pastime: they are a positive help in equipping a Royal child for future public duties. The need for a degree of acting skill by members of the Royal Family has never been greater than it is today and those members who come over best on television are people like Charles who enjoyed acting in school plays. On school stages they learned the art of timing as well as developing the art of making their voices heard in the back of a hall.

Less extrovert than Andrew but more academically ambitious than Charles was Elizabeth's youngest child, Edward. He had the good fortune to grow up more distanced from the Throne than his elder brothers – he was third in line of succession – and so suffered less from both public interest and speculation. He had his fair share of rough and tumbles at his prep school but by the time it was his turn to go to Gordonstoun the rarity value of having one of Elizabeth's sons at the school had begun to diminish. A quiet and studious boy, more prone to moods than his elder brothers, he found his own level with more serious-minded fellow pupils and had the added advantage of having Andrew to support him when they were both at Gordonstoun during the early part of Edward's school career.

While Andrew and Edward still had to face the problems of school, the maturing Charles and Anne were facing the problems of adolescence – problems which were to be accentuated for both of them because this was now the swinging sixties and the birth of the so-called permissive age. Everything in society was changing, the old standards did not seem to obtain and the new freedom which youth was demanding made it even more difficult for the teenage Royals to find their feet. At sixteen Charles appeared to be a somewhat vague-looking youth, rather gauche and very much an unknown quantity: his sister Anne had begun experimenting with trendy clothes. Despite a certain sophistication which developed as a result of their unusual background at home where they met world statesmen and conversed with exceptional men and women from all walks of life, the guests of their parents, they nevertheless remained extremely naïve about many of the more ordinary but important aspects of growing up.

One of their great problems was that they had discovered from bitter personal experience that any minor escapade in which they had been involved had often been blown up out of proportion when it was related to the public; therefore, as teenagers they had become extremely wary and disinclined to take anyone into their confidence unless it was a trusted relative. Fortunately for them there was a woman of wide-ranging talent to whom they could safely turn with their difficulties and be sure of receiving wise guidance.

She was their grandmother the Queen Mother, to whom Charles, and to a slightly lesser degree Anne, always unburdened themselves, knowing that in her they had both a patient and understanding listener. The time of year when they could talk for hours was during the family summer holiday at Balmoral when their grandmother could always be found at Birkhall, her eighteenth-century country house built in white stone lying slightly north of the River Muick and about eight miles from Balmoral Castle.

4

A Family Holiday

THE EXODUS FROM Buckingham Palace to Balmoral is planned with almost military precision. Titularly in charge of the move is the Lord Chamberlain, Lord Maclean, the most senior member of the Queen's Household. His post is not hereditary and Maclean, a life peer who has held the job since 1971, is a great personal friend of Elizabeth. They have many common interests: he is also a Scottish landowner whose home is on the Isle of Mull and both he and the Queen are extremely knowledgeable not only about Scottish estate management but also about Highland cattle. It is from his offices in St James's Palace, only a short walk from Buckingham Palace, that Lord Maclean controls the vast computerised Household indexes without which the modern move to Balmoral would be very difficult.

His right hand aide is Lieutenant Colonel Sir Eric Penn, a retired Grenadier Guardsman who holds the title of Comptroller of the Lord Chamberlain's Office, and between the two of them, with the aid of experienced Household officials, they are responsible for the transfer of all vital papers, documents and secret hot-line arrangements from the moment the red and gold Royal standard is lowered over Buckingham Palace. Big cases of Royal personal paraphernalia go north by train from Paddington Station and by road and these contain many items which could be considered strange if one did not know the multiplicity of hobbies and interests of various members of the Royal Family.

For many people do not realise that there are at least three Royal artists, Philip, Charles and Andrew, who have all had their works exhibited, and especially on holiday love the opportunity to paint in watercolours; this means that the paraphernalia of their hobbies all add to the Royal luggage sent to Scotland. There are also favourite dog baskets and blankets and much-gnawed favourite toys. Even Royal horses go to Balmoral for the Royal holiday; they go from Windsor Castle along with saddles, the inevitable fishing rods and the unlikely bicycles.

One thing which, not surprisingly, escapes public knowledge is the sombre fact that wherever Elizabeth or a member of the Royal Family travels they must always have near at hand suitable mourning apparel in case a death should occur. This may be of any famous personage in the world and would involve the English court in a period of official mourning. Men must always have a black tie and a black armband with them.

Packing for the Royals is a meticulous business and has been developed into a fine art as a result of many years of travelling the globe. Cases which contain Elizabeth's clothes are numbered in special order and packed in such a way that when she is going away for days or weeks at a time there is never a last-minute search for a particular item. Contents of cases are itemised, neatly recorded and indexed so that a particular pair of shoes or a special dress can be ready in minutes if necessary.

Lightweight items such as blouses and underwear are carefully laid between thick sheets of tissue paper and folded with such expertise that despite long journeys there are never signs of creases. For her two-month stay at Balmoral the amount of holiday wear the Queen takes north, while it is considerable, is by no means as vast, say, as when she goes on a foreign tour and has to change clothing three or four times a day. A great amount of everyday wear like tartan skirts, twin sets, summer dresses, sturdy shoes, wellington boots, slippers, jackets and mackintoshes are a part of a wardrobe that remains permanently in her Scottish home.

The one time in the year when the Queen shows some sign of flagging and the lines of middle age seem more marked than usual, often making her look drawn and tired, is towards the end of July when she has almost completed the long, taxing and tiring round of spring and summer engagements. She is not a sun worshipper, hot climates drain her energy and even normal warm English summer days take an extra toll; there are days when she is often on her feet for long spells at the handshaking open-air receptions and garden parties which are all part of her summer ritual. As the days of high summer draw nearer and the end of July is in sight, an air of combined excitement and impatience is felt at Buckingham Palace.

Great trunks and cases are brought up from basement store rooms, filing cabinets are locked and the Palace Housekeeper, who possesses a master key, waits for the message that the Queen's twelve-roomed private apartments in the north wing overlooking a great expanse of green lawn are to be closed. This is the longed-for moment every year in early August which officially launches the Queen's summer holiday when she begins the first leg of her journey north to Balmoral, boarding the Royal yacht *Britannia* which, after various informal calls in the Western Isles, finally docks in Aberdeen.

The journey on the Royal yacht, an extremely comfortable but not ornate ship, is the very first chance to relax on the holiday and since none of the family are ever seriously seasick, there are no qualms if bad weather is forecast. After dinner on the first day everyone makes for the cinema, a highly popular feature of life on the *Britannia* during the holiday trip. Once, while the Royal party were seated in the small cinema, there was a sudden heavy lurch and Elizabeth, Philip and three other members of the family in the front keeled over like a falling row of cards. Amidst much laughter the Royal party on the floor sorted themselves out and Elizabeth declared, 'This is funnier than the film.'

The journey over, the much-longed-for holiday at Balmoral begins. It is at this not so very old baronial castle, with its pale granite turrets framed by dark pinewoods, that the Queen, for about eight weeks, enjoys more personal freedom than at any other time in the year. Balmoral stands in her privately owned Scottish estate set in the heart of the heather-clad hills and the rugged mountains of Deeside in Aberdeenshire. It covers more than 40,000 acres and embraces some of the most spectacular scenery in the Highlands. Elizabeth, for two glorious months, is not only a sovereign but laird as well and comes into her own as a country landowner.

There are always about thirty people staying in the house, made up of members of her family and most intimate friends. It is traditional for the Prime Minister of the day to spend a weekend with Elizabeth at Balmoral and there may be rare occasions when members of the Privy Council have to travel on official business but Elizabeth sticks inflexibly to her rule: only under very exceptional circumstances are visiting dignitaries ever allowed to drive through the great iron gates and intrude on a holiday life-style that has hardly changed with the passage of the years.

Elizabeth is always very happy at her other private estate, Sandringham, the vast mansion south of the Wash in Norfolk, but if she had to make a choice it would be Balmoral she would select as her permanent residence. As she grows older and gradually hands over more and more responsibility to Prince Charles, it is here in the Scottish Highlands that she will spend more and more of her time. Elizabeth's love affair with the Highlands, because that is essentially what it is, has been lifelong, just as it was for much of her great-great-grandmother's life.

Queen Victoria first saw Balmoral in September 1848

when the Royal doctor advised her to enjoy some bracing air: as a result her husband, Prince Albert, bought a four year lease on Balmoral House, then a small country mansion. When the lease expired Albert bought the Balmoral estate for £32,000, had the old house demolished and in its place designed and built the present castle. He gave it a fake Scottish baronial style complete with keep, towers and turrets. Many Victorian critics dismissed it as eccentric and architecturally too reminiscent of the sort of German schlosses Albert had once known in Germany. But these remarks in no way upset Victoria and her husband for whom Balmoral remained their 'dear paradise'. Victoria's first impressions of Balmoral, which she recorded in her diary, were to stay with her all her life. She wrote: 'It was so calm and solitary, it did one good as one gazed around, and the pure mountain air was most refreshing. All seemed to breathe freedom and peace and make one forget the world and its sad turmoils.'

It is essentially this same freedom that means so much to Elizabeth today. More than a hundred years later she finds the peace on this vast estate for which she constantly yearns but so seldom finds. Elizabeth on these visits is, of course, retreading ground which has been so familiar to her for so many years. She first knew Balmoral when she was a few months old and went there when her grandfather, George V, was in summer residence. This stern King who had very little sense of humour and never really liked children and simply loathed babies, was completely captivated by his first granddaughter, Elizabeth, and was sometimes even known to unbend enough to push her in her pram.

Far from the 'big house' Elizabeth walks for hours on end with dogs at her heels and quite alone. This sort of isolation cannot be repeated for her anywhere else in the same way, not even at Sandringham. She really is, for once, almost as free as the air, pausing to stop and talk with woodmen, foresters or whoever else she may accidentally bump into on the estate. Then again, relaxation comes more easily at Balmoral since there is an easier acceptance of her presence: estate workers and their families are less in awe of her and this is one of the reasons why so many Royal servants have, over the years, been recruited at Balmoral.

It is surprising just how many Royal servants who hold down jobs as personal servants and meet Elizabeth at an intimate level are of Scottish origin: many of them came from small Scottish communities and entered Royal service by spotting a short advertisement for domestic staff inserted in Scottish newspapers and guardedly stating 'Housemaid wanted for large country residence'.

It is only in comparatively recent years that servants as well as members of the Royal Family have enjoyed real comfort at Balmoral. Edward VII referred to it as 'a Highland barn with a thousand draughts' and it remained a basically cold and chilly house until shortly after the Second World War when George VI and the Queen Mother made the first really serious attempt to modernise the house by improving the long-out-of-date kitchens with their stone-flagged floors and old-fashioned ranges. They installed hand-basins in bedrooms which still had the old-fashioned basin and jug washstands that had been in use since Victoria's day.

To the joy of the family modern bathrooms were put in, an improvement which meant a great deal to Elizabeth especially when she compared it to Windsor Castle, then an extremely uncomfortable place where even in the Private Apartments she had no running water in her room and had to use a hand-basin that was kept in a cabinet. When at last she had a bathroom of her own at Windsor, one that she was to use for many years, it was so small and poky that she had to climb into the bath from the back.

Although George VI and the Queen Mother started modernising Balmoral no dramatic structural changes were made and as soon as you cross its threshold and enter the hall with its magnificent and sweeping stairway, you are at once conscious of its Royal and Victorian past. On your right on a small table is a guest book bound in red leather which since Victoria's time has annually recorded the arrival of Prime Ministers and such dignitaries who for official reasons have been allowed to visit Balmoral. At the foot of the great stairs there stands a life-size white marble statue of Prince Albert complete with dog and gun. This statue has not always been regarded with great reverence by younger members of the family and it is not unknown for him to be found sporting a bowler hat. No monarch since Victoria, and this includes Elizabeth, has ever seen fit to change the numerous downstairs rooms with their tartan-clad walls and original Lanseers.

When the Prime Minister of the day makes the annual visit to Balmoral they discover a new Elizabeth, a warm and welcoming hostess who goes out of her way to see that they too enter into the full swing of outdoor activities. Nevertheless, Sovereign and Head of Government still address each other as 'Prime Minister' and 'Ma'am'. Away from London pressures and with the Prime Minister entering into the holiday spirit of Balmoral, monarch and senior minister can learn much about each other that never emerges at their regular weekly meetings which, if they are both in London, are held every Tuesday evening shortly after six o'clock at Buckingham Palace.

In her dealings with her Prime Ministers – and Mrs Thatcher is the eighth of her reign – Elizabeth is believed to have been deferential to the wider experience of Sir Winston Churchill and Anthony Eden; charmed by the old-world courtesy of Harold Macmillan and thoroughly at ease with Sir Alec Douglas-Home. She also got on extremely well with Harold Wilson but was less at ease with Edward Heath.

Her relations with James Callaghan seem to have been cordial but it is generally accepted that the Premier with whom she has relaxed most at Balmoral is Mrs Thatcher, her husband Denis being among the few guests to enjoy the Balmoral golf course. This sport simply does not interest the Queen and her family. Prime Ministers and their spouses visiting Balmoral for the first time are always cheerfully told by Elizabeth, 'I'm afraid there are rather a lot of dogs.' And at some point in the day they may bump into her, with a headscarf over her head and obviously pre-occupied, carrying bowls of chopped meat for the corgis and labradors who are constantly at her heels, both outside and inside the house.

For Charles and Anne, Balmoral was always a place of sheer enchantment, especially during their teenage years when they were allowed to stay up late for dinner and enjoy the parties. A certain amount of school holiday work had to be done but for the most part their days were spent joining in all the outdoor activities with the rest of the family – swimming, barbecues, riding, and fishing being the most popular. But Elizabeth has always taken the attitude that young children should stick to regular nursery routines, eating at their proper times and always being tucked up at their usual time.

Not until a Royal child was twelve was he or she allowed in the Balmoral dining room for dinner, and then only on certain nights of the week. One thing Elizabeth also insisted upon was that a growing child, after an exciting day on the estate, should never get overtired by being allowed to stay up too late. Charles and Anne never tried to push their luck since they knew there were no exceptions to this rule. During their teenage days at boarding school, the summer holidays were the longest period in the year which Charles and Anne spent continuously with their parents whom they addressed, as they still do, as 'Mummy' and 'Papa'.

What really makes Balmoral a joy for Elizabeth is not so much the house as its setting – the heather-covered hills which lead beyond to the high ground of the Gelder Burn culminating in the rugged peak of Lochnagar rising to a height of 3,786 feet with, most of the year, its mantle of snow. This peak gave its name to Prince Charles's best-selling fairy story, *The Old Man of Lochnagar* which he wrote for his brothers, Andrew and Edward, when they were little boys. The Balmoral estate is so huge that Elizabeth can escape from the big house into a totally different atmosphere and one of utter informality at any time she chooses; tucked away on the estate are remote old shooting lodges and cottages which she can use when she wishes and to which she sometimes disappears with Philip and a few friends.

Her favourite hideaway is 'The Glassault' beside Loch Muick, an isolated cottage lost in the heart of woods and moorland and first enjoyed by Queen Victoria. Here, without servants to fuss or bother them, she and Philip have barbecue parties, taking it in turns to share the task of cooking the food sent up in hampers from the 'big house'. These isolated cottages on the estate are only very sketchily furnished and on chilly days when it is really too cold to eat on the moors, a wood fire is lit and the party eat indoors. Water is carried from a nearby burn and Elizabeth, always a stickler for orderliness, makes sure that everything is always tidied up and the floors swept carefully before the Land Rovers set off again for the castle and the Queen Mother's residence, Birkhall. Only Elizabeth's closest intimates ever share the pleasures of The Glassault but even here, when there is such an easy and intimate relationship, Elizabeth still remains the living embodiment of sovereignty and no one, not even childhood friends, would ever make the serious mistake of being over-familiar.

It is true to say that even the most fabulous hotel in the world could not offer the unique enchantment and variety of fun that can be had at Balmoral during the summer months and yet there are friends of Elizabeth who travel north to join her with more than a little apprehension in their hearts. No one can set off for a holiday at Balmoral with the notion that it is going to be a summer break when he or she can sometimes sit back, have a snooze and put their feet up. On the contrary, once Elizabeth has got over her initial fatigue – and this usually takes five or six days – then life at the Castle really is very hectic. Elizabeth is the only person at the Castle who has breakfast in bed but even then she is up most mornings by eight o'clock and seldom if ever goes to bed until well after midnight. Life is so active that visitors, young and old, simply tumble into their beds at night utterly exhausted.

The day begins when guests help themselves to a hearty breakfast from an array of silver dishes from sideboards around the dining room offering traditional fare of eggs, bacon, sausages, kippers; there are deliciously mingled smells of freshly ground coffee (tea for those who want it) and a wide variety of home-made Scottish bread. Before he married Lady Diana Spencer and lived in his three-roomed Private Apartments in Buckingham Palace Prince Charles always preferred to eat alone – but never when he was at Balmoral. He has always had 'crazes' for breakfast dishes and after one foreign tour, for example, he developed a passion for ugli fruit but this fad, to the relief of his staff, soon faded. Prince Charles has spells when he refuses tea or coffe and will only settle for fruit juices.

Even at the breakfast hour at Balmoral conversation is lively with caustic and ribald remarks, often coming from Philip about some item of news he has heard on the radio or read in a paper, with everyone joining in. No matter what the weather is like, and Balmoral is notorious for heavy mists, when the Queen finishes her correspondence and morning State papers she is out and about, usually around 10.00am, and will, if the mood takes her, invite anyone she chances to meet in a corridor or a hall to join her in a walk which often lasts a good two hours. Over the years a number of out-of-condition guests have had their legs sorely tested trying to keep up with Elizabeth's spanking pace. Sometimes she goes by Land Rover to the starting point. She is a fast and sure driver behind the wheel and with six or more labradors in the back she will call out, 'Anyone coming with me?'

One of the great outdoor joys for Elizabeth is a Balmoral picnic, a quite different affair from the intimate parties at The Glassault, and which she plans herself down to the last detail. She chooses one of her favourite places, somewhere in the hills or lower ranges of the mountains, and everyone who is staying in the Castle sets off by Land Rover in casual clothes, some of their outfits looking as though they have seen better days. The food, crockery and cutlery are packed in hampers, taken to the picnic point by Land Rover and from then on Elizabeth and her family and friends are left quite alone without a servant in sight. Elizabeth, always in a skirt and never in trousers and always wearing her familiar three strings of pearls, takes complete charge of the picnic and not only opens all the hampers but serves everyone herself. She always gives huge helpings and no sooner has someone got an empty plate than she goes over to them saying, 'And now for seconds. . .'

The Royal picnickers, sitting on rugs, eat off plates resting on their knees and tuck into a splendid feast which offers game pies, pork pies, mutton 'puddies' (a Balmoral lamb speciality) various sorts of cold meats and home-made pickles. No hard spirits are offered but there is an ample supply of bottled beer and soft drinks. There is always plenty of fresh fruit and cheese but the sweet that always tempts regulars to Balmoral is made from an old Scottish recipe and tastes very much like cold Christmas pudding made with beer.

Elizabeth is a meticulous person and after a picnic she conducts 'tidying up' in an almost schoolmistressy sort of way. She personally puts everything back into its proper place in the hampers and that includes anything that has not been eaten. No food is ever wasted: in this she is like every economical housewife – leftovers can be depended on to turn up next day in another form. Meat remnants, for example, make their appearance in shepherds pie or rissoles. The great complaint – if it is a complaint! – among Elizabeth's friends is that despite the almost continual exercise in one form or another, they always find they have put on weight at the end of a stay at Balmoral and they blame this on the food.

97

Cold weather never stops a picnic and Royal guests with quite minimal appetites find they are more than easily persuaded by Elizabeth to tuck in. Curiously, Elizabeth and her family are never put off by cold winds: they are all an extremely hardy lot. The Queen Mother, even though she is in her 'eighties' almost relishes a chilly day. When she is in London before the summer holiday she enjoys lunching in her garden at Clarence House and often when there is a chilly wind blowing, she will provide stoles for her luncheon guests but refuse one for herself. A man who had lunched with the Queen Mother and two ladies-in-waiting in the garden at Clarence House once found that although he had a suit on he was quite cold but the Queen Mother in a silk dress and big picture hat seemed quite oblivious to the weather. She is just as unperturbed about the climate at Balmoral although she will sometimes settle for a much worn mac and a floppy rain hat.

The start of the grouse season brings with it more great outdoor activity, shooting sorties taking on the character of a military manoeuvre with guests piling into shooting breaks and Land Rovers – always seemingly full of labradors – and vanloads of beaters. After hours in the open air guests go back to Balmoral with less than an hour to change for dinner. From that point on, one item of food appears constantly on the Balmoral menu after the 'Glorious Twelfth' when everyone eats grouse so often that in the end their appetite for the bird begins to pall: there is grouse pâté, grouse pie, cold grouse, hot grouse – and guests are always given a pair of grouse to take home with them at the end of the holiday. While a quantity of grouse goes to Smithfield Market a lot is sent for distribution to Scottish hospitals. Apart from grouse a gastronomic delight of Balmoral is the dessert of raspberries and strawberries which grow prolifically on the estate.

One agreeable aspect of a Balmoral holiday for Elizabeth is that there is a constant change of faces. Most guests stay for about ten days and it is the regular change of personalities that she enjoys with everyone knowing each other so well that there is never any need for introductions. Guest accommodation is in a private wing and married couples each have their own bedroom and a sitting room where displays of rare flowers, sometimes gardenias, are chosen by the Queen. Bathrooms are sometimes shared by several guests and are all pure Victoriana with large baths and huge taps and mahogany loos flushed by old fashioned handles.

As one lot of guests depart before lunch a new group arrives for the grand tea which is served every day in the drawing room at four o'clock when Elizabeth pours out the tea herself. The teacups are huge – larger than average breakfast cups – and the mid-afternoon fare both at Balmoral and Birkhall is a really splendid Scottish tea offering scones, biscuits and cakes of every kind. The Queen is now a reasonably good cook and on picnics often prepares Scottish pancakes herself on a hot griddle.

From the point of view of Elizabeth's friends, Balmoral has one decided advantage over Sandringham in that when they go through the great door they enter the hall and, after being greeted there by an Equerry, they always have time to powder their noses or have a quick wash and brush up before they encounter their Royal host. At Sandringham there is no entrance hall and guests step straight into the drawing room from the porch to find themselves walking into the midst of a Royal tea party. As one man told me,

> You don't get time to do a thing except run a hand through your hair, and pull yourself together. Then you find yourself walking straight up to the Queen. You bow and start making what you hope is sensible conversation. The first time I ever went to Sandringham, which was a long time ago, this happened to me and I simply couldn't stop my cup rattling in the saucer.

Because Balmoral is the most private Royal retreat, the summer holiday period is the only time in the year when the Court Circular, the stiff daily record of the official activities of Elizabeth and her family published in *The Times* and other serious newspapers, never publishes a list of house guests. So jealously guarded is Elizabeth's privacy during August and September that it merely states that 'The Queen has arrived at Balmoral House' meaning that Elizabeth and the Court have moved into official residence for a time.

The holiday at Balmoral emphasises better than anything else the strange role of members of the Royal Household, men and women who know more about the private life of the family than anyone else. They work for Elizabeth and her relatives in their separate Households, year in and year out, and although they cope well in London where protocol is well defined, they face their sternest test when the same jobs are transferred to the far more relaxed and intimate atmosphere of Balmoral. While they remain hand-picked servants of Elizabeth and the family, when they are in Scotland they are constantly in much closer everyday contact with the sovereign and her relatives and are almost *en famille*. So they walk a curious tight-rope whereby they become friends and intimates as well as super hand-picked employees.

It is rare for the wife or husband of a household official to be invited to Balmoral. Exceptions are only made when that person is related in some way to the sovereign or has been a close friend since childhood. All in all, Balmoral represents a curious and extra strain on courtiers since besides carrying out their official duties, they have to be in excellent form, amusing at the right time, using their high degree of sophistication at all times, witnessing the interplay between members of the Royal Family and being part of the scene without ever making a wrong or ill-timed remark.

Group Captain Peter Townsend described this situation most succinctly in his book, *Time and Chance*, when he wrote, 'I felt as if I were on a stage, playing a part, a minor one, in a wonderful comedy, human, colourful, animated and at times intensely moving with an extra-ordinary varied dramatis personae.'

Unlike Townsend, most Equerries have some link with Royalty: usually a member of their family has held a previous Royal appointment of some kind – it may have been a grandparent, parent or cousin, close enough to have established some affiliation with the family. The post-war experiment of King George VI which brought people like Townsend into the Household did not last long: he was one of the few men appointed a temporary Equerry not picked for his family connections but for his wartime RAF fighting record. Townsend was fortunate in that he adapted perfectly to the job but today the men and women who surround Elizabeth as members of her Royal Household on this most private holiday, all people with the ideal background, still admit to some degree of strain.

Physically the days at Balmoral are demanding and when the first day of the grouse shoot dawns no matter whether they are stalking, beating or shooting, the days can be both exhilarating and exhausting. No sooner is the shoot over than everyone, sportsmen and spectators, gather in the drawing room with its heavy Victorian furniture and bay windows looking out over the distant hills, for pre-dinner drinks. The splendid Balmoral evenings begin in earnest when, followed by her family and guests, Elizabeth leads the happy procession from the drawing room and into the dining room at precisely 8.45pm.

Elizabeth, without a tiara, wears one of her favourite gowns and Philip and some of the other men of the Royal Family are kilted in the blue and green Royal Stuart tartan and wear black buckle shoes. Male guests who are entitled to follow the Royal example wear the tartan of their own clan, the married men with tartan-sashed wives at their side. Other guests are in formal black dinner jackets. The Balmoral tartan of red, black and lavender, designed by Prince Albert, is seldom worn these days. Philip and Charles both own a number of kilts specially tailored to prevent high winds from causing any embarrassment.

The dining room is not large and the noise from the pipes as the pipers march round the table is deafening but while guests wince as the pipe music blasts their ears, Elizabeth only registers great pleasure. All take their seats with Elizabeth and Philip sitting opposite each other in the centre of the long dining table and it is the habit for conversation following Elizabeth's cue to be directed to one end of the table and then to the other. Shortly before the meal is over the pipers re-enter the dining room playing traditional Scottish airs like 'Flowers of the Forest' and 'Scotland the Brave'.

Old-fashioned tradition is still maintained and when the four-course meal is over the men remain to take port and smoke cigars while the ladies retire to the drawing room. When Elizabeth gets up all the men, including Philip, rise to their feet and incline their heads. Elizabeth remembers that in the past when her mother led the ladies out of the dining room, she always paused first to curtsey before her husband, the King.

Many nights there is dancing, often lasting from 10.30pm until two o'clock in the morning with scarcely a pause between one gay and rousing number and the next. As one man who loves Balmoral told me,

> I honestly don't know where the Queen gets her energy from. She knows all the intricate steps and is very light on her feet. One minute you will see her almost breathless after a reel and then she will be up again ready for the next. I remember once I was so tired after an extremely active day that I glanced at my watch and thought, 'Well, it's one o'clock and she must be going to bed soon.' But not on your life! She was dancing away until two o'clock in the morning and was up bright and early as usual the next day.

Some evenings are relatively quiet after dinner when Elizabeth and her guests play cards – Canasta is popular – and Princess Margaret plays the piano, choosing

102

ballads and modern songs that she knows are Royal favourites. Among those in the party you will sometimes find two very happy couples from the hamlet of nearby Crathie where Queen Victoria's faithful servant, John Brown, is buried in the church graveyard. They are the local doctor and minister and their wives for whom these Balmoral evenings are a pure delight.

Elizabeth always attends the hour-long Sunday morning service at 11.30am at the small red-spired kirk of Crathie set on a hill. From the pews set aside for the Royal Family in the south trancept they can see the marble busts of earlier sovereigns. The Royal party listen to a simple service and rise to their feet with the rest of the congregation when the Queen's favourite hymn is played, 'How Bright These Glorious Spirits'.

It was once possible for the family, when Charles and Anne were very young, to stroll in Crathie village (population 519) with its scattering of granite houses graced by tall trees, its Lochnagar distillery which makes malt whisky, and Strachan's shop, the grocer-cum-post-office: unfortunately crowds are now so great when the Queen is in residence that this minor pleasure is denied her and even the short journey from the castle to the kirk has to be made by car.

The Queen Mother never stays at the Castle; she has her own house Birkhall, about eight miles away, but still on the Balmoral estate. It is a not over-large, tall, white three-storied Queen Anne house overlooking the River Muick. Throughout the summer holiday there is constant coming-and-going between Birkhall and the Castle. In contrast with the Castle, with its pages and footmen, there is a minimum of formality at Birkhall. The Queen Mother and her late husband planned the lovely sloping gardens of Birkhall when they were Duke and Duchess of York: it is essentially an old-fashioned garden, in parts very steep with beds filled with huge clumps of perennnials – great masses of Glove Thistle in beds eight yards in depth and over six yards long and Giant Himalayan Lilies growing in profusion. It has a great advantage over the Castle in that it is only six hundred feet above sea-level and therefore much warmer, and flowers and vegetables come into season much earlier.

Princess Margaret always stays with her mother at Birkhall in the same way that she stays with her at Royal Lodge, Windsor, when the rest of the family are at Windsor Castle. Less energetic than most members of the Balmoral party, Margaret in recent years often dodges out of the very arduous sport of red-deerstalking: this is an all-day affair when the party treks for miles and miles into the hills behind dour and determined ghillies often fighting off swarming flies and mosquitoes which have bedevilled Balmoral for generations and against which no repellent ever seems satisfactory.

One of the gayest nights of the holiday is the Ghillies' Ball held in the Castle ballroom hung with curtains of the Royal Stuart and Balmoral tartans when everyone who has the right to wear it dons full Highland dress. Until the early hours of the morning ghillies and their wives and members of the large estate staff dance their way through one reel after another, partnered by members of the Royal Family and any close Scottish friends from Deeside and Aberdeenshire who may be there for the evening. Without exception all members of the Royal Family are good dancers, basically because dancing lessons were de rigueur when they were all little children.

The one person who had to take a crash course in Highland dancing was Philip who, when he was first invited to Balmoral before his engagement to Elizabeth was announced, found himself a wallflower at a ghillies' ball and very much put out because he could not lead the dancing with her because he did not know the steps. It took him six lessons to get the hang of it all.

For Philip, Balmoral has nostalgic memories indeed. It was in the library of the Castle that he first approached King George VI about his engagement to Elizabeth: he knew he had been thoroughly 'vetted' and approved but the King, so close to his elder daughter and dismayed at the thought of 'losing' her, while he tacitly accepted the idea told a bitterly disappointed Philip that any thought of an official engagement would have to be shelved for at least six months. It was to Birkhall that Elizabeth and Philip, unable to find any real degree of privaty at Broadlands, Lord Mountbatten's Hampshire home, fled for the remainder of the honeymoon where, although the weather deteriorated and it rained a great deal, they found peace and quiet.

Royal lovers have always found sanctuary in Balmoral. It was there that Princess Margaret and Lord Snowdon were first toasted by Elizabeth and her family when they became unofficially engaged, well before the official announcement was made that took the whole world by surprise; the Duke and Duchess of Kent spent their honeymoon at Birkhall; it was at the Castle that the Prince and Princess of Wales sought and found quietude after their engagement had been announced. Shortly after their betrothal Prince Charles had to go solo on a five week tour of New Zealand and Australia; when he returned to Britain in order to avoid a public reunion he and Lady Diana were reunited at Balmoral, which provided the haven they needed.

Not all parties are held in the castle: the Queen Mother, who has her own distinctive style of party-giving, has a special 'do' for all her grandchildren which is always held on a September evening at Birkhall. The drawing room, the largest room in the house, is cleared of furniture – which is stored in a tent outside – and invitations go out to the children of friends in the neighbourhood and once again there are reels, this time danced to the music of a three-piece band from Aberdeen.

One of the delights of the estate for Royal children has always been three small summer houses in the grounds of Birkhall where generations of youngsters have played and explored under the loving but ever vigilant eyes of the Queen Mother. One of the summer houses is on top of the mound above the house and near apple trees; the second is down by the River Muick and the third is hidden among trees off the main garden. Elizabeth once told a friend, 'We used to have our tea one day here and another day there, and it was quite fun deciding where we would give a little tea party or be invited to a little tea party. Sometimes Princess Margaret would do the honours, and sometimes I would.'

A generation later Charles and Anne discovered the fun to be had in and around the little summer houses of Birkhall. Of the two, it was the boy who developed an extraordinary closeness with his grandmother. The Queen Mother recognised his shyness, a problem she not only knew and understood – for years she had helped and encouraged her acutely shy husband to surmount it – but also realised just how great a disadvantage it would be for Charles in the future if it were not overcome. The powerful link that was established between grandmother and grandson was responsible not only for building up Charles's self-confidence but also gave him the special outlet he desperately needed in schooldays.

Since childhood Charles always found it easier to discuss his deeply personal problems with the Queen Mother rather than with either of his parents and it was at Birkhall that he first told her of his unhappiness at school and pleaded with her to intervene on his behalf with Elizabeth and Philip. In her calm and quiet way the Queen Mother explained what he really already knew – that there could be no going back and that, come what may, he would have to stick to the rigours and endure the sense of loneliness he experienced.

While perhaps not as close to the Queen Mother as her brother Charles, Anne nevertheless shared in his deep affection for her. Their implicit trust in their grandmother was of tremendous consequence to them both since, unlike ordinary children, neither of them could ever bring themselves to confide either in the relatively few boys and girls who were the children of their parents' friends or were of their own age at school.

Therefore the problems of adolescence, difficult for children in all walks of life, were always far greater for Elizabeth's growing-up elder children.

Charles lived in an all-male society during term time and when he was on holiday he spent almost the entire time with adults. While he had great respect for a father intent on advancing his son beyond his years – teaching him to drive a Land Rover when he was only twelve – Philip was not the sort of man this hesitant son ever approached on personal worries let alone sexual doubts. As the sixties developed, when public attitudes were changing in a most dramatic way, Charles remained emotionally retarded and there was not the slightest hint that he was going to develop into a self-assured man and the world's most eligible bachelor.

Even when he was eighteen, still preparing for his A-levels and old enough to reign as King in his own right if anything happened to Elizabeth, he had never had a girl friend, never invited a member of the opposite sex on any outing and had certainly never asked his parents if he could invite a girl home, whether to Buckingham Palace or any of the other Royal residences.

His only close contact with growing up youngsters of his own age belonged to Lord Mountbatten's large family of grandchildren and closest to him were the Hon. Norton Knatchbull, now Lord Romsey and heir to the Mountbatten title, slightly older than Charles, and his two elder sisters, Lady Joanna Knatchbull and Lady Amanda Knatchbull, all children of Mountbatten's elder daughter, Lady Patricia Mountbatten – now Countess Mountbatten of Burma – and her husband, John, Lord Brabourne, the film producer. Then there were the three young daughters of Mountbatten's youngest daughter, Lady Pamela, married to the interior decorator Mr David Hicks, but their children, Edwina, Ashley and India Hicks, were only little girls when Charles was growing up.

Adolescence was all so much easier for his tall, good-looking, extrovert brother Andrew who, from the age of thirteen, had a constant succession of girl friends, the first he encountered at Gordonstoun and who came from solid professional homes. This boy had no emotional hang-ups and made history in the Royal Family by taking one or two current girl friends to stay at Balmoral and Windsor. It says much for the Queen who, although initially taken aback at the proposition, did not hesitate when Andrew asked her if he could invite Kirsty Richmond, the daughter of a widowed nurse, to Sandringham for the New Year: her answer was in the affirmative. What is astonishing is that of all the young girls Andrew introduced to his family, not one of them let him down and either spilled the beans or boasted about their relationship with him in public. Mrs Richmond described Andrew as 'a very well mannered and nice boy' and 'not any different to most other boys of his age'. Andrew was certainly sexually more precocious and knowledgeable in his early teens than Charles ever was in his early twenties.

As a direct result of being so close to Andrew – they overlapped at Gordonstoun for two years – the Queen's youngest child, Edward, benefited enormously. He grew up emotionally less introverted than Charles and yet far less of an extrovert than Andrew: over all, he was a decidedly well balanced boy. He had the advantage that when he went to Gordonstoun, not only had the novelty of having a Royal Prince worn off but he had been less subjected to public curiosity and was thus able to make friends with fellow pupils of both sexes.

Because of Andrew's easy manner with girls and because he made no effort to conceal his hankering after the bright life, he was soon labelled 'Randy Andy', much to the Queen's annoyance and concern. Edward, equally popular at school and mature for his age but far less interested in girls, was able to proceed with his own quiet conquests without anyone being any the wiser.

For the Queen's only daughter, Princess Anne, the problem of coping with adolescence was quite a different matter.

108

5

The Swinging Sixties

WHEN SHE WAS a plump and bossy schoolgirl longing for
the day when she would be old enough to leave
Benenden and break out on her own into the world of
the swinging sixties, Princess Anne always secretly
sought to emulate her mother's younger sister, Princess
Margaret, her stunningly elegant and witty aunt who
seemed to have everything going for her. Yet try as she
might, Anne was never destined to achieve that elusive
Royal charisma which both her mother and grandmother
personified and which Princess Margaret fleetingly captured in her twenties and early thirties. From the time
that she was a little girl Anne had a certain charm but
this was something she could turn on and off at will: if
she felt like it, she would sit at a family dinner table and
even when close friends of her parents were present she
would keep up a stony silence throughout the meal. At
other times in a better mood she would be the life and
soul of a party and go out of her way to be pleasant.

This moodiness in her make-up has always been with
her and it is a misfortune that in repose her face can often
look sullen, emphasised by a pouty lower lip, so that she
often appears bored when in fact she may be quite
enjoying herself. Added to this are other strong character traits inherited from her father which make her more
outspoken than any of her three brothers and this again

is a disadvantage since her abrupt and direct manner sometimes unintentionally wounds or hurts her listener. Essentially she is a very private person and is at her best with small groups of people, friends she trusts and knows well enough to be completely at ease and with whom her ambivalent attitude to her Royal position never manifests itself.

Both Elizabeth and Philip went out of their way to humour their only daughter as she was growing up and they had great hopes that some of the stubborn and difficult traits in her temperament would be rubbed off when she went to school and found herself part of a larger community and mixed with other girls. She was given an enormous amount of personal freedom during the holidays and at that time, before Royal security had perforce to be tightened up, she was allowed to indulge in many whims: the last thing her parents wanted was for Anne to complain, as she often did, that she was like a bird imprisoned in a gilded cage and so she was given every opportunity to find outlets beyond Palace walls for her surplus energy.

She took ice-skating lessons at the Richmond Ice Rink, went sailing with her father on board his yacht *Bloodhound* and when she was thirteen her father found her a more than apt pupil when he taught her to drive in the private grounds of Windsor Castle and Balmoral. In her growing-up days she was frequently at cross-purposes with Charles who often wearied of her taunts and jibes and rather than fight back would turn away disconsolate.

It was apparent to those close to her that there was from the very beginning a marked similarity between Anne and Princess Margaret in that they both, at some deep psychological level, resented the role of being 'number two', a role that was driven home to both of them more and more forcibly as they grew older and one with which they had inevitably to come to terms. Neither of them really succeeded in totally overcoming a certain resentment and envy for their elder sibling and it is interesting to note that both Anne and Margret were rather spoiled as children in that they were allowed to indulge in tantrums and flashes of temper without always necessarily being scolded or reprimanded. In each case sympathetic Royal parents fully understood the great divide that separated the second child from the heir and sought to find ways and means of controlling aggression and petulance without being too heavy-handed.

It was probably Anne's salvation, as well as her great good fortune, that she found her great and all-absorbing passion in life when she was very young and never once veered from her powerful and driving ambition to become one day a famous horsewoman. This was an enormous relief to Elizabeth and Philip, who realised during Anne's early teenage years that the best thing was to allow her total freedom to mess about in stables, going around as she always did in old jeans and a denim cap. All Anne's surplus energy in her spare time during her last two years at school were devoted to the finer arts of schooling and dressage of horses, and shortly before she left Benenden at the end of the summer term in 1968 she acquired her first thoroughbred horse, Purple Star, and in her first adult event she came seventh in the Novice Class of the Windsor Horse Trials.

She began 'eventing' – that is, competitive riding – but she was not just an average horse-mad girl, she was absolutely and utterly dedicated to equitation. With her natural rhythm in the saddle – an essential for good riding – especially across country, she began to spend more and more time preparing for competitions, always intent to go all out and win. She had no interest in being placed second or third – she felt she had been second too long in her life. While she could often be mistaken for a stable lad in her scruffy clothes in the Royal Mews, Anne was always immaculately turned out in jodhpurs and jacket when it came to eventing.

Strangely enough, when she was about sixteen, it was Princess Margaret as much as Elizabeth who began to

111

develop in her niece a critical faculty about clothes: and gradually Anne built up a sensible but limited wardrobe. Instead of having clothes sent to Buckingham Palace 'on approval' as was the custom of her older relatives, when she finally left school she busied herself shopping for trendy off-the-peg clothes which she bought in some of the multiple-chain-stores and boutiques in King's Road, Chelsea, where she used the changing rooms just like any other customer. Elizabeth never debunked the miniskirts, the long boots and outlandish hats that resulted from some of these shopping expeditions and although Elizabeth's eyes often almost popped out of her head when she inspected some of her daughter's purchases, she nevertheless gave her full approval for Anne to go ahead and experiment with clothes.

The freedom which Elizabeth gave Anne in the selection of modern gear paid dividends since her daughter soon developed a clothes sense which was to be of tremendous help to her when she left school; she was able to overcome the usual difficult transition period from ending school life and entering public life without passing through a gauche or awkward stage. She moved smoothly and in a very short time from being a far from fashion-conscious schoolgirl into becoming a well-groomed nineteen-year-old with a decided flair for uncluttered bright clothes and imaginative hats, among the first of them being a striking large-brimmed black sombrero.

Elizabeth and Philip worked closely together in the upbringing of their children and they had to use all their combined skill and tact in their handling of Anne. While Elizabeth saw to it that the growing girl had a real sense of freedom, Philip endeavoured to channel her outgoing and active spirit in other directions as well as equestrian pursuits. She was constantly with him at polo matches, and on his yacht at Cowes where she always called in to lend a hand and where, as a result, she became a skilled crew member. In their times together there is no doubt that Philip helped Anne to accept with better grace the difficult situation she found herself in as being number two all the time.

Another activity which for a time had captured Anne's interest was tennis. As a tennis player she won golden praise from Dan Maskell, the great coach, who gave Anne lessons on the court at Buckingham Palace. In his view she was undoubtedly Wimbledon material if her enthusiasm for riding had not superseded all other ideas. He once said, 'Her accuracy and competitive sense made her an excellent pupil. She was very exact.'

When she left Benenden and knew little about make-up her practical approach to all problems was demonstrated when she decided to go to a professional beautician to learn how to apply make-up properly. Equally, she rejected the idea that she should indulge in the luxury of a hairdresser visiting the Palace to create a coiffeur for her on the few occasions she accompanied her parents on 'teach-in' public engagements. Typically, she decided to do her hair herself. In her positive fashion she said she preferred to experiment herself since her hair seldom went the same way twice and so one week she would be seen with her hair hanging loosely over her shoulders and the next week in a soft and becoming bun.

Elizabeth and Philip were both disappointed when Anne did not make the grade for a place at university which could have led her to enter one of the liberal professions. Anne tended to evade pressing questions about what she wanted to do with her life and although she once registered a vague interest in veterinary work this idea gradually faded as her absorption in horses increased. It was a big step towards driving her own horse boxes on motorways when she passed her driving test at the first attempt, and two months after her eighteenth birthday she was given a blue Rover 2000. This meant that she could drive herself where she wanted but always with the proviso that when she was out in the evening she was back at the Palace by midnight and always with an escort. Elizabeth saw to it that with very few limits imposed upon her, Anne was as free as she could possibly be.

She kept pace with all that the 1960s offerd in the way of new entertainment and in the soundproofed Palace sitting room she shared with Charles she tuned in to the music of the Beatles and other pop groups who enthralled her just as much as other girls of her age. To her regret she unhappily could never go to see a live pop show: it wasn't that such an expedition was forbidden by her parents but they felt, and Anne agreed, that her presence could cause further burdens for organisers at overcrowded pop concerts.

Anne's friends were mainly young people from wealthy families with solid aristocratic backgrounds and for the most part their common link and interest was horses and eventing, subjects which dominated not only their conversation but their lives. Although she was an easy mixer with anyone who belonged to this world she very rarely came into contact with people outside this closely knit group. She never had the chance to acquire the common touch as Charles did so successfully at University and later in the Services.

She was not in any sense a domesticated girl – her life had been all against it and she very much took for granted that there was always staff to prepare meals and deal with humdrum matters like laundry. Despite the challenging atmosphere in which she was brought up, constantly meeting VIPs from all over the world and occasionally being invited to join one of her mother's informal Palace lunches where professional people from all walks of life were drawn together, Anne, unlike Charles, was not politically orientated and although she had a good mind she never attempted to stretch it to the maximum. Nevertheless, she gave value for money in her exchanges at official receptions and appeared to be precisely what she was, unusually well informed for her age but singularly lacking in any real interest outside the world of horses.

She proved a good and reliable trooper when she accompanied Elizabeth and Philip on some of their

114

public engagements during the year after she left Benenden and although it was tacitly understood that she would soon have to take her fair share of Royal duties, she hoped that that day would be put off as long as possible, allowing her as much time as possible to ride. It was finally put to Anne by her parents that this hobby-for-the-rich was simply not on as a full-time occupation and, much to her surprise and astonishment, she was launched into public life almost without warning and with extraordinary suddenness.

This happened when Philip suddenly discovered that because of an unusual pressure of engagements he could not possibly go down to Pirbright in Surrey to present the traditional leeks to the Welsh Guards on St David's Day on 1 March 1969. All the other senior members of the family were busy and so the proposition was put to Anne that she should stand in for her father. That first public engagement turned out to be a tremendous success. Anne knew immediately what she would wear for the military occasion – a bold wide-brimmed green hat with a gorgeous looking suit to match and full of confidence and accompanied by one of Elizabeth's ladies-in-waiting, she set off from Buckingham Palace to go solo while still short of her nineteenth birthday. The novelty of being saluted and greeted in her own right pleased her, and after inspecting a guard of honour, pausing here and there in time-honoured fashion to have a word with first one soldier and then another, she was a decided hit at a lunch in the regimental Mess when senior officers who had been with her said afterwards that she was 'a very jolly girl'.

Anne was outgoing and enthusiastic throughout the day and was spontaneously cheered when she left and there was not the slightest clue given that one day, and not so very far ahead, she would find many of these public duties not only repetitious but boring into the bargain. That summer Anne carried out nearly thirty public engagements, culminating in a two-day visit to the 14/20th King's Hussars in Germany where she drove a fifty-ton tank. All seemed to be well on the professional front with Anne only registering occasional irritation when any official duty seemed likely to conflict with horse trials and competitions. On the emotional front she continued to enjoy the company of the same group of friends and was hardly ever seen with any one particular man.

Words she used herself much later explain in two sentences what riding has always meant to her: 'It's the one thing that the world can see I do well that's got *nothing* to do with my position, or money or anything else. If I'm good at it, I'm good at it – and not because I'm who I am.' Always Anne was driven by a sense of having to prove herself and could never have uttered the light-hearted but telling words spoken by her brother Charles when, soon after he had entered public life, he said he enjoyed it all enormously, adding, 'I'd probably have been committed to an institution long ago were it not for the ability to see the funny side of life.'

Anne could never accept that there was a funny side to life as a Princess: that was the heart of her problem. But the world of serious competitive riding has always attracted people who not only ride hard but also play hard and it was here that Anne found her fun. They have their own jokes and a fair amount of horseplay and schoolboy pranks are all part of their social scene. At parties Anne would always join in the laughter while watching the antics. Since dedicated eventing com-petitors usually come across each other when they start regularly entering competitions in their teens, friend-ships are struck up early in life and they get to know one another very well – not surprisingly many of them marry fellow competitors – as Anne was to do.

When she was only a little girl, just six, Anne often filled a great gap in the difficult and trying days when Princess Margaret was bent on establishing a new life-style after her final break with Peter Townsend in 1955. Margaret had always had a good rapport with children and she found one of her outlets in taking her young niece on occasional visits to pantomimes or theatrical entertainments for children. She enjoyed listening to Anne babble away ten-to-the-dozen about daily activities which, until she was thirteen, were confined to the school room at Buckingham Palace where she and two friends, Caroline Hamilton, eldest daughter of the Dean of Windsor, and Susan Babington-Smith had lessons.

Anne was never short of news for her aunt: there was, she said, the notion that a Frenchwoman, Mademoiselle Bibaine de Roujoux, was going go spend a month at Balmoral to help her and Charles with their French (a notion subsequently put into effect); there was the bother of trying to keep still for A. K. Lawrence who was to make a sketch of her head for Elizabeth. So far she had only managed one flight in a helicopter and only one flight in an aeroplane from Dyce in Scotland to London Airport and she was busy pressurising her father for more adventures in the air. For a bemused Princess Margaret this was all in striking contrast to the circumscribed wartime childhood she had shared with Elizabeth.

One day when Anne was having tea with her grandmother, the Queen Mother, and Princess Margaret at Clarence House, the home they both shared in The Mall, Anne commented that 'someone new' had taken her photograph with Charles. She said Elizabeth and Philip were both very pleased with the pictures and that she, Anne, didn't think they were at all bad either. The photographer, she said was 'very nice' and 'not fussy'.

The man behind the camera that day in 1957 was Anthony Armstrong-Jones and this first assignment from Elizabeth came as a result of his formal application to take the official coming-of-age pictures of the soldier Duke of Kent. They were so good that Elizabeth decided that Armstrong-Jones should be invited to take official pictures of Charles and Anne in the grounds of Buckingham Palace, pictures that showed not only flair and imagination but were also a complete break with the previously accepted traditional and formal Royal poses of the past.

To Princess Margaret and her mother the name Armstrong-Jones meant nothing at all: and yet that first photographic session with Anne and Charles was to be one of their first talking points when Princess and photographer met for the first time, quite by chance, nearly two years later. They were both invited to a private dinner party given by a mutual friend, Lady Elizabeth Cavendish, a lady-in-waiting to Margaret, at her home in Cheyne Walk overlooking the River Thames at Chelsea. This initial encounter was to be the start of a courtship which, to say the least, bore absolutely no resemblance to the staid and at times almost formal build-up to the betrothal and marriage of Elizabeth and Philip, second cousins, a decade and a half earlier.

When she was a little girl Margaret used to stamp her feet in temper when she was refused anything and she usually got what she wanted: in many ways that demanding trait was still part and parcel of her basic nature when she met Tony. Although she had suffered many doubts and experienced great sadness when Townsend moved out of her life, she nevertheless could still be almost as imperious as her great-great-great-grandmother, Queen Victoria, when she was displeased. As a little boy Tony also hated to be frustrated but learned a new degree of patience when a bout of polio, which left him with one leg slightly shorter than the other, confined him to bed for the best part of a year. As a man he was ambitious, successful and intolerant of those people who either did not provide him with stimulation and new bursts of adrenalin or had not achieved fame in their own field.

That first meeting of Margaret and Tony could not have been better timed. Both had a gap in their lives which each thought the other could fill. They had each met their match, a sparring partner who, each felt, in one way or another could be tamed to their individual way of thinking. Margaret was bored not only by the ultra-conformist suitors who pursued her, dancing attention upon her every whim, but also by her Royal workload for which she had not only lost much of her enthusiasm when it was really demanding but which she also found increasingly monotonous, while Tony in his turn, was eagerly seeking a fresh challenge and new fields to conquer.

The Welsh-born Armstrong-Jones, with his celtic streak of sentimentality and his background of Eton and Cambridge, was already well established as a personality in the emerging semi-bohemian world of the media and television with its developing personality cult. He offered Margaret from the start of their relationship what was tantamount to pure and simple excitement spiced with a conspiratorial sense of fun, the like of which she had never known in her life before, not even with Townsend. Armstrong-Jones had the natural instinct and commonsense to recognise that if his relationship with Margaret was to progress at all, then it would only flourish in an ambience totally removed from the world of elegant country houses where she had been accustomed to spending weekends when she was not at one of the Royal residences.

It was almost a stroke of genius on his part that when he decided they must be able to meet somewhere they could be certain of total privacy and on *his* ground not hers, he chose to rent a small and scruffy two-storied dockland house in Rotherhithe in the East End of London, owned by a bachelor friend who, delighted by Tony's offer to redecorate the house, agreed to let him have it for a tiny rent. For weeks Tony spent all his spare time stripping bare the walls of the little house and making them good, and painting everything white in the one large upstairs room with a bay window overlooking the Thames, a room whose furniture consisted of an old dresser, two small cupboards, an old square table, four chairs, a bookcase and a wooden rocking chair. Not only the curtains were white but so was the china.

For Margaret who had been both moody and taciturn for a long time, her first glimpse of what was to become known as 'the little white room' was the start of an

119

adventure that could hardly have failed to capture her imagination, so utterly original in concept and in total contrast to the formality she had grown up with all her life. For Tony, who had always had great charm and appeal for women in all age groups, the zest with which he entered into the chase brought out all his sense of the bizarre and he probably considered one of his greatest early triumphs to be when he persuaded the Queen's sister to ride pillion on his motor cycle. Secrecy added spice to their romance and for several months their growing closeness was only known to the Queen Mother, vicariously entering into the spirit of a romance which was obviously transforming her younger daughter.

In those so-happy early days both Margaret and Tony each utterly absorbed and intrigued by one another, stifled the more wilful aspects of their characters and relished every minute of their time together in secrecy which added so much spice to the romance. It was the last place in the world where anyone would have thought of looking for the Queen's sister – in a derelict neighbourhood where the closest social amenity was a fish and chip shop. When they were quite alone and preparing a meal for themselves, Margaret wearing an apron as she cooked steaks on a gas stove that had seen better days, and Tony uncorking red wine and preparing his own special salad dressing, they had achieved the impossible: they were just two people who, away from the panoply of protocol and regality, were falling in love.

The Queen Mother had also found wonderful hours of escape in the Rotherhithe hideaway, stepping out of her Rolls-Royce which left her at the corner and walking unescorted down a mean street to Tony's front door, incredibly never once being recognised. There, in the little upstairs room, she would join the couple in their meals throwing her own fair share of chicken bones out of the window and into the river. Margaret's new relaxation and happiness was commented upon by several members of the Royal Family and it was finally decided that the Queen Mother should tell Elizabeth about the deepening relationship between her sister and the photographer. It was felt that at all costs it must for the time being remain a secret – but someone else, who lived not very far awayin an elegant mews house in South Kensington, knew something of what was going on and was to be confided in at a very early stage.

He was Tony's father, Ronald Armstrong-Jones, an urbane and sophisticated Queen's Counsel who, although he was aware that his son was seeing a great deal of Princess Margaret, never thought it would come to anything and was almost totally absorbed in preparation for his third marriage which was to be to twenty-eight-year-old BOAC air hostess Jenifer Unite, a bright and amusing girl of considerable talents and a brilliant pianist of concert standard.

In January of 1960 Ronald, who had suffered from asthma for many years, was taken ill and sent to the King Edward VII's Hospital for Officers in Beaumont Street. One Monday afternoon his fiancée was rushing up the hospital steps when she bumped into Tony and his sister Susan, now Lady de Vesci: Tony seemed his usual relaxed self and told her, 'Don't worry too much about Daddy. He'll soon be well again.' When Jenifer opened the door of Ronnie's bedroom, her arms filled with flowers, she sensed at once that something had happened. To receive his visitors, Ronnie was dressed in his usual immaculate pinstripe blue suit with a crisp bow tie but as the door opened he did not walk over and kiss Jenifer. He was standing with his back to her staring out of the window with his hands resting on the radiator. As shafts of sunlight crossed the room he slowly turned towards Jenifer, his face very serious, and said, 'I have just heard the most fantastic piece of news which I cannot possibly tell you. I have pledged my word to tell no one.' Jenifer was taken completely aback but made no attempt to press her fiancé. Although privately her mind was in a whirl of speculation she could not have guessed the truth.

She was kept guessing for four days after Tony's visit to the hospital. Ronnie telephoned Jenifer from the hospital to say he would be home at the mews house the following day.

'I'll come and pick you up,' she said.

Ronnie replied cautiously, 'It would be better if you waited for me at the Mews. I will be there at 10.30am. Please make sure you are there before I arrive.'

The next day, a cold bleak January morning, Jenifer went to collect Ronnie's coat from the cleaners and was in the mews house early to make sure there was a good fire and hot coffee ready when he came in. She heard Ronnie's key turn in the front door lock and with him, to her surprise, was Tony and his sister. They all kissed each other. Jenifer had no sense of impending drama, but as she was about to ask them if they would all have coffee – less than a minute after they had entered the house – Tony said, 'Jenifer, I've got something to tell you. Would you like to come outside in the car with me?'

She looked questioningly at Armstrong-Jones senior who signalled her to do what she had been asked. Still puzzled by the strange performance she turned to follow Tony into the Mini outside and found it even odder when Tony said, 'Would you mind winding up your window.'

He took out a packet of French Gauloise cigarettes, lit one and in a most casual voice said, 'I've got some news for you. I'm going to marry Princess Margaret. The news must not leak out until we are ready to announce it. You know what happened to Peter Townsend. I don't want that to happen to me.'

Then came the thunderbolt. 'We would like you to get married before us, that is, if you don't mind. The Queen thinks it would be better.' The words scarcely made sense to the bewildered Jenifer and it took a time for her to fully realise what was going on; then she and Tony went back into the house. Ronald Armstrong-Jones and Jenifer agreed to advance their wedding and decided they would be far away in Bermuda on their honeymoon

122

when the official announcement of Tony's and Margaret's engagement was made from Buckingham Palace.

It was just over a year after the wedding at Westminster Abbey, in May 1960, the culmination of the most rewarding and happy time in Margaret's life, that Ronald Armstrong-Jones began to feel a certain uneasiness about the future of his son's romance. The more he got to know and understand Princess Margaret the more he feared that she and his son were too alike, both headstrong and both with very positive opinions of their own and that their similar temperaments might clash.

He loved to entertain them at his lovely two hundred acre estate at Bont Newydd in North Wales five miles from Caernarvon. Here stood the love of his life, Plas Dinas, the seventeeth-century ancestral home of the Armstrong-Jones family with its pink-washed walls covered with Wistaria. When he was in residence the Welsh Dragon flag was always flown from a flag pole at the end of an avenue of glorious beech trees. He was captivated by the way Princess Margaret always addressed him as 'dear father-in-law' and found himself quite relaxed in the presence of Elizabeth. He soon discovered that Elizabeth was extremely observant: during her sister's wedding she had noticed that under his gorgeous robes one of the high church dignitaries had worn a pair of hunting boots. 'The poor dear probably found them the most comfortable thing he could wear since he was on his feet so long,' she said.

Ronald Armstrong-Jones was enchanted by his new daughter-in-law and described her like this: 'Her outstanding features are her skin and her eyes. Her complexion is absolutely fantastic and her eyes are blue, blue, blue. She really is very tiny and I am always surprised by her smallness, and her voice is so light and pleasant.'

There were nevertheless sides to both Margaret's and Tony's characters which caused Ronnie a certain amount of disquiet and when he went to Kensington Palace for an early evening drink or a quiet dinner by candlelight with his son and daughter-in-law he found their tendency to bicker, however mildly, a distinct annoyance. When the couple went to spend weekends at his Welsh home they seemed happy and relaxed but the attempts of one partner to try and dominate the other, often over small issues like what programme to watch on television, upset him.

One evening Ronnie went round to see Police Constable Williams, a prominent figure in the local chapel choir at Bont Newydd and asked him if he thought he could get a choir together as a surprise for his daughter-in-law. Williams was delighted with the idea and arranged for the local brass band from Llanrydd to accompany the choir and just as dinner was over, Princess Margaret heard the first strains of Welsh music. There was *Cwm Rhondda* and *Men of Harlech* David of the White Rock, and the rich voices of the choir poured in through the open windows from the terrace outside.

There were tears in her eyes as she turned to her father-in-law and said, 'I simply must go out and say "thank you",' and as she did so, there were enthusiastic Welsh cheers from the choir and brass-band for 'Mr Tony's lady'. Armstrong-Jones Senior noticed how much more relaxed Margaret seemed to be away from London: whereas there she had a small appetite at Plas Dinas she ate everything except potatoes – which she never touched. At Plas Dinas her breakfast – always served in bed – consisted of orange juice, Welsh ham, fried eggs and tea. Of an evening, nothing pleased her more after dinner than playing paper games such as Consequences. Ronnie said it was his opinion that Princess Margaret would have probably developed along quite different lines if she had married someone much older than herself.

At Plas Dinas she often joined in barbecues which Ronnie held at a little cottage he owned on the Menai Straits and here, with a hamper packed with steaks, butter, bread, lettuce, olive oil, potatoes and plenty of gorgonzola cheese, he was always very much the master of ceremonies. He would never use charcoal for fires and being what he called an expert in the fire-lighting business, always cooked over hot wood ashes. It was on these open-air jaunts that Ronnie, so much older than his wife Jenifer, Tony and Margaret, would send them all looking for driftwood.

One day Margaret and Tony returned to Plas Dinas late in the afternoon carrying two huge sackfuls of pebbles they had collected in three back-breaking hours in the Estuary and Margaret cheerfully told Ronnie, 'We're going to put them in our garden at Kensington Palace. They will make a lovely path because they are all the same colour.'

One night Ronnie did not feel well and went upstairs to bed leaving Jenifer, Tony and Margaret to enjoy a cold supper of home-made pâté, cold ham and cold chicken. After the meal, as the three of them were all busy talking, Ronnie called down, 'What *are* you all doing?' The trio trooped up to the older man's bedroom and curled up in chairs listening fascinated to his tales about Welsh village life. As he looked across at his daughter-in-law he speculated on what would have happened if her father, George VI, had lived. He felt that George VI would have undoubtedly never mishandled the Townsend affair and would certainly have given his blessing to his marriage to Margaret if that is what his younger daughter had really wished. He knew that Margaret still missed her father dreadfully. What were the words she had used to describe him? 'He was the most important person in the world to me. Never a day goes by but what I think of him.'

Ronald Armstrong-Jones met his son regularly for lunch and was impressed by the way in which Tony had fitted into the Royal life-style while at the same time finding it possible to continue his career as a photographer with the *Sunday Times*. As the Snowdon marriage progressed, first with the birth of a son, David, Viscount Linley, in 1961 and then a daughter, Lady Sarah Armstrong-Jones, in 1964, Ronald Armstrong-Jones put aside his earlier forebodings and listened fascinated as Tony recounted how he had become the unofficial photographic adviser to the Queen and Prince Philip, both expert photographers in their own right. He also got on very well with other members of the family who were beginning to establish their own marriage patterns, each with their own very different ideas about the way in which they saw their future within the ranks of the Royal Family.

6

The 'Second Eleven'

THE QUEEN IS extremely proud of the way in which she has fashioned her 'Second Eleven' – the team of men and women in the Royal Family who do not always have star billing but who nevertheless perform a vital supporting role in the business of modern monarchy.

One man who epitomises the strength of these lesser-known Royals who guard their private lives most jealously is the thirty-eight-year-old Duke of Gloucester, a cousin of the Queen who never wanted to become an active member of the Royal Family and never evenexpected to become a Royal Duke.

For many years he was a bachelor who lived in an unpretentious Victorian terrace house in Camden Town overlooking Regent's Park Canal and drove to work on a 99cc Honda motor cycle. As an architect he spent a fair amount of time working at his drawing-board planning conversions of houses and flats, but he much preferred the outdoor life, clambering over scaffolding, talking to builders, plumbers and electricians. His professional business card simply gave the name of his firm, Hunt Thompson Associates, and his own name: 'Richard Gloucester, M.A., Dip. Arch. RIBA'.

As the younger son of a Royal Duke, a Prince in his own right and a cousin of Elizabeth, he decided never to use his title on the grounds that it would not benefit anyone, least of all himself, and he was convinced that people would think, 'My goodness, this chap's a Prince and we'd better not upset him,' or have the opposite reaction, 'Who does he think he is, waving his HRH at us?' He was the son of one of the most forward-looking women in the Royal Family, Princess Alice, Duchess of Gloucester who, even when Royalty was very rigid in its attitudes before the Second World War, nevertheless decided to break with long-standing tradition and have her children in a nursing home – Lady Carnarvon's nursing home in Portland Place. And when they began to grow up it was in a normal family atmosphere when the children joined in and were listened to about discussions on their eduation.

Thus, the first son, William, after Eton, elected to go to Stanford University in California and Richard, who also went to Eton, decided he preferred Cambridge. Princess Alice was re-inforced in her modern outlook with the knowledge she gained from her husband, the late Duke of Gloucester – one of the four sons of the martinet George V – of how the sons suffered from the disciplinarian and extremely rigid attitude of their father. Richard, the present Duke of Gloucester, grew up a serious, earnest, bespectacled man, accustomed to a tightly-knit and warm family atmosphere and more than relieved at the prospect that he would never have to play an active role as a Royal. This he saw as the predestined lot of his elder brother William, heir to the Dukedom.

William, as their father grew more frail, had regretfully decided on his own initiative that it was time to give up his personal freedom as second consul in the Diplomatic Service in order to take on the responsibilities, not only of looking after the ailing family estate of Barnwell in Northamptonshire, but of helping Elizabeth, already hard pressed by her task of finding enough experienced members of the Family to carry out Royal engagements. The brothers were different both in temperament and looks. Whereas William was proud, athletic and every inch the dashing Prince, Richard was intense, reserved

The Queen Mother and a local resident chatting over the fence at Sandringham
TIM GRAHAM

Prince Andrew and Prince Philip enjoying a joke at a tree-planting ceremony at Dartmouth Naval College TIM GRAHAM

The Prince and Princess of Wales at the Grand National TIM GRAHAM

The Prince and Princess of Wales at Craigowan Lodge on the Balmoral Estate TIM GRAHAM

The Prince and Princess of Wales watching polo at Cowdray Park TIM GRAHAM

Master Peter Phillips REX FEATURES

Princess Anne and Captain Mark Phillips REX FEATURES

Prince Edward with his Labrador, Frances TIM GRAHAM

Prince Andrew, ex-King Constantine of Greece and Lord Lichfield at a clay pigeon shoot in Chester TIM GRAHAM

Prince Charles tries out a mini motorcycle to the amusement of onlookers TIM GRAHAM

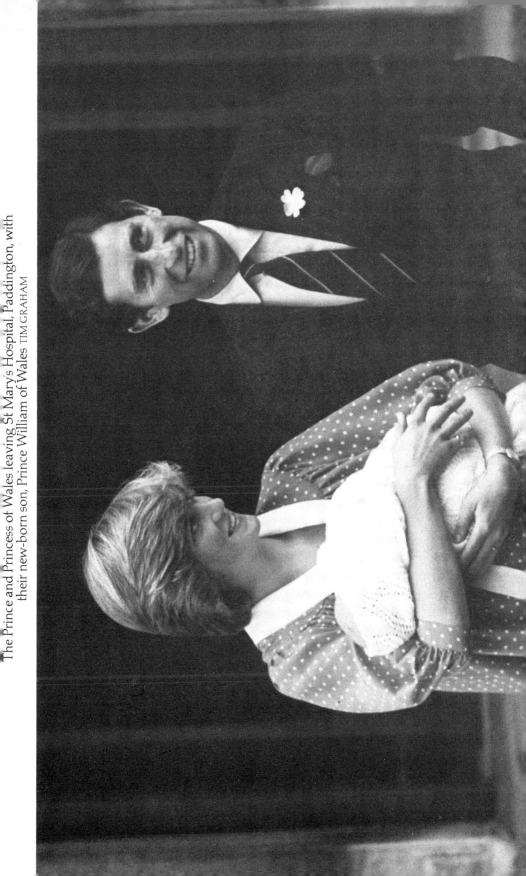

The Prince and Princess of Wales leaving St Mary's Hospital, Paddington, with their new-born son, Prince William of Wales TIM GRAHAM

Prince Edward and Princess Margaret at Clarence House TIM GRAHAM

to a point that worried his mother and utterly dedicated to his career, determined to climb to the top in spite of, and not because of, his distinguished connections.

Essentially he was a person who merged into most backgrounds with easy and practised anonymity, and if any man was happy with his lot then that man was Prince Richard of Gloucester. His cautious nature was best judged by his attitude to marriage: when he was an undergraduate at Cambridge he was invited to a tea-party at Magdalen College, and having nothing better to do that summer afternoon in 1965 he went along. Also invited was a tall, slim and fair-haired Danish girl studying at the Cambridge Language School who only decided to go along to the party at the last minute because her girl friend did not want to go alone.

Richard was intrigued by Birgitte van Deurs, with her slight but attractive Scandinavian accent, and she in turn warmed to the undergraduate's quiet modesty. As they got to know each other better and she returned to live with her divorced mother in Denmark, Richard flew regularly by tourist class across the North Sea to visit her in Copenhagen. Missing Richard, she returned to England and took a job as secretary at the Danish Embassy, but since both of them were so cautious by nature and neither of them were prepared to rush into any serious commitment, it was six years before they became official-ly engaged.

Richard was an enthusiastic photographer and the first engagement gift he made to his somewhat astonished fiancée was a Leicaflex camera like his own, commenting that now they could both swap lenses. After this came the very special and most unusual engagement ring, its principal feature is what is known as a 'Cat's Eye', a rare calcedonic quartz which resembles the pupil of a cat's eye. It was set in diamonds and Richard had taken the cat's eye from a set of studs given him at his christening. From her future mother-in-law, Princess Alice, Birgitte received a diamond brooch which Princess Alice had been given by her husband when Richard was born.

Because of the seventy-two-year-old Duke of Gloucester's failing health, Richard and Birgitte had a low-key and quiet wedding at the local parish church, which could be reached on foot via a narrow bridge leading from the Barnwell estate.

In the role of best man was Prince William, gradually re-accustoming himself to life in England: he had first been Third Secretary on the staff of the British High Commission at Lagos, Nigeria, before being transferred as Second Secretary (Commercial) with the British Embassy in Tokyo. He had enjoyed a free and easy private life which he felt was second to none and his Royal duties were virtually nil, limited to occasional appearances on the balcony of Buckingham Palace when he was home on leave. He found his real personal freedom and enjoyment in the skies and when he climbed into the cockpit of his own private aircraft and soared into the clouds, he could fulfil his deepest yearnings. In 1972 it was put bluntly to William, still a bachelor, that the ranks of the Royal Family were so undermanned that it was time he reconsidered his future since his services were urgently needed at home. To close friends he admitted, 'I've spent my time running away from what I knew was inevitable: a full time job as a Royal Prince. Now the time has come when I know I can't run away any longer.'

At heart William was not cut out for public life as a Royal – he was essentially a loner and very much a private person who, like his younger brother Richard, abhorred the thought of living in a goldfish bowl. As he once told me,

It is almost impossible to describe to you what it is like to be a member of the Royal Family. In essence, what it boils down to is this: you can never be your real self. Just to know you are Royal inhibits you. It wasn't that anyone ever said to me, 'You are a Royal Prince and you must act like one.' I simply knew that whether I liked it or not, I was automatically separated by my heritage from the rest of the world.

130

That was one of the frankest statements ever made by a Royal about 'being Royal'.

Prince William made what friends recall as a very moving speech at the Barnwell reception for Prince Richard and his Danish bride which revealed not only his joy at the happiness his younger brother had found but also his own regret at the role he felt fate had cast for him as a future Royal Duke. It was clear that he deeply envied Richard and his new sister-in-law, so obviously devoted to one another, as they set off for their honeymoon near Loch Ness in Scotland, to return afterwards to the terraced house in Camden as 'Mr and Mrs Gloucester'.

Three months later, on a warm summer afternoon in August 1972, Prince William of Gloucester plunged to his death in the blazing cockpit of his Piper Cherokee plane at the start of an air race near Wolverhampton. When the terrible news was broken to Birgitte her first words were, 'But what is going to happen to my Richard? I don't want him to change.'

Just what was going to happen to Prince Richard was immediately a matter of grave concern, not only to his young bride but to his mother, to the Queen and to senior members of the Royal Household. In the past Richard had made it abundantly clear that he was determined to live a free and independent life without participating in Royal duties. Unlike most of the other members of the Royal Family, his closest friends were men of his own age whom he had met at Cambridge, and who were drawn from very different social backgrounds to his own. Four of them became partners in the firm of architects and were the sort of people he enjoyed taking home to Barnwell, not a large house by Royal standards, but with its estate, nevertheless a mansion.

For a considerable time after William's death it was very much touch and go as to whether Richard Gloucester would, as his mother desperately hoped, accept his new Royal responsibilities or completely opt out of the role which had been put on his shoulders with such shattering suddenness. No pressure was ever exerted on Richard by the Queen to make up his mind one way or another, but one thing is certain: during his period of doubt he discovered a great affinity with Charles, and without at first committing himself in any way, began to show some interest in the problems that had faced his late brother in trying to make the family estate a going concern and, very much aware of his mother's growing worry, began to accept some official engagements.

Princess Alice, always one of Elizabeth's key supporters in taking her share of Royal duties, knew that it would be a daunting task to persuade Richard to change his life-style and she was both surprised and fortunate in finding a strong ally in her new daughter-in-law. With Birgitte at his side, Richard gave up his Camden house and moved into the family grace-and-favour apartment in Kensington Palace, with its two lovely sitting rooms, a bedroom and a magnificent hall, the main rooms overlooking the trees an sweeping green lawns of Kensington Gardens.

For a time he continued his job as an architect, fitting in engagements as and when he could but nevertheless managing to carry out seventeen Royal 'jobs' during his difficult winter of decision in 1972 and 1973, the last winter before his father died. He discovered a certain fun and achievement in the Royal work and revealed a sense of humour that surprised many people. He once found himself dressed up in oilskins and crawling along a Roman sewer beneath the streets of York with the Lord Mayor in front of him. When he noticed that the elastic in the trousers of the gentleman in front had given way he said, 'My Lord Mayor, do you know your trousers are falling down?' Replied the Lord Mayor, 'Yes, sir, but what can I do about it here?'

Birgitte had a strong and positive personality on home territory but found herself on less sure ground in public, and disliked making speeches. In the mid-1970s when she was guest of honour at the Women's Travel Club in London she spoke for less than a minute – the shortest ever Royal speech. She has made great progress since then and when she was at a State banquet in the Solomon Islands to celebrate Independence Day, she startled everyone by joining in a hula-hula, swaying to the throbbing drums with a grass-skirted dancer wearing war paint. Her kindly and understanding mother-in-law was enchanted when she heard about Birgitte's spontaneous gesture, which indicated a gradual increase in self-confidence that had taken a long time to develop.

This young Duchess developed an easy manner, discovering how to solve minor Royal problems like keeping a tiara in place with hairpins. Because her husband was Commandant in Chief of the St John Ambulance she decided to do voluntary work for the organisation and, without any carpet being laid out for her, drove her own Mini to their Grosvenor Crescent headquarters to take a first-aid refresher course and later, nursing examinations, holding the strong belief that everyone should have sufficient knowledge to cope correctly when faced with accidents. Over the years, and only after several miscarriages, she gave birth to three children, Alexander, Earl of Ulster, Lady Davina and Lady Rose, the latter days of pregnancies often being extremely trying since she was ordered long spells of rest.

The Duchess is very much involved in the day-to-day running of Barnwell where there are three live-in staff, a footman, a butler and a cook. This sounds very formal but in fact it is a house without ceremony and where the children run about everywhere in a totally relaxed atmosphere. Birgitte's lady-in-waiting, Mrs Louise Wigley, once confessed, 'When we work the children are all about us, even on our laps.' The crunch will come for Birgitte when the issue of sending the three children to school has finally to be determined: she dislikes the British boarding-school system and, like most Continentals, abhors the tradition of sending children away from home at any age. Her husband, like his late brother, went to Eton and was happy there, and would probably

133

like to continue this tradition when Alexander is old enough to go, but whether he will win through will depend largely upon his wife, who will take a great deal of persuading to change her firmly held views.

The Gloucester household is far from being spartan, but is run on strictly economic lines and they manage with what is regarded as a minimum Royal staff when they are at Kensington Palace on weekdays: their private secretary has his own two secretaries to help him, and Birgitte has her own correspondence secretary. The Palace, known as KP to the Royal family and members of their Households, groups together round a courtyard the homes of Princess Margaret and Prince and Princess Michael of Kent. In all there are up to thirty residences within the building, including a complex of flats used by senior Royal aides and grace-and-favour cottages mostly used by retired Household officials and which, with their small white railings fronting small green lawns, give it the air of an old world village.

Everyone, including the Gloucesters, lives there rent free, and there has always been a tacit understanding between all the Royals living there that they all respect each other's privacy: as a result there is comparatively little coming-and-going between relatives who may live next door to one another. Occasionally they bump into each other but apart from a brief 'hello' there are no lengthy chats during these encounters. No member of the Royal Family would ever dream of 'dropping in' on another relative without first checking that a visit would be convenient: even Princess Margaret telephones her mother at Clarence House before going round, just as the Queen Mother rings up the Queen before she ever sets forth for Buckingham Palace.

All members of the Royal Family are competent photographers but the professional runner-up after Lord Snowdon (technically no longer a member of the Family – and bearing in mind that Lord Lichfield is not an immediate member of the Royal Family) is Richard Gloucester, and before she had children it was often his wife who helped him process films in his darkroom.

Richard used his photography to help him with his job as an architect and has always been proud of his 'before' and 'after' pictures of housing projects and developments in which he was involved. He has published a book of photographs on statues, *On Public View*, and London scenes, *The Face of London*. His last book was *Oxford and Cambridge* with the text written by Hermione Hobhouse. Did anyone recognise Gloucester and start taking pictures of *him* when he was going round the colleges? He told an interviewer,

> Good heavens, no. Not even the porters. They would politely chuck me out of those parts of the colleges which were not open. That was mainly a problem in Oxford, where they don't open the colleges to the public until the afternoon. I had to pretend I was a student visiting someone.

These words reveal a curious aspect of Gloucester's character: although he knew that he could always pull rank if he ever wanted to do so, he really did seem to get a kick out of his self-imposed anonymity. His wife Birgitte is held in great affection by the Queen who is very grateful to the Danish girl for her part in bringing Richard 'out of his shell'.

Prince Charles is also close to the Gloucesters and before his marriage to Lady Diana Spencer found them such good company that the trio sometimes went skiing together. The friendship between Charles and Richard surprised many members of the family who at first did not recognise the qualities in Richard which appealed to Charles. Essentially what Richard had to offer the Queen's eldest son was the sort of person he always needed but seldom found in his bachelor days – someone with whom he could relax and drop all formality. Richard always gave Charles straight questions and in a strange way could tease and pull his second-cousin's leg without ever giving offence.

In evaluating Richard Gloucester, a Prince of the blood

Royal, one can only look back on the predicament of his father, a shy nervous son of the over-strict and uncommunicative George V, who longed to have a normal army career and command his regiment (the 10th Hussars) only to find his progress constantly blocked or deflected by his Royal obligations. Even as a schoolboy Richard was well aware of his father's longing for a private life that was always denied him. Prince William also sought personal freedom in a professional career only to be drawn into his Royal obligations by an innate sense of loyalty to his cousin, Elizabeth, and another loyalty to his frail and ageing mother who was increasingly unable to cope with the problems of the family estate on her own.

That Richard overcame the reservations he shared with his father and brother is undoubtedly due to the very real love and support he had from his wife and it is fair to say that without this Danish girl to support him immediately after William's death, it is highly probablethat he may never have joined the Royal fold and faced up to the responsibilities with which he copes so well today.

The Gloucesters, like the Kents and Ogilvys, are men and women who belong to Elizabeth's 'Second Eleven' and are vital to her not only because she trusts them implicitly but because none of them long for 'star' status, like some of their senior and wealthier relatives epitomised by Princess Margaret in the older generation and Prince Andrew in the younger generation, who really do bask in the world spotlight and would be lost without it.

What is especially interesting is that by top strata standards none of the 'Second Eleven' Royals are rich: admittedly they all live in comfort and there are no complaints, but there is certainly no sign of regal affluence in any of their lives. Princess Alexandra – her grandfather was King George V and her uncle was King George VI – grew up having to watch her pennies and although she is married to a successful businessman, the Hon. Angus Ogilvy, younger son of the Earl of Airlie, neither of them have ever made any bones about the fact that they are not flush with money. They have a full-time cook but, as Alexandra is quick to point out, even a cook has days off and she is both efficient and capable of working on her own in her large kitchen in Thatched Cottage, a lovely five-bedroomed house hidden by trees and leased from the Crown Estate Commissioners in Richmond Park.

Here, seven mile south-west of the centre of London, with herds of fallow deer grazing peacefully in the two thousand acres of parkland and wild herons circling overhead, the Ogilvys have lived for almost twenty years, enchanted by the five-bedroomed house with its large bay windows looking out over woods and sweeping lawns. In the early days of their marrige the couple were convinced that Thatched Cotage would prove not only too expensive but also too large, with its suite of five fine reception rooms, four bathrooms and a large double drawing room.

Knowing the financial predicament of her cousin and of Ogilvy's relatively limited income ('I work for every penny I earn'), Elizabeth suggested they should take over one of the grace-and-favour residences in Kensington Palace but Ogilvy, a proud man intent on living without outside help, gently refused the offer saying, as was very true, that the longer they stayed in Thatched Cottage the more they loved it. At first they were short of furniture and, apart from tables, chairs and a few other small pieces from Ogilvy's bachelor flat in Culrose Street, they were more than grateful for those wedding gifts which could be used to fill up empty spaces, especially several lovely items given by his grandmother, Mabel, Countess of Airlie, who had been a Lady of the Bed-chamber and close friend of Queen Mary for more than half a century.

Angus Ogilvy had grown up in the wartime years and had gone straight from Eton into the Scots Guards so despite the fairly close connections his family enjoyed with Royalty, he himself had had relatively few long encounters with the Royal Family. Restless and unable to readjust to civilian life or make up his mind about his future career, he astonished everyone by joining the Merchant Navy and signing up on an old freighter bound for the Baltic ports. His spell at sea was short-lived: for twelve days in one of the worst North Sea gales in years, he was continuously seasick and that was the deciding factor – he gave up the Merchant Navy. His thoughts turned to commerce and after his return home he joined an insurance broker, a job which was to lead him to a financial group in the City where he found his natural outlet in the world of banking, insurance and the stockmarket.

He first met Princess Alexandra through a coincidence. He visited the Kent family home – Coppins, near Iver in Buckinghamshire – to advise Alexandra's widowed mother, the Princess Marina, Duchess of Kent, about her pending tour of Malaya where Ogilvy had served with the Scots Guards. While he was at Coppins he met Alexandra who was home on holiday from Heathfield, the girls' public school near Ascot.

The couple's next encounter, which was to change both their lives, was many years later at a weekend house party given by Lady Zia Wernher, one of Elizabeth's closest friends: this was in 1957 at a time when many people in the family were convinced that Alexandra would fulfil her Greek-born mother's great hope and marry Crown Prince Constantine of Greece. Alexandra was already twenty-one, and although she accompanied her mother on many visits to Athens, she developed no real affinity with Greece, and the more Constantine was pushed in her direction, the less and less interested she appeared to be and the more she was seen in the company of young Army officer friends of her brother, Eddie, Duke of Kent, then at Sandhurst.

When they were only children Alexandra – Alex as she was known to friends and family – and Eddie were already well aware of their mother's overriding ambition and desire for them both one day to marry into one of the European Royal families, and as they headed towards maturity so the pressure became greater. But what Princess Marina had not counted on was the close friendship of brother and sister, Eddie being only a year older than Alex, which brought them both into contact with each other's close and non-Royal friends. People like Ogilvy with his almost confirmed bachelor life style, who was at once an exciting, heady and heavyweight intellectual encounter for her daughter.

Ogilvy's courtship of Alexandra can be likened in some ways to that of Margaret and Armstrong-Jones in that each man intrigued a Royal Princess by his independent bachelor life-style which at the time of meeting neither man seemed inclined to throw overboard in favour of marriage. Over long months Ogilvy wined and dined Alexandra and at the flat he then rented in Park West, a large block on the Edgware Road, she mingled with his wide group of friends, many from the City. He always escorted her home to Kensington Palace by taxi. At that time Alexandra's workload was increasing year by year and her ability to cope alone on strenuous tours, both at home and abroad, meant that she was frequently out of London for days at a time, leaving Angus footloose and fancy free – but always he was waiting for her when she returned.

What made Ogilvy hesitate to propose to Alexandra was that he could not see any satisfactory future for them both within the Royal Family set-up: he personally loathed the idea of taking part in public duties of any kind, let alone Royal duties, and yet at the same time he could not see how Alexandra could withdraw from those Royal duties if she agreed to marry him. Sometimes Alexandra stayed with Angus's family at Airlie Castle in Scotland, and sometimes Angus was invited to lunch or dinner with Alexandra at the Queen Mother's Windsor home, Royal Lodge. It was not until November 1962, when they were both invited as house guests of the Queen Mother at Birkhall, that the problem was finally resolved: Angus secretly proposed and was accepted and the couple agreed that they would both continue with their own independent careers – provided Elizabeth agreed.

Back in London and before the official announcement of the engagement was made, Princess Alexandra climbed into the driving seat of her black Mini and having made an appointment to see her cousin in Buckingham Palace, officially asked permission to marry Ogilvy. Like Armstrong-Jones, Ogilvy was offered an Earldom but refused it on the grounds, as he told friends, that 'I don't see why I should get a peerage just because I have married a Princess.' Fiercely independent, Ogilvy subsidised his wife's royal duties out of his own pocket – and these were costly: it was not until about ten years after the marriage that Elizabeth, unaware of the financial strain on Ogilvy, finally increased her cousin's allowance to a more realistic sum.

For anyone marrying a relative of the Queen there can be no suggestion of impropriety in public at any level and in 1976 when a Government report criticised one of the many firms with which Ogilvy was associated he at once resigned from all his boardroom appointments – he held at least seventeen directorships. Even though he was not personally involved in any way, Ogilvy gave up his City appointments saying it was 'the honourable thing to do'. He felt this drastic action was the only course open to him because his wife was a member of the Royal Family: in fact, there was absolutely no reason for him to resign at all. He subsequently joined Sotheby's, the famous firm of fine art auctioneers as adviser-director in their Finance Department.

Ogilvy has never had robust health and for years has been dogged by chronic back trouble and numerous new methods of treatment and rest cures have failed to ease his long spells of severe pain, which he tolerates with remarkable patience. As a father, one of the major concerns he shares with his wife is the upbringing of their two children, James and Marina, on what he calls

140

'ordinary lines'. Ogilvy once said,

> It is very difficult making sure that they develop on ordinary and sensible lines when they belong to such an august family on their mother's side. When they go back to school after Christmas or summer holidays other children quite naturally ask them what they did and where they went and they can only say that they spent the holiday with the Queen at Windsor Castle or Balmoral.

This same problem presents itself, only in triplicate, to Alexandra's brother, Eddie, Duke of Kent, and his hauntingly beautiful wife, Katherine, whose major concern in life are their three children, George, Earl of St Andrews, Lady Helen Windsor and Lord Nicholas Windsor: they are without doubt three of the most scholastically brilliant children in Elizabeth's growing young family; there are especially great hopes ahead for their son and heir, George, Earl of St Andrews, the only member of the Royal Family ever to have won an open scholarship to Eton where he went as a King's Scholar. If the Duchess had had her way, the Kent family would have been larger but a seven-month miscarriage in 1977 not only put paid to any more children but was such a shattering personal blow that it took her many months to get over the sudden loss of her child.

As a team the Kents are yet another example of Elizabeth's reliable and enduring 'Second Eleven', essentially a reserved couple who jealously guard their private life in their London grace-and-favour home in York House at St James's Palace. They, too, have no background of inherited wealth. For twenty-one years the Duke was a full-time army officer and his official pay was only boosted by limited investments. His wife had no private income either, although she inherited £100,000 when her father, Sir William Worsley, a former Lord Lieutenant, died at the family home in Malton.

In the early 1970s their financial situation was so severely stretched that the Kents finally sold the family home, Coppins, because they simply could not cope with the overheads and were grateful to Elizabeth not only for the grace-and-favour apartment in St James's but also for Anmer Hall, a four-bedroomed house in the grounds of Sandringham as a place where they could escape from London at the weekends. It took Eddie Kent two years to persuade Katherine Worsley, daughter of an East Yorkshire squire and former Member of Parliaments to marry him because she said – and she meant this – she did not feel she could face up to life as a Royal Duchess, and furthermore her great ambition was to be a teacher.

Eddie first met his future bride at a County ball when he was stationed at Catterick in North Yorkshire in 1957 and their growing friendship was viewed with some concern by his mother, Princess Marina, who, worried by her eldest son's playboy image and not at all sure that he was ready for the responsibilities of marriage, urged him to wait a while. Eddie Kent finally took matters into his own hands during the Royal Christmas of 1958, and while on a short leave from his Regiment in Germany.

He was spending Christmas with the Royal Family at Sandringham when he sought out his cousin Elizabeth and asked her permission to leave the party on Boxing Day to drive to Hovingham Hall near Malton in East Yorkshire to see Katie. Eddie's suit was at last successful and they were married in York Minster in June 1961. The Queen Mother voiced the opinion of many members of the Family when she said about Katie, 'She is just the right girl for Eddie.' And of course the Queen Mother was right.

From the start Katie had a steadying influence on her impetuous and fun-loving husband who in many respects resembled his father, an Air Commodore in the RAF who was killed in 1942 when the Sunderland flying boat, taking him to inspect crews stationed in Iceland, crashed into the side of a mountain in Caithness. In his youth he, too, like Eddie, had cut a dashing figure in the society of his day. As the years went by, happily immersed in the cocoon of family life provided by his essentially home-loving wife, Eddie Kent, with the tradition of Eton and Sandhurst and a commission in a smart cavalry regiment (Royal Scots Greys), settled down and acquired a new and purposeful dignity.

He had talents which were unsuspected; at Sandhurst he won the Modern Languages prize and passed a stiff examination as a French interpreter and at the Staff College at Camberley passed out in the top ten. From the Staff College he went to the Ministry of Defence, donned a bowler hat and carried an umbrella, but he revealed to Lord Mountbatten that he was no longer happy with his life in the Army, declaring that he was more interested in electronics than tank warfare.

What had really upset him dated back to 1971 when, as a Major in command of a Squadron in the Royal Scots Greys, he was unceremoniously recalled from Ulster after a tour of only three weeks. It was felt in Whitehall that as a cousin of the Queen, no matter how dedicated a soldier he was, he could not be made an IRA target. Kent felt he was being restricted at a time when his role in the Army really mattered and believed it to be an untenable situation that his contemporaries continued to serve in Ulster while he was prevented from doing so. Spurred on by Mountbatten and encouraged by his wife, he told the Queen of his dilemma: she urged him to look about and find the sort of job he really wanted and when the vice-chairmanship of the British Overseas Trade Board came up, a civilian job, he seized it with both hands.

Top men in the industrial and commercial world had a jolt when they met Eddie Kent for the first time: they found him to be not only shrewd but a man with very much a mind of his own. His overseas work was greatly assisted by his ability to switch languages so easily – a relic from his Sandhurst days – revealing a fluency which put to shame most of the British exporters he encountered. If Eddie Kent still remains an underrated member of the Royal Family it is because it is possible that he underrates himself.

143

Like other members of the Royal 'Second Eleven' he accepts that he will never have any of the charisma of men like Charles and his brothers but nevertheless he gives the impression of being a strong man when he is seen at his best, square-shouldered and in the uniform of a Lieutenant-Colonel greeting the world's VIPs at London Airport on behalf of Elizabeth. His wife's severe depression and near nervous breakdown, following the death of her unborn baby when she was in her forties, seemed to age him considerably but in those difficult days he was a tower of strength.

If anyone ever worked a near miracle within the ranks of the Royal Family it was the extrovert Princess Michael of Kent, an ash-blonde, sensationally beautiful six-footer who, in a matter of a year or so, made a great splash on the Royal scene and caused not inconsiderable eyebrow raising among her new in-laws. Her husband, Prince Michael of Kent, was a confirmed bachelor noted for his string of conquests. He met his match when as an officer in the mechanised cavalry – once the 11th Hussars – he encountered the striking Baroness Marie Christine von Riebnitz who was a Catholic and a divorcee.

It was only after consultation with the Archbishop of Canterbury, a special meeting of the Privy Council and a petition to the Pope, that Elizabeth was able to give her permission for them to marry. Because of the Act of Settlement of 1701, which forbids marriages between a member of the Royal Family and a Catholic, their wedding had to be celebrated in the Town Hall of Vienna, a civilian ceremony instead of a religious one. The marriage also meant that Michael had to renounce his succession to the Throne – he was sixteenth in line – but it did not mean that any children of the marriage, who would be brought up in the Church of England, would forfeit their rights of succession.

A debonair, highly sophisticated man of the world, his presence at dinner tables was eagerly sought by hostesses wherever he went and he did not earn his label as a super playboy for nothing. Off duty he devoted himself to some of the most dangerous sports in the world and for a long time his passion was competing in international bobsleigh races, at which he had several near accidents. He took part in powerboat races and once again almost broke his neck. His real enthusiasm was motor racing and he drove in scores of gruelling rallies and won many trophies, even though he was up against drivers far more experienced than himself.

Like his brother Eddie, he managed on his Army pay and had just enough private money to keep a small house going in London. He seldom carried out Royal engagements but always helped out on the infrequent occasions when Elizabeth urgently required a stand in: for example, at the funeral of President Fakhruddin Ali Ahmet in India in 1977 when costs for his trip were borne by the Queen. All the family were convinced that Michael was a confirmed bachelor who would continue to lead a strictly non-Royal life so that when Marie Christine, bubbling over with self-confidence, captured his heart, they were utterly taken aback.

The couple were head over heels in love but Prince Michael was nervous to the point of fear about approaching the Queen and asking her permission to marry. Like so many other members of the family when they found themselves in a serious quandry, he telephoned Lord Mountbatten in his London home in Kinnerton Street and asked if he could see him on an 'important and personal matter'.

Twenty-four hours later and over an early evening drink in Mountbatten's small but gracious sitting room, with its pale blue walls and its centrepiece of a low glass-topped table which charted Lady Mountbatten's world tours betwen 1921 and 1939, Prince Michael and Marie Christine explained their anxiety. The younger man asked Mountbatten if he would consider making the first move by interceding on his behalf with the Queen who, he feared, might be against the marriage because Marie Christine was a divorcee.

Mountbatten's counsel was that they should keep

their love for one another secret for the time being and said that as soon as the right opportunity presented itself, possibly at one of his weekly tête-à-têtes with the Queen, he would raise the matter with her. Mountbatten added that although he did not want to raise false hopes, he felt that provided the Queen did not feel she was being rushed into making a decision, he could see no reason why she should not give her blessing to the match. To his chagrin and considerable irritation, Mountbatten found himself up against a surprising amount of opposition to the marriage in Court circles and Prince Michael and his future bride spent many anxious weeks before they learned that Mountbatten had worked his usual miracle and that the outcome of his talks with the Queen was a happy one.

Before returning to London at the end of their honeymoon Prince and Princess Michael spent a few days in Paris where they had a strange encounter. Marie Christine, who had been brought up on the dramatic love story of the uncrowned King Edward VIII and the American divorcee, Mrs Simpson, had always longed to meet the now very old and sick Duchess of Windsor. Impressed by Marie Christine's charm and sincerity, the Duchess's French physician, Dr Jean Thin, allowed the couple a brief glimpse of the former sovereign's widow in her private room in the American Hospital in the French capital. The door was quietly opened and Prince and Princess Michael saw the sleeping figure of the Duchess of Windsor. They were the only members of the Royal Family to have asked to see her for many years.

In a relatively short time after their marriage Marie Christine made it clear to one and all that she simply loved being a Royal Princess, adored the Royal round and was ready to take on any amount of hard work. Although the couple were not on the Civil List and therefore received no money from the State, they managed to clock up no less than fifty engagements in the first year, a year in which Princess Michael also had her first baby, Lord Frederick Windsor. To the disquiet of some of her husband's relatives, she stepped out in style wearing stunning clothes that completely outshone both Princess Margaret and Princess Anne and her easy and gracious manner endeared her wherever she went.

At first her name did not appear in the Court Circular but, undismayed and content, she graciously accepted one invitation after another, efficiently carrying out her jobs – albeit with an occasional giggle here and there, the most infectiously happy mistake she could have made. Her outspoken and direct approach did not always go down well with senior Household officials: when she attended one of her first fashion shows instead of giving a formal and unrevealing Royal glance, she made earnest notes about striking outfits that impressed her. She never minded freely admitting that she was sometimes nervous before engagements and once said, 'I always say a little prayer, "Please don't let me make a gaffe."'

Mountbatten was charmed by her poise and open manner and went out of his way to help and guide her during that first year. Mountbatten was a man who constantly looked ahead and believed that if the Royal Family was to move with the times then more men and women with the Royal prefix HRH should be allowed to take full time jobs either in industry, or any other field that interested them. So it was with very real enthusiasm that he learned that Prince Michael was anxious to leave the Army and take up a full-time job. Once again it was Mountbatten who broached Prince Michael's desire for a change in life-style with the Queen, and by 1979 he had put his desk job at the War Office behind him, donned a civilian suit and moved into the City.

When they are in London Prince Michael and his wife live with their two children in charming grace-and-favour apartments in Kensington Palace with the Prince and Princess of Wales, Princess Margaret, the Duke and Duchess of Gloucester and Princess Alice, Duchess of Gloucester, as their neighbours. Princess Michael is a wealthy woman in her own right and after spending many months searching for a second home in the country, they finally settled for a small Georgian house in Gloucestershire within easy distance of the Wales's home, High Grove near Tetbury and Princess Anne at Gatcombe Park.

Prince and Princess Michael proved themselves to be a highly complementary couple, desperately anxious to succeed in their Royal role. The first real accolade came in 1981 when the Queen invited them to represent her at the Belize Independence celebrations. They are now members of the Queen's much valued 'Second Eleven' – men and women like the Duke and Duchess of Kent, the Duke and Duchess of Gloucester and Princess Alexandra and Mr Angus Ogilvy, people to whom she can turn, secure in the knowledge that they will never let her down.

7

Uncle Dickie

OVER THE YEARS the Queen and Prince Philip have achieved a remarkably happy private life of their own. Apart from Sundays and holidays, there are very few days in the year when they are not working and like other married couples in their age group, they have each developed their own particular style of leisure and relaxation.

When a working day is over, there are many evenings when Elizabeth, quite alone, sits back in an easy chair, the *Radio Times* and *TV Times* close at hand, watching television programmes or a video film on her 26in. screen, waiting for Philip to come in from one of his many engagements. The first positive indication that Philip is home is a sudden scurry of corgis in the direction of the hall of their private apartments as Philip, sometimes in uniform but mostly in dinner jacket, returns full of news and ready and eager to recount in minute detail his experiences of the evening, knowing full well that he has an expectant listener who wants to know 'everything'.

Here, in total privacy, in a high-ceilinged sitting room with a large bay window, a room which also doubles as Elizabeth's study, they can talk themselves out for just as long as they like. Without a servant in sight and relaxed in a comfortably cluttered room, with magazines and books all over the place and two water bowls for the dogs in the hearth – the whole scene bearing not the slightest resemblance to the ornate State apartments on the same first floor of Buckingham Palace – they often stay up exchanging views and news until after midnight. The Queen can unload her personal experiences of the day, knowing that the one person who can understand the pressures of work, which sometimes leaves her physically and mentally exhausted, is Philip. He can always be relied on to see the funny side of her life and cheer her up.

What these easy exchanges symbolise more than anything else is the real strength of what is, by any standards, a most extraordinary marriage, extraordinary in the sense that from the beginning in 1947 both partners knew it Had to work. They were both sure and secure in their love for one another: but at the same time they must have accepted that although they could make mistakes in the future, could sometimes be at cross-purposes with one another, at no time, either by so much as a glance or a gesture, could any private differences between them ever be indicated in public. No matter what the years held in store, neither of them could ever contemplate any form of separation or the break up of their union. They were married for life – like it or not.

These blunt facts have to be borne in mind in any attempt to assess the relationship of the Queen and Philip, both in their own ways determined and strong-willed people, each with a stubborn streak and very positive minds of their own. This makes it all the more remarkable that, apart from the occasional ups and downs from which no married couples are immune, their marriage has developed into a tremendously powerful and mutually supporting unit. Their open life-style has been such that it would have been impossible to hide any serious cracks in the relationship and such differences of opinion that they have experienced have, for the most part, been of a relatively minor nature.

All their children have confirmed that while they have

witnessed gentle leg-pulling and arguments between their parents, they have never witnessed outright quarrels or serious bickering of any kind. Nevertheless, over the years there have been sharp exchanges at times and senior members of the Royal Household are quick to spot certain cool or icy moments as the pair stride out into the quadrangle of Buckingham Palace and step into their waiting car. These moments of mutual irritation blow over very quickly.

Long ago the Queen and Philip came to the conclusion that since they had to carry out many separate engagements in their different work spheres, their schedules had to be planned not only to achieve maximum efficiency but also to allow for individual likes and dislikes. For the most part Philip finds racing tedious and cuts his attendances at meetings down to a minimum. He is without a doubt a technocrat and a politician manqué and prefers to gravitate towards people like the Ferranti brothers and men of their stimulating ilk, in order to pit his wits against challenging minds. Such cut-and-thrust encounters have little appeal for the Queen who prefers to charge her mental batteries during her regular encounters with eminent statesmen and diplomats both from home and abroad and, say, in her regular Tuesday meetings with the Prime Minister of the day at Buckingham Palace. The Queen does not enjoy evening functions like dinners, which so often take place in rooms filled with cigar smoke with long speeches following heavy meals, so the couple decided it would suit them both better if Philip, who thoroughly enjoys making after-dinner speeches and is in his element during brisk exchanges at such soirées, accepted this sort of invitation leaving the Queen free to follow her own pursuits.

So, although certain first nights and galas remain inescapable, the Queen nevertheless manages to enjoy quite a number of evenings at home doing exactly as she pleases – having her mother, sister or a friend to dinner, catching up with official homework, reading or, if she feels like it, curling up in an easy chair and watching television. She occasionally relaxes by listening to records of taped music when she is alone.

The Queen has long been resigned to the fact that her husband could never share such relaxed hours even at the end of a long and busy day: he is a workaholic, the sort of man who could only watch television if he were doing something else at the same time, either swotting up reports or making notes about a forthcoming speech, keeping half an eye on the screen. His restless nature and addiction to work is possibly one of the most trying aspects of her marriage with which the Queen has had to come to terms.

As her husband, searching for a fulfilling and satisfying role for himself as Consort, espoused one cause after another, often inflicting punishing schedules on himself, the Queen discovered early in her reign that all her protestations were in vain: she recognised that there was no way of changing Philip unless she wanted a frustrated man on her hands. By giving him his head to pursue his own interests – many of which did not interest her at all – no matter whether they took him to a regimental dinner at the Dorchester or winged him to some far distant part of the globe to see a new technological project for himself, both of them benefited. They come together not only as husband and wife but as friends who stimulate one another by not always sharing the same interests and by not always living in each other's pocket.

Both have excellent memories and if one of them is uncertain about a date or place the other acts as an accurate prompter. Philip has a remarkable visual memory and can remember names and put them to the right faces and when he has any doubts he can always turn to his private card index system – now very large indeed – which meticulously lists details of people he has met over the years. They are kept up to date so that when Philip meets these people again, often after a long interval, he can put questions like, 'How's your son George doing these days?' 'Been doing any more timber felling lately?' People are left astonished. 'Fancy him remembering that,' they will say. If anything, Elizabeth probably has the edge on Philip when it comes to a factual memory. She has caught out numerous politicians in her time: she reads all her official papers meticulously and Sir Harold Wilson, former Labour Prime Minister, freely confessed that she remembered things which had completely escaped his own phenomenal memory.

Since both their diaries are made up many months in advance, both the Queen and Philip always know where each of them is at any given moment in the day. However, they do occasionally have secrets from one another and the greatest of all was the one which the Queen kept from Philip when they celebrated their Silver Wedding anniversary in 1972. For this very special occasion the Queen decided to give her husband a very special present – a private 'den' of his own which he could use during the summer holidays at Balmoral and where he could work without interruption. She spent many weeks pondering over her idea and finally designed a special chalet containing all the gadgets she knew he loved – an easel for his painting, bookshelves, a special table for microscopes, and so on. Unbeknownst to Philip, this carefully planned 'den' was secretly put up on the Balmoral estate not very far from the Castle and it is said that there were tears in Philip's eyes when the Queen first showed him the secret present she had so lovingly planned for him.

The closeness that has developed between the Queen and her husband has been a gradual process over the years and the person who, from the beginning, had the greatest influence on their marriage was Lord Mountbatten whose true role within the Royal Family was only fully understood by a very few people. He was in the unique position of having known both the Queen and Philip intimately since their infancy: he knew and understood their individual make-up inside out – probably better than either of them did themselves. No mean psychologist in his own right, he was very much a father figure to both of them and it is no exaggeration to say that Mountbatten gave the Queen and Philip a personal insight that neither of them would ever have achieved without him. In their unique roles as Sovereign and Consort, they faced one major hurdle in their marriage from the time Elizabeth succeeded to the Throne in 1952: neither of them had anyone – other than each other – to whom they could turn and talk freely about deeply personal matters. Both needed someone whom they could trust absolutely and whom they both respected, for a 'second opinion'.

Apart from the weighty matters of State which the Queen had to share with her Ministers, she was constantly faced with family issues of one sort or other which had to be resolved. Some were relatively simple decisions to be reached as to whether a certain relative should or should not be given a grace-and-favour home but others were of a far more complicated nature involving long-term plans concerning the family as a whole or the Queen in particular.

It was here that Mountbatten filled a tremendous gap in the Queen's life and performed a role which no-one suspected. The Queen, for example, while she had close friends from childhood whom she trusted implicitly, could never, in her role as head of the family, seek advice from them on issues which troubled her, issues she felt were for her and her alone to decide. It was then that she would turn to Mountbatten.

She was close to her mother, who could be relied upon to be helpful in all circumstances but the Queen needed someone far more objective on matters that were often essentially personal. In addition there was a certain barrier between them that applies in most mother-and-daughter relationships, a hesitancy to reveal all. There was also Princess Margaret, but here again, although they were completely free and honest with one another, Elizabeth's younger sister simply did not have the knowledge or breadth of vision to act as a sounding board if and when the Queen needed to talk herself out; Princess Margaret had never been involved in matters of State, except for her routine duties of a Privy Counsellor, and not infrequently was directly involved in domestic anxieties which faced the Queen.

Mountbatten, 'Uncle Dickie' to all the Royal Family, had been an integral part of the British monarchial structure all his life, and was the one person, apart from her husband, with whom Elizabeth could discuss anything and to whom she could always turn for help. No one ever spoke more frankly to the Queen than this wise man with his vast reservoir of knowledge and experience both inside and outside the sometimes rarified atmosphere of the family and the men and women who comprise the Court and the Establishment.

From Mountbatten she received, as did other people in his very intimate circle, not so much hardline positive advice but rather a carefully reasoned résumé of the issues facing her which made it easier for her to weigh up the various pros and cons of a situation and so enable her to reach her own final decision. It was Mountbatten's habit, after his retirement as First Sea Lord in 1965, to leave his small but elegant three-storied house in Kinnerton Street, just off Belgrave Square, at seven o'clock once a week and drive himself in his ageing but beloved Jaguar the short distance to Buckingham Palace to see the Queen, usually staying for three and a half or four hours. In their relaxed time together over dinner, the Queen was able to air any subject under the sun.

On his side, Mountbatten was able to supply her with the sort of information which would otherwise have never reached her ears. As Mountbatten was on first-name terms with almost everyone who mattered both in public and political life, he was able to keep her up-to-date on developments in many fields and recount topical news about the quirks and foibles of men and women in public life. In what he termed his 'gossips' with the Queen, Mountbatten was able to brief her on private and current lines of thinking in many quarters, highly valuable information which could not have reached her from any other source.

In their different ways, these two people both loved Philip deeply and so without hesitation they could discuss him freely together, laughing at some of his escapades or deliberating on matters they knew to be uppermost in his mind. In Mountbatten, a man of immense talent and sound practical commonsense, a brilliant conversationalist and world famous in his own right, the Queen found her true mentor; he was her guide and philosopher.

Mountbatten always went out of his way to have an extremely amusing piece of 'gossip' ready that would make the Queen roar her head off – she has a very hearty and infectious laugh in private – something that she could store up ready to bring out at her next meeting with a Minister or some other official. It was Mountbatten who was the first person to reveal to the Queen that he had discovered that she possessed a title of which she was completely unaware: that of Duchess of Normandy.

Senior members of the Royal Household were aware of Mountbatten's closeness with the Queen and so while he was therefore greatly admired, he was also, to a very great extent, secretly feared at many levels. Nothing escaped his vigilant notice and if he was ever aware that anything was amiss within any of the Royal establishments, he did not hesitate to tell the Queen if he felt it was in her interest to be made aware of the situation. Holidays are the times of the year when the Queen is most easily accessible to members of her family but, even then, many of them are hesitant to raise some personal issues and so it was that while he was alive nearly all of them, with the exception of the Queen Mother, at some time or other sought the advice of Mountbatten before they made any direct approach to the Queen.

After members of the family had been to Broadlands, his seat in Hampshire, and got their worries off their chests, Mountbatten would wisely bide his time until what he considered to be the most judicious moment to broach the problem with Elizabeth had arrived. He rightly felt that he was doing the Queen a great service in saving her from being troubled over minor problems when she had other more important things on her mind, small problems which were nevertheless often of very real   conse-quence to a relative. He also knew he was drawing her attention to family matters about which she might otherwise have remained totally unaware.

When he was with the Queen, Mountbatten always addressed her as 'Lillibet', but when he was talking to members of the Royal Family he always referred to her as 'The Queen' even, say, when he was talking to his son-in-law, Lord Brabourne. Only a very few close relatives and contemporaries ever call Elizabeth by her Christian name: even to Mountbatten's two sons-in-law, Lord Brabourne and interior designer David Hicks, she remains 'Ma'am' just as she does to Captain Mark Phillips, the Duchess of Kent, the Duchess of Gloucester, Angus Ogilvy, the Princess of Wales and Princess Michael of Kent.

It was not only Elizabeth who relied so heavily on Mountbatten. He was also Philip's greatest friend and intimate apart from Elizabeth, but the relationship between the two men was different in that Mountbatten was less gentle with his nephew and never minced his words whenever he thought this necessary. Philip may have been the First Gentleman in the Realm but Mount-batten throughout his life still represented parental authority for the nephew he had brought up from youth into manhood and when it came to a showdown of any sort it was not always Philip who won the day. There were sulky spells which lasted for weeks when Philip stubbornly refused to talk to his uncle because Mount-batten had been to blunt with him. Undoubtedly, without Mountbatten to turn to and to be relied upon always to give straightforward answers to straightfor-ward questions, Elizabeth and Philip both individually and together would often have felt very lost indeed, as would other members of the family.

Mountbatten was meticulous in the extreme and was accustomed to living a highly organised life. He was always punctual. He was always totally briefed before he made any speech or attended any gathering and he expected members of the Royal Family to be equally punctilious and equally efficient. As younger members of the Royal Family began to take on public engagements he would encourage them when he thought they were doing well or suggest greater care or ways and means of improvement if he felt they were not adding up in his eyes. As the Duke of Kent, Princess Alexandra and others in their age group began to take on more responsible duties, sometimes representing the Queen abroad, he would carefully go over their plans for foreign tours, often completely altering schedules, pointing out that if engagements were changed and timing tightened up more personal appearances could be included in the trip. It was his proud boast that when pushed, he could shake eighty hands a minute.

During the hard-pressed working years in the first decade of her reign, Mountbatten's constant eagle eye over the activities of her large family was indeed a blessing for the Queen. By then Prince Philip was travelling some 80,000 miles a year and delivering at least eleven major speeches in that time, and he too was more than content to know that his uncle was acting in loco parentis when he was abroad. It was at this time in their marriage that Philip avoided the serious mistake he had made when he embarked on an unusually lengthy trip through the South Atlantic covering 40,000 miles and was away from London and Buckingham Palace from October 1956 until early in 1957 – missing the traditional Christmas. Because the tour lasted so long there was damaging gossip and rumours of a rift in the marriage which distressed the Queen and her husband: the truth was that Philip had longed for such a temporary escape from public life.

As Robert Lacey in his biography of Elizabeth II wrote,

'Her husband's resentment at the truncating of his naval career took the form of long hours in the *Britannia*, like his expedition in the winter of 1956–7 when he could exploit the chores of his role as consort to recapture something of his carefree days at sea.'

The Queen had fully understood and freely accepted Philip's longing for a break and the fact that she could never indulge herself in any similar form of escape did not deter her from encouraging him to explore new territories. They talked regularly to each other by telephone and when they were reunited in Lisbon, Philip was refreshed and invigorated and the Queen all smiles at what was a joyful reunion. It was at once both tragic and ironic that her determination never to make Philip feel shackled, to urge him to satisfy his longing for personal adventure, should have boomeranged on them both in this way.

Those people who know the Queen well can easily recognise a moment of displeasure. She does not have to utter a word. She has a certain steely and withering look described by friends as 'a look which makes anyone on the receiving end wish the floor would open and swallow them up'. One person for whom Elizabeth had only deep warmth and affection and who witnessed the empathy which flowed between the Queen and Philip as they matured was an old lady who spent long weeks living in a second-floor suite in Buckingham Palace from the early days of the reign until she died in 1967. She had always been a regular visitor to the Palace and yet she remained almost unknown to everyone except senior members of the Royal Household and members of the Royal Family.

She was Princess Alice of Greece and Denmark, the mother-in-law to whom Elizabeth was utterly devoted and with whom she spent long hours sitting spellbound as she listened to stories of a European Royal past. Unlike Elizabeth's own mother, the Queen Mother, Princess Alice, whose German father became a naturalised Englishman, was linked by marriage to nearly every

159

Royal house in Europe and her reminiscences of the splendour of Royal days she had known in childhood in Russia, Germany, Sweden and Denmark would go on for hours. The daughter-in-law and mother-in-law established a remarkable rapport.

Elizabeth went to great lengths to see that Philip's mother was happy, always making sure that there was a tiny posy of cut flowers on her breakfast tray, always popping into her suite with some titbit of news or other. Yet at the time of Elizabeth's marriage to Philip in 1947, only two years after the end of the Second World War, Princess Alice was kept well in the background and was never seen on any official wedding photographs. This strange situation arose because there had been a tacit understanding between George VI and the Government of the day that Philip's German connections – and they were very strong – should not be stressed but rather played down as much as possible: anti-German feelings were still running high in Britain and so it was that apart from her mother-in-law, none of Elizabeth's German in-laws were invited to the great ceremony in Westminster Abbey. For many years afterwards Philip's three elder sisters to whom he was devoted – Margarita; Theodora, known as 'Dolla'; and Sophie, known as 'Tiny' – always slipped quietly into England and their visits to one of the Royal residences, usually Balmoral or Buckingham Palace, went unannounced and unnoticed.

For a very long time Princess Alice, a great-grand-daughter of Queen Victoria, and herself born at Windsor, would only come to England to visit her son and daughter-in-law under a cloak of near secrecy. Slender, tall, with a striking carriage and the same quizzical eyes and smile of Philip, she lived for many years in Athens with The Sisterhood of Martha and Maria, a community of working sisters she founded in 1948. Throughout those years, while staying at Buckingham Palace, she would wander around London in a grey suit or grey coat and a convent style grey headdress, without ever being recognised. She travelled everywhere by bus and underground, shopped in Selfridges and Boots, often strolling among office workers relaxing in the sunshine of summer days in Hyde Park and St James's Park, only to return to the Palace to regale Elizabeth with tales of her encounters and adventures.

Over the years Elizabeth became utterly devoted to her mother-in-law who had the same stubborn streak of independence inherited from her by Philip. When Princess Alice decided, despite pleas from Elizabeth to stay longer, that it was time for her to return to Athens, she always waved aside any notice that she should travel to London Airport by limousine and be received in the VIP lounge used by the Royal Family. She made her way by airport bus and checked in her own luggage which she had labelled herself and she flew back to Athens tourist-class without any fuss at all.

As she grew frailer and tired more easily after an operation in the London Clinic, she finally gave in to the Queen who had been pressing her to come and live permanently in Buckingham Palace. As she told her friends, 'With Elizabeth and Philip near me, I knew I had really come home.'

The Queen was indeed fortunate that her closest senior relatives, her mother, the Queen Mother, her mother-in-law, Princess Alice, and Lord Mountbatten, not only liked children but could all communicate with them at any age level so that when she was away with Philip on long tours she knew that these wise and loving members of the family would more than compensate for her absence. Prince Charles and Princess Anne both undoubtedly benefited from the times spent with the two grandmothers and Mountbatten to the extent that regular partings from their parents were never the wrench they might have been if they had been ordinary children with ordinary parents.

8

More Babies

As a child, the Queen had always yearned for a baby brother and to belong to a big family. When she married Prince Philip in 1947 she made it abundantly clear that she hoped to have a large family herself. It was only her early accession to the Throne in 1952 that caused the long gap between the birth of Prince Charles in 1948, Princess Anne in 1950 and that of her third child almost a decade later.

It was in the mid-afternoon of Friday, 19 February 1960 at the age of thirty-four that the Queen gave birth to her second son, Prince Andrew, the first child to be born to a reigning monarch since Princess Beatrice, Queen Victoria's last and ninth child, in 1857. Since it was considered undesirable for the Queen to be confined in a hospital, Prince Andrew, who weighed 7lbs 3ozs uttered his first cries in the enormous bathroom of the Belgian Suite of Buckingham Palace which had been specially converted into a delivery room. While the early months of pregnancy had not been easy because the Queen allowed herself to get over-taxed and over-tired, she soon regained her usual good health after a period of compulsory relaxation and the birth was simple and straightforward.

She was sitting up in bed, reading her 'boxes' and drinking tea a few hours later and in the months that followed the Queen found she had more time to spend in the Palace nursery than had ever been possible when Prince Charles and Princess Anne were still very young and she was immersed in learning and perfecting the intricacies of queenship. So determined was the Queen to spend as much time with Prince Andrew that she cut back her public duties as far as possible in order to be able to spend as much time as possible with him, regularly putting him to bed, reading him stories, generally playing with him for long spells and carefully and lovingly teaching him the letters of the alphabet herself.

Both she and Philip were convinced that they had unwisely and unwittingly allowed Prince Charles and Princess Anne to be over-exposed to the public gaze when they were toddlers and this policy was rapidly swung into reverse with the arrival of their third child who, for the first year of his life, was only seen in public once and in that time only two official photographs were ever issued. The Queen was convinced that maximum privacy would allow Andrew to develop more on the lines of an ordinary boy and if, like Charles, he showed a natural tendency towards shyness, this would not be exacerbated by the presence of crowds. As it turned out, Andrew was different in almost every way to his elder brother and almost from the time he could walk revealed a powerful streak of self-confidence combined with an ability to get into mischief at the slightest opportunity.

The Queen achieved enormous satisfaction from her new term of motherhood and four years later, with the succession now more than assured, she finally realised her great desire for a family of four children with the birth of her last child, Prince Edward, who was born five days prematurely in Buckingham Palace in March 1964. For the first time after the birth of any of her children, the Queen was advised by her doctors to take things more easily for a while and this was one of the rare occasions in her life when she was off work for two full months – previously only heavy colds or occasional bouts of sinusitis ever caused her to take sick leave, but even then she always did her official 'boxes'.

With the arrival of Prince Edward, the Queen was sure of herself, very much in command of her job and so moved into one of the happiest and most satisfying periods in her life, bringing up what she liked to call 'my second family'. By then Charles was away at Gordonstoun, trying to adjust to the spartan life and Princess Anne had settled down well at Benenden, so whatever spare time the Queen had was concentrated on nursery life again. She always regarded children's birthday parties as being of supreme importance and whenever one was being celebrated she always did her best to make sure that her official engagements were planned so that if she could not be present the entire time, she could join in the fun for at least an hour or so. Like her mother and sister, she was always in her element surrounded by exuberant and excited little girls and boys.

It was Princess Margaret, however, who always gave what the Queen considered to be the jolliest parties for the growing band of Royal children – her sister how had two children, a son and daughter, the Duchess of Kent also had a son and daughter and in the same year that Prince Edward was born, Princess Alexandra gave birth to her first son. When Elizabeth's nephew, David, Viscount Linley, celebrated his third birthday Prince Andrew was one of the fifteen very young guests invited to Princess Margaret's home in Kensington Palace.

Shortly before six o'clock, just like all the other parents, the Queen arrived to pick up her son, only hours after she had attended the State Opening of Parliament with all its pomp and pageantry, and she looked around eagerly for a glimpse of Andrew. Young as they were, the tiny tots already automatically knew that when they greeted the Queen for the first time they must bow or curtsey, and also perform this act of fealty before her sister. As a footman opened the door of her home in Kensington Palace one non-Royal four-year-old was greeted by Princess Margaret, her arms out-

164

stretched, who kissed the little boy on both cheeks. As soon as he was released he gave Princess Margaret a broad smile and then politely piped up, 'Hello, Ma'am,' and dashed into the party which was being held in the garden room at the back of the house overlooking the lawns.

All the furniture had been taken out and chairs had been put around the room with a slide and a small roundabout in the centre. Chatting away in another room was a group of nannies all in crisp white uniforms. Royal birthday parties usually began about half past three and after handing over their child for the party, mothers were not expected to return until six o'clock, by which time the children were always absolutely exhausted. The one Royal relative who resisted any hints that the party was for children only was the Queen Mother, who nearly always stayed from start to finish, listening to all the excited chatter and pausing to wipe an occasional sticky hand or helping a toddler get to her feet after taking a tumble.

It is noticeable that while Royal children never interrupt the Queen when she is talking, at these parties they would nevertheless rush up to her and, at the appropriate time, tell her about their afternoon. All the children were given the same present, for instance a bottle of fruit drops. Parents would come and collect their children who would put on their coats and, clutching their bottles of sweets, line up in Princess Margaret's hall with its floor made from Welsh slate. When Princess Margaret came to say goodbye, all the little girls – none of whom could have been more than five years old – made perfect curtseys and all the little boys made solemn bows. It is at these birthday parties, where all parents are either very close to members of the Royal Family or Royal themselves, that Royal children begin to strike up their first friendships which last for life.

Most of the children later go to the same preparatory and public schools and share in family celebrations of one kind or another, christenings, confirmations, weddings, silver weddings and so on. So it is that when they grow up Royal children always find themselves mixing with men and women they have known since nursery days, the few people with whom they can completely relax and with whom they can be totally at ease, their Royal status causing no inhibitions whatsoever. This pattern has been established for generations and even today remains very much the same. From their earliest days the family bond is all-powerful and from babyhood onwards, Royal children not only spend Easter, summer and Christmas holidays together but also share many weekends in the year, especially in the late spring and early summer months when, with their parents, they join the Queen and Prince Philip at Windsor Castle.

They grow up with the same good manners drilled into them from the time they can walk, acquire a similar voice intonation and soon begin to overuse the word 'one' – 'One feels that', 'One expects to' – a word that seems quaint to other people but which is accepted by them without question. Because they grow up in such a closely knit group, there has always been great hesitation, particularly on the part of the Queen's children, to make any real attempt to break out of this cocoon-like atmosphere, even when they reach teenage years.

During schooldays Prince Charles, Princess Anne, Prince Andrew and Prince Edward did not invite school friends 'home' since this would have presented the Queen with precisely the burden she sought to escape at holiday times – freedom from everyone outside the family, young or old. And equally on their side, Royal children looked forward to their holidays in much the same way as the Queen – to be alone with their parents and members of the family.

The great fun for Elizabeth in the 1960s, however, was the pre-school days of Andrew and Edward during a decade when six Royal cousins and second cousins were born in a period of six years – David, Viscount Linley and Sarah Armstrong-Jones, the children of Princess Margaret and Lord Snowdon, were born in 1961 and 1964;

166

George, Earl of St Andrews and Lady Helen Windsor, son and daughter of the Duke and Duchess of Kent arrived in 1962 and 1964; and James and Marina Ogilvy, son and daughter of Princess Alexandra and Mr Angus Ogilvy appeared on the scene in 1964 and 1966. The childhood days of Andrew and Edward were in striking contrast to that of any other Royal generation, including their elder brother and sister, Charles and Anne.

The Queen's attitude towards the upbringing of her 'second family' was far more flexible and both boys, for instance, often piled into a saloon car from the Buckingham Palace Mews and accompanied by a detective and a nanny went down to south coast resorts. They splashed in the sea, made sandcastles and even queued up for icecreams on promenades and although they made odd encounters with other children, no-one was ever aware of their identity. Unlike Charles and Anne, their photographs seldom appeared in the newspapers and so they were never immediately recognised on sight.

Their nursery regime was generally more relaxed – 'Mrs' Helen Lightbody's role had been taken over by a much gentler personality, Miss Mabel Anderson, who had joined the Queen as an assistant nanny well before her accession. Miss Anderson, warm and outgoing, is the only single woman known to have refused the courtesy title of 'Mrs'. The Queen worked far more closely with Miss Anderson than she had done with 'Mrs' Lightbody and while Andrew and Edward were always kept to a strict timetable, they were allowed far more freedom for play and games in the Buckingham Palace gardens where they had a sand-pit and a caravan in which to romp about on wet days.

It was very apparent early in his life that the most extrovert of the Queen's children, bubbling over with energy and constantly getting into one adventurous scrape after another was Andrew. It was never difficult to know when he was around: there was always noise. In almost every way Andrew was the complete antithesis to Charles who had been extremely reserved and dogged by shyness until he reached manhood. Prince Philip's three sisters always said that Andrew's mischievous and often downright naughty behaviour reminded them very much of their brother at the same age. It was fortunate that from the time of Andrew's birth until he went to school, the Queen, despite her tours abroad, nevertheless spent far more time with him than she had with her other children. He was wilful and his mother is credited with handling a potentially difficult child with great skill and insight.

Whenever he got into scrapes it was the Queen who gently rebuked him and in his early formative years she allowed Andrew – and later Edward – to play with his toys on the floor of her study, seldom being whisked back to his nursery because members of the Royal Household had business to discuss. With one sharp word the Queen could always silence Andrew but nevertheless his pranks became legendary: he climbed trees and scaffolding and ended up with cuts and bruises, fell into the lake at Buckingham Palace and when trying to carry out a balancing trick in front of younger cousins tumbled many times into a fountain in the grounds of Windsor Castle. He hid behind damask curtains in the Palace and jumped out to startle the first passer-by and Prince Philip once ended up at a film premiere with a black eye as a result of being on the receiving end of a playful wallop from his son.

It was more than somewhat of a relief for the Queen and Philip to discover that in Prince Edward, their youngest and last child, they had to cope with far less of a handful than Andrew. Even so, Andrew did his best to egg on the smaller boy into one sort of mischief or another. His influence over Edward, despite his inherent bossiness, was never really great since the younger boy, quieter by nature and far more self-contained, was not easily enticed or lured into escapades which did not appeal to him. Before they went away to school both Andrew and Edward were taken on regular sightseeing trips in London, again always accompanied by Miss

Anderson and a detective. These outings to museums, exhibitions, skating rinks, cricket matches and historic places of interest like the Tower of London, the Guildhall and even Madame Tussauds were regarded as a huge success because once again, the children were never recognised, not even on buses or the Underground.

Theirs was by no means the sort of 'ordinary' upbringing the Queen originally had in mind, but it was nevertheless a vast improvement on the relatively restricted childhood days Prince Charles and Princess Anne had known. Andrew and Edward, like their elder brother and sister before them, accepted their privileged life, with its palatial homes, a magnificent yacht, the ever-present footmen and pages and all the routine pomp of Palace life as the norm – they had known nothing else. It says much for the Queen's personal influence over these two boys that, when they finally had to face the harsher world of school life, they fared far better than either Charles or Anne. They both proved easy mixers and were more than able to stand up for themselves.

Prince Edward had the added advantage that after Prince Andrew went to Heatherdown preparatory school in the autumn of 1968, he still had three more years as the one remaining child living in Buckingham Palace with his parents. He had lessons in the Palace schoolroom with six other children, including two cousins of the same age, Lady Sarah-Armstrong Jones and James Ogilvy. Edward's great advantage, however, was that both parents devoted an enormous amount of time to their youngest son and lavished great affection upon him. Although he was for so long the centre of attention for the Queen and Prince Philip, Edward never showed any signs of being a spoiled child and in the absence of the demanding and rumbustious Andrew, thrived in the calm and quiet atmosphere of the Palace.

He benefited enormously not only from the very close relationship he enjoyed with both parents but also from his occasional encounters with the great and famous who went to the Palace. Because he was quiet and well behaved he was often allowed to shake hands with and chat to visiting dignitaries and bedtime was often extended. By the time he became a day boy at Gibbs, a preparatory school in Kensington, he was a far better adjusted seven year old than either of his brothers or his sister were at the same age. His really close companion who went with him to Gibbs was James Ogilvy and the two of them became almost inseparable.

Princess Margaret's two children, David, Viscount Linley and Lady Sarah Armstrong-Jones, did not grow up in anything like the splendour of Buckingham Palace: nevertheless, their home in Clock House in Kensington Palace, with its fine furniture, splendid works of art, had all the trappings of monarchy and wherever they went with their mother, the trio were always received with curtseys and bows. Lord Snowdon did what he could to counteract this side of their life, and saw to it that they were never over-indulged at home: toys and clothes were made to last, they made their own beds and everything had always to be put away in its proper place at the end of the day.

From the time they were born, Lord Snowdon was intent upon making his children fully aware that despite their Royal connections, they would both have to fend for themselves when they grew up. In this he had the full support of Princess Margaret who never made any bones about the fact that she does not regard her children as being 'Royal' in any way. But this was easier said than done and, in turn, Princess Alexandra and her husband, Angus Ogilvy, the Duke and Duchess of Kent, the Duke and Duchess of Gloucester and Prince and Princess Michael of Kent all had to face the same hazardous problem in bringing up their children.

In their family homes, James and Marina Ogilvy; George, Earl of St Andrews, Lady Helen and Lord Nicholas Windsor; Alexander, Earl of Ulster, Lady Davinia and Lady Rose; Lord Frederick and Lady Ella were all watched over by nannies and the time they spent with their parents was very much the same as for any other child in their upper-class income group. Parents, by example, urged them to work hard and play hard and discipline was on easy lines. The Ogilvys, the Gloucesters and the two Kent parents would talk at great length to close friends about their determination that their children should grow up as 'ordinary' children and one day in the future be allowed to choose careers for themselves and enjoy their own particular brand of life-style. At times they were obsessed by the problem.

Unfortunately for the parents, their desperate desire for their children to be brought up on 'ordinary' lines was to be foiled time and again by the wonderful holidays spent at one or other of the Royal homes: even at a very early age they witnessed first hand all the glitter, the ritual, the pomp and splendour that sur-rounded Elizabeth and she, after all, was either their aunt, as in the case of Princess Margaret's children, or their second cousin, as in the case of the Ogilvy and Kent children.

Angus Ogilvy, a very down-to-earth businessman, often freely admitted that he could never offer his children a holiday anything like as exciting as the summer months with the Queen at Balmoral. He could take them to Airlie Castle, the ancestral seat of his family, but much as his children loved this Scottish sanctuary, it could never compare with Balmoral. And there was nothing to compare with Windsor Castle, Sandringham or the Royal yacht *Britannia*. The anxiety felt by Ogilvy and his wife was shared equally by Princess Margaret and her husband, the Gloucesters and the Kents: interestingly, all the children had one Royal-born parent and one commoner parent and yet all the parents were unanimous in their view that the Royal connections must be played down as much as possible.

If the Queen herself was anxious about the future of her growing family, she gave no indication of it. Her greatest concern was over her son and heir, Charles, Prince of Wales, who was moving towards his last term at Gordonstoun, academically a plodder, very much a loner, slow to mature and still, as he had always been as a little boy, so desperately anxious to please.

9

Charles at University

ONE OF THE most difficult jobs in the world is to bring up
a modern Royal Prince, especially an Heir to the Throne,
and one of the most formidable tasks that faced the
Queen and Prince Philip was the higher education Prince
Charles should receive when he left Gordonstoun. They
consulted many people including eminent academics,
senior members of the clergy and Government ministers
in their earnest search for a solution to the problem.
Eventually, and with Charles's full approval, it was
decided that he should go to Trinity College, Cambridge.

The man who was to play a role of great consequence
at that time in Charles's sheltered life was the late Lord
'Rab' Butler who was invited to tea at Buckingham Palace
to sort out issues that would be involved if Charles went
to University. Butler was a broad-shouldered, slightly
hunched man with greying sideboards and high fore-
head and as he sat drinking tea opposite Prince Charles
and Prince Philip in a Palace drawing room, would have
been a daunting character for the most brilliant intellect
to encounter. It would have been hard, indeed, to find a
more distinguished academic and politician than Butler,
a man whose qualities earned him the label 'The best
Prime Minister Britain never had' – he had twice been
pipped at the post for Number Ten Downing Street.

On that chilly January afternoon in 1967, as Master of

Trinity College, Cambridge, Lord Butler could well have made the hesitant and uncertain school-leaver, eighteen-year-old Charles, feel even less confident than he already was. But Butler, who had previously been Chancellor of the Exchequer, Lord Privy Seal, First Secretary of State, Deputy Prime Minister, Foreign Secretary and Minister of Education, was able to establish an immediate rapport with the young man in front of him, an Heir to the Throne whose apparent lack of self-confidence at that time was giving rise to very real anxiety, not only to Elizabeth and Philip but also to people at Government level for whom Charles remained an unknown quantity.

He was quiet and retiring, his manners were impeccable, he was not in the least bit bold and never seemed to assert himself. He was however an unusually attentive listener and when his interest was sufficiently aroused, he talked well, kept to the point of an argument and revealed a clear and lucid mind. What puzzled many people, Butler included, was that Charles did not seem to have inherited any of his father's strong and forceful characteristics and whenever they were together it was his tendency always to let Philip hold the floor. He rarely interrupted except for an occasional 'Well . . .' 'Perhaps . . .' – and seldom got further.

Charles did not break his usual pattern that January day and, hands folded on his knees, remained quietly in the background for the most part of this all-important tea-party when Philip was very much in charge. It lasted about two hours and the impression Butler gained of the younger man made him determined to break the hold he felt that Philip had on his son. The trio were meeting to discuss and iron out problems before Charles was launched into the next stage of his education by becoming an undergraduate at Trinity College the following October. What Butler endeavoured to do at the tea-party was to get as much out of Charles as possible about his own views about his future life at Cambridge.

The matter of Charles's University career had been the subject of endless discussions over a period of more than a year between Elizabeth and Philip and their advisers. One marathon dinner at which the matter was debated had included among those present the Archbishop of Canterbury, Michael Ramsey, Prime Minister of the day Harold Wilson, Lord Mountbatten, Dr Robert Woods, Dean of Windsor and a close friend of the Queen and Sir Charles Wilson, chairman of the Committee of University Vice Chancellors. One person who did not attend the dinner, however, was the subject of the great debate, Charles himself.

As he sat now with Charles and his very forthright father in Buckingham Palace Butler, who was a happily married family man with two sons of his own, felt great personal sympathy for Charles who he realised had reached a vital point in his young life. The next three years at University would either make or break him and Butler realised that if only he could gain the boy's complete confidence and trust a great deal could be achieved. Ironically, no one has ever fully recognised just how much Butler did achieve during the three years when he literally had Charles in the palm of his hand: it was Butler's tact, wisdom and great understanding that made Charles the man he is today.

As the Master of Trinity sat with Charles and his father that day he knew that the boy had made only two strong personal points about his future. He had made it clear that he wanted to go to University and that he wanted to be allowed to live in college. Although Charles had positively declared he wanted to go to University he had to wait almost a full year before his parents were finally convinced that this was the right course. Such were the anxieties about him that, although Charles did not know this, even Philip joined in the opposition to the idea that Charles should attempt to take a degree – something which privately Butler was prepared to move heaven and earth to see that he did.

Looking back and in hindsight, it is incredible that so many people, including his own parents, had such little confidence in Charles to the point that they were convinced that he would fail his degree. One eminent educationalist went so far as to inform the Queen and Philip bluntly, 'Whatever you do, don't let him risk exams.' Charles's scholastic record at Gordonstoun had in no way been outstanding and he left with two poor 'O' levels, a standard which many critics claimed did not entitle him to a University place. Yet Butler had been privately impressed by a distinction Charles had gained in an optional paper when only six per cent out of 4,000 candidates had gained such distinctions.

He rightly felt that in his present situation, being widely considered as potentially poor University material by almost everyone who surrounded him, Charles had indeed reached a vital crossroads and felt that Trinity could make Charles, provided he had a free hand. But even at the tea-party the Master of Trinity had to use all his skill in persuading Charles to come out of his corner and speak frankly about his own view about the subjects he would like to take at University.

It so happened that in his last year at Gordonstoun and as a result of his two extremely happy terms at Timbertop, the country annexe of Geelong Church of England Grammar School in Melbourne, Australia, Charles had developed a very real interest in anthropology and had even written a short essay on the subject.

Charles had always harboured a deep yearning to see Australia and it was at his own personal request that a suitable school was found for him there: Timbertop, sometimes called the 'Eton of Australia', with its emphasis on self-reliance was finally decided upon by the Queen and Prince Philip because it had a fine record of integrating boys from very different backgrounds and had the added merit of allowing pupils a great deal of free time in order to follow their own special interests. During Charles's six months in Australia his interest in anthropology was fanned by the keenly observant headmaster, Thomas Garnett, who recognised that the boy was generally far more enthused by the past than the future; Charles told him how he had spent long hours by himself in the caves of Morayshire, with bats fluttering around his head, searching for traces of past civilisations. When Butler asked Charles what subjects he would really like to take at Cambridge he received an unequivocal answer: anthropology and archaeology.

This was not the reply Philip had hoped for: as a man predominantly interested in scientific developments and modern technology, he had next to no sympathy with his son's leaning towards ancient cultures and regarded Charles's very evident increasing preference for the arts more as a misfortune than anything else. Philip was convinced that Charles should channel all his scholastic abilities into studying the British Constitution and he was backed up in his view by almost everyone who had entered at some point on the long debate about Charles going up to University. Not only had Prime Minister Harold Wilson supported this line but so had Sir Charles Wilson.

While Philip stressed the necessity for Charles to immerse himself in the subject of the Constitution, quoting Professor A. V. Dicey, a famous constitutional lawyer at length, Butler fixed his hooded eyes on Charles who had quietly listened to all the points that were being made. Then Butler, with all his innate powers of skill and persuasion spoke for a considerable time about the necessity for Charles to be given at least the chance to enjoy his work. That could only be achieved by choosing subjects which really appealed to him – like anthropology and archaeology. Butler put his case well, stressing that the complex subject of the British Constitution could well be shelved until a later date in Charles's Cambridge career in order to give a chance to concentrate on something that really appealed to him. Charles kept nodding and saying, 'That's exactly how I feel.'

Philip listened attentively. It was not that Philip wanted to force his son into studying a subject he did not like but, bearing in mind all the advice he had received over so many months, he did not feel that Charles had time to indulge in any subject that was not specifically aimed at preparing him for the job that lay ahead of him. Philip knew that Elizabeth wanted Charles, as soon as he was sufficiently prepared and old enough, to be initiated by her personally into many active issues of State with which she had to deal. The last thing she wanted was for Charles to be like his great-great-great-uncle, King Edward VII who, as Prince of Wales, never saw a State box until he was sixty when his mother, Queen Victoria, died.

Elizabeth's great hope was that as a result of personal tuition, Charles would be fully fledged in the workings of monarchy and ready and equipped to take over if anything happened to her. If only for this reason, Philip continued to press for the Constitution to be given the number one priority in Charles's university curriculum. It says much for Butler, whose family had maintained a consecutive tradition at Cambridge as dons since 1794, that at the end of the afternoon anthropology and archaeology were in and the Constitution was out – at least temporarily – and Butler had won a great battle for Charles, the true significance of which was never fully realised at the time.

After what had been decidedly unsatisfactory and often unhappy years at school, Charles was now being given a chance to relax and enjoy his first year at Trinity, to be able to delve into subjects that really fascinated and intrigued him instead of at once burying himself in the heavyweight issues of the Constitution. Butler, in his wisdom, came up with a suggestion that appealed to both Elizabeth and Philip: Charles was to reserve an option to switch to history at the end of his first year.

The tea-party ended on a happy note with Charles in a more cheerful mood but leaving Butler brooding over the responsibility he had accepted. Despite his enthusiasm, Charles had a daunting task ahead of him: if he managed a degree it would be achieved entirely on merit. When the time came for his University paper to be marked no-one would know the identity of the candidate. Butler knew that failure on Charles's part to win University honours would reverberate not only round the country but within the Royal Family itself and the damage it would do to the eighteen year old's personal ego was too appalling to dwell on.

In the next few months before Charles turned up at Trinity, this time without being escorted by either parent, Butler made it abundantly clear to both Elizabeth and Philip that Charles should not only be allowed maximum freedom during his three University years but also that his official duties should be kept to an absolute minimum. Promises were duly given that Charles's life would be interrupted as little as possible but to Butler's chagrin it was not to work out like this at all.

During the still settling down period at Trinity he had to attend his first State Opening of Parliament and within two months he was winging his way to Melbourne to attend the funeral of Prime Minister Harold Holt. It soon became very clear to the Master of Trinity that the pattern of serious hours of swotting would be constantly broken and that unless Charles put the time at his disposal to maximum use, it would be a miracle if he achieved the vital degree. It was in these early days that Butler, personally very fond of the immature Charles, pulled a master stroke which was eventually to lead to a change in Charles that took everyone who knew him, even his parents and relatives, by complete surprise.

In a nutshell it was Butler – and Butler alone – who was responsible for transforming Charles from a plodding, home-loving, hesitating and uncertain youth into a poised man with a mind and will of his own. What Butler did was to have a copy made of a key to a side entrance to his Master's Lodge which led directly into his private study. This meant that Charles could meet Butler privately whenever he wanted and without the rest of the University being any the wiser. Butler told Charles that there was no need for him to telephone in advance and that he could use the key whenever he wanted. At first Charles hesitated about taking advantage of the offer and so Butler launched an initiative by suggesting that whenever he felt like it, Charles should join him for an hour or so in his study about six o'clock in the evening.

As his first term progressed, so did his relationship with the elder statesman, who was at heart very much a family man. For Charles these chats, which usually took place in the evening or over lunch at the weekend, were the most invaluable and rewarding experiences of his young life and were undoubtedly directly responsible for moulding him into the man he is today. Throughout his growing up and adolescent life Charles had always had an ambivalent relationship with Philip: no man could have been a better father in the sense that his sole goal was to make Charles stretch himself to the maximum both physically as well as mentally.

This often made him appear to be a far too demanding and over-critical parent, characteristics which tended to send Charles into moods of gloom rather than spur him on to greater achievements. Butler was well aware of this strong hold that Philip had on his son and in his own way was determined to devote his time to breaking the umbilical cord which still tied Charles, at eighteen, too closely to his family. He regretted that Charles had easy access to Sandringham, Elizabeth's private home in Norfolk only a short drive from Cambridge, which meant that whenever he felt alone or that things were becoming too difficult, he could go to the family home and once again find himself in known and familiar surroundings. Butler urged him to remain within the University as much as possible and this, for the most part, is what he did.

During his early weeks at Cambridge it became obvious to Butler that Charles, while apparently quite relaxed, was again coming up against the problem he had found during his schooldays – undergraduates were giving him a wide berth for fear of being accused of currying favour – and so the Master stressed upon Charles how important it was for him to take more initiative himself and join and take part in some of the many societies the University had to offer.

It was not in Charles's nature to push himself and it was to a considerable extent an unnerving experience for him to enrol at the Cambridge College of Arts and Technology to keep up his skill at pottery, which he had first learned at Gordonstoun. Twice a week he cycled over from his college rooms (his bicycle was numbered T4444 – T for Trinity) and found himself happily working away alongside housewives, secretaries and bank clerks all taking the same night-school class. He integrated well and spurred on by Butler who wanted to boost his still flagging self-confidence, decided to try and join the Trinity College theatrical group called the Dryden Society.

When Charles approached the secretary, Anthony Kirwin, he was bluntly told that he would only be considered after he had been auditioned. That meant he had to prove himself with a mime, extemporary acting and prepare a modern speech. Charles was not in the least abashed or put off: he had had years of experience clowning and fooling in family charades and he felt that would stand him in good stead. It did; after his audition, undergraduate producer John Parry complimented him on his good timing, and was later relieved to discover that Charles was very good with his ad-libs when fellow actors dried up.

When the society staged Joe Orton's play *Erphingham Camp*, Charles had his experience of slapstick when he was hit in the face first with a custard pie and then with a toilet roll. In the final scene when he had to read a sermon he was momentarily at a loss because he could not find a 'dog collar' in the Society's props. He solved the problem by going round to Trinity College chapel and borrowing one from the Dean, the Reverend Harry Williams.

Butler's constant urging to Charles that he should mix as much as possible paid dividends: he became friendly with Hywel Jones, the son of a Welsh minister who was President of the Trinity Students' Union and had rooms leading off the same staircase as Charles. Jones, now a management consultant, would discuss politics with Charles until the early hours of the morning and both men were surprised by the other's openmindedness.

It was such encounters with men of all political spectrums, when Charles did not have to look over his shoulder to see who was listening, that began to bring out the best in this late developer. To his delight, but without giving away his surprise, Butler at one of their evening meetings heard Charles ask, 'Would it be all right for me to join the University Labour Club?' Butler's reaction? 'Hell, no it wouldn't.' He told Charles, 'Cambridge is full of these parties. You must enjoy yourself while you're at University but you mustn't join anything political.' This was yet another indication to Butler of his charge's naïvety in thinking that he could become associated with a Labour Club, which was tantamount to joining the Labour Party. Nevertheless when the first term ended in December both Elizabeth and Philip saw early but positive signs of change in their eldest son.

Because of the Royal population explosion in the early sixties, with the team of nannies and nursery maids it brought in its wake, that was the second Christmas holiday the Royal Family had spent at Windsor instead of the inconvenient-for-children Sandringham House, and it was there that Charles's parents noted a welcome new jauntiness in his manner and although parental eyebrows were occasionally raised at certain comments by Charles which seemed to have a left-wing flavour about them, it was regarded as a good sign. As the Queen Mother remarked to an old and close friend, 'Charles really is coming out of his shell, isn't he?'

He proudly announced that he was becoming quite a good cook. At Cambridge where he received much the same treatment as any other freshman, he did have one or two advantages. He did not have to share his rooms although he was one of six who used the same bathroom on Staircase E of New Court, a tranquil corner of the college overlooking the River Cam. What he could enjoy – something denied other undergraduates – was a small kitchen area where he was able to entertain on what was a pretty modest scale. He enjoyed shopping immensely and in his beige corduroys and inevitable sports jacket he became a familiar figure among the Cambridge market stallholders and local shopkeepers. He always paid cash for everything he bought and once mildly complained, rightly, when he found he had been short-changed.

In view of Butler's stricture that Charles's studies should be interrupted as little as possible, he received relatively few visits from members of his family, but whenever the Queen or the Queen Mother were in the vicinity of Cambridge – which was not often – they could never resist a quick visit to his rooms, seldom if ever being recognised as they quickly crossed the great quadrangle where once Francis Bacon, Isaac Newton and Lord Byron had walked. Charles, with his small 'fridge and two-ringed gas stove, could always be relied upon to provide a quick hot dish – usually eggs served in one form or another.

In June 1968 Charles completely confounded the critics who said that he was not bright enough for Cambridge; he came through his first-year exams with flying colours, just missing a first-class pass: a place in Division I of Class II of the Archaeology and Anthropology Tripos. These results surprised everyone – except Butler who privately voiced the opinion that he was convinced that Charles had a greater academic bent than either of his parents or, for that matter, any other senior member of the Royal Family he had met. He was confident that Charles would, at the end of the next two years, take a full Honours course and emerge with a First in the favourite subjects he had chosen – archaeology and anthropology. Instead, Charles decided to study the British Constitution. 'Why?' asked Butler. 'Because one day I may be King,' replied Charles.

Then to Butler's downright fury, just when Charles's mind was maturing and he was eagerly proceeding towards more advanced work, he was snatched away from Cambridge in April 1969 and sent to the University

183

College at Aberystwyth. Critics claimed that the proposal was totally indefensible on educational grounds: Aberystwyth could add nothing to the education he was already receiving at Cambridge. A widely held view at the time was that Charles was being sent there to appease the swelling sentiment of Welsh nationalism. What the critics did not know was that Charles was to be Invested as Prince of Wales at Caernarvon Castle in June 1969, and both the Queen and Philip considered this the right time to launch their son officially into public life. At Aberystwyth the Prince could establish his first contacts with the Principality and in a nine-week crash course endeavour to learn the rudiments of the Welsh language so that he could make a speech in that language.

It was at Aberystwyth University College, at a time when Welsh nationalism was widespread, that Charles met the outspoken Welsh patriot, Edward Millward, who was to be his tutor. Charles found that he could politely hold his own in debates with the versatile Millward and often managed to score some well timed points. Millward stuck to his principles and only addressed Charles as 'Mr Windsor' but their relationship ended in mutual respect with Millward saying, 'Goodbye, Sir' and his pupil warmly shaking his hand and saying, 'Goodbye, Edward'. Theirs might have proved an uneasy relationship but Millward was very impressed by the young man's open manner and determination to master the Welsh language even if it meant studying until the early hours of the morning. Millward was a gifted and natural teacher who pushed Charles hard in the crash course which even included a collection of Welsh rugby songs that Charles managed to learn off by heart.

Only one or two people knew that the break with Cambridge, which was to last for several months, was to cause Charles more than a considerable amount of heartbreak. What he had enjoyed for the first time in his life was freedom to entertain anybody he liked and when he liked. But there had been too many notorious stories surrounding two previous Princes of Wales, albeit many years earlier. First there had been Edward VII who since a youth had enjoyed his paramours and extra marital activities; and then there was Edward VIII, with his open affairs with married women culminating in his blind and obsessive love for Mrs Wallis Simpson. Perhaps for this reason the Queen and Prince Philip never went out of their way to encourage Charles, now that he was older, to invite girls on Royal holidays.

Until long after he left Gordonstoun at eighteen, Charles had enjoyed next to no contact with the opposite sex apart from relatives or daughters of his parents' friends whom he had known since childhood. Who knows, he might have been bolder if, as a young adolescent, he had had somewhere to take a girl and be left in private with her: as it was any friend he ever wanted to see more of had to stay under a resplendent roof and face the daunting prospect of critical assessment, never outwardly manifested, on the part of the Queen and shrewd and clever cross examination by Philip.

There had always been a tacit understanding between Charles and his parents that he was at school to work and their interpretation of play meant healthy outdoor sports. Neither parent was ever deliberately unkind but at some subconscious level they were undoubtedly fearful of escapades of former Royal princes ever manifesting themselves again, and Charles was very much aware that no nonsense of that kind would ever be tolerated. He was just as much haunted by the ghost of his Uncle David, the late Duke of Windsor who abdicated for love in 1936, as were other members of the family who seldom mentioned his name.

Even members of the Royal Family older than Charles and well down the line of succession like Prince William of Gloucester were affected by the Duke of Windsor spectre. William, a dashing and glamorous man who had his fair share of short-lived affairs, specifically blamed the spectre of his uncle David for the fact that at thirty-two he had himself never married. He once said, 'I just can't afford to make a mistake like Uncle David. Nor can Prince Charles – he is in an even worse position than I am. It would be unthinkable for any member of the family to marry the wrong sort of person and then be involved in a divorce.' That was before Princess Margaret, for whom the Queen always leant over backwards, was given her sister's permission to go her own way and end her marriage to Lord Snowdon in a 'quickie' divorce in 1978.

Not surprisingly and from a very young age, Charles remained inhibited in the presence of girls and it was not until he enjoyed his first steps of real freedom at Cambridge that he made his first hesitant attempts at dates. Rab Butler longed to see him mix easily with people from varying backgrounds and although the young man gravitated almost naturally towards men from old established families, he broke new ground when he joined various Cambridge societies and began to invite small groups of undergraduates back to his rooms for a beer or a glass of sherry. He found it easier to talk to girls in these intimate groups when conversation turned easily to University chat and gossip. For once he could join in the common groans, moans and laughter over shared University experiences.

He was an excellent mimic and as his confidence built up so he became more relaxed, less guarded and accepted for what he really was at that time – just another undergraduate anxious to get a really good degree but fearful lest he might not. Charles was both shy and diffident and blushed easily when he made his first approaches to girls who, to his apparent surprise and delight, were only too happy to have him as an escort. Charles, at nineteen, had the manners of an old-fashioned courtier, that is, until he fell head over heels in love for the first time in his life with the sparkling and sophisticated twenty-three-year-old Lucia Santa Cruz, whom Rab Butler had appointed to help with research on his political memoirs *The Art of the Possible* which he was then preparing.

Their first encounter was when Charles paid one of his regular evening visits to the Master's private study and Lucia, daughter of the Chilean Ambassador to London, was filing some papers in an outside office. That was to be the first of many happy times when Charles and Lucia sipped sherry with Butler who, as he watched the friendship grow, sometimes discreetly excused himself. During his belated and very first serious romance, Charles was able to collect Lucia in his car, and entertain her privately or with other friends in the elegant but small farmhouse on the Sandringham estate which was used from time to time by members of the Royal Family in preference to opening up the 'big house'.

Although Butler later denied that he 'slipped' Lucia a key to the Master's Lodge so that she and Charles could meet without the news being open gossip across the length and breadth of Trinity, there is no doubt that he looked upon their friendship in a fond and paternal light. He thought the twenty-three-year-old Lucia well able to care for Charles with great gentleness without, at the same time, getting too emotionally involved herself. Charles has always recognised his debt to Lucia in those growing-up days and they remain good friends to this day.

Butler was content and relieved that in more ways than one, the Prince was at last beginning to mature and spread his own wings, no longer constantly saying 'Papa thinks . . .' or 'Papa says . . .'. Significantly he acquired a new air of authority, he walked purposefully and held his head high. The long hours spent in the company of Butler when Charles was given the benefit of his personal views on all manner of things from poetry to his assessment of political figures were indeed bearing fruit.

Although all the major preparations were well in hand, it was not until 22 June 1969, a mere week before his Investiture, that Charles flew from Aberystwyth to Windsor Castle to join the family which had gathered to finalise last-minute arrangements. Charles was tense and nervous at the prospect of the Investiture with its ritual and all that it represented when for the first time in his life he would be the star in a pageant that was to be watched on television by millions all over the world. The man who was to boost his morale enormously was Lord Snowdon, eighteen years his senior, and someone he had always liked and admired. In many ways it was Snowdon, appointed Constable of Caernarvon Castle by the Queen, who temporarily replaced Butler as Charles's confidante during the days leading up to the great ceremony.

Princess Margaret's husband was a romantic modernist who had masterminded much of the pageantry and introduced spectacular innovations, even to the point of persuading the Queen not to wear very high heeled shoes so that instead of treading on a traditional red carpet she could walk on grass without sinking into the ground. It was Snowdon, with his quiet manner and the impressive assurance that he had acquired since his marriage to Princess Margaret nine years earlier, who rehearsed Charles for long and patient hours over the majestic ritual and with his easy sense of humour took the edge off the younger man's increasing nervousness.

It was a Snowdon touch of near genius that, minutes before the great ceremony began and Charles was waiting in the wings and the fine Welsh voices swelled into the first verse of 'God Bless the Prince of Wales', he made sure that his two young children, David, Viscount Linley, eight, and Lady Sarah Armstrong-Jones, only five, suddenly appeared and ran straight into Charles's arms, completely dispelling his mounting tenseness.

The young man, who wore a light gold crown on his head and who will long be remembered for the deeply moving moment when he placed his hands between Elizabeth's and said, 'I Charles, Prince of Wales, do become your liege man of life and limb and of earthly worship, faith and truth I will bear unto you to live and die against all manner of folks,' bore little resemblance to the uncertain youth who only two and a half years earlier had met with Lord Butler over tea and sandwiches to discuss his future.

The following summer, only four months short of his twenty-second birthday, Charles was a man, as it soon became abundantly clear not only to Elizabeth and Philip but to the rest of the family as well. Not only was he Earl of Chester, Duke of Cornwall, Duke of Rothesay, Earl of Carrick and Baron Renfrew, Lord of the Isles and Great Steward of Scotland, he was also Charles Mountbatten-Windsor, BA (Hon). Butler had done his job well. No man could have done better. What Charles now wanted was action, to qualify as an RAF pilot and feel free in the air; to sail the high seas with the Royal Navy.

In a very different way but with a positive style of her own, his sister Anne was pursuing her own independent life in other fields.

10

Hurdles for Anne

PRINCESS ANNE MAY well have grown up into a Royal misfit if it had not been for her love of horses which developed into a passion for the showjumping circuit. She reached the crossroads in her young life when at eighteen she left Benenden school and was still uncertain about her future, lacking sufficient 'A' levels to gain a place in a University and showing little enthusiasm at the prospect of carrying out Royal engagements.

Her real break came when it was put to Mrs Alison Oliver, trim, fit and in her early thirties one of the most brilliant women in the British showjumping world, that if she could manage to take on one extra pupil she would not be wasting her time. At her training stables at Brookfield Farm near Warfield Park, covering eight hundred Buckinghamshire acres, she hesitated before nodding her head and saying, 'I'd very much like to meet the girl first. Then I'll let you know.'

Mrs Oliver, married to showjumping champion Alan Oliver, was above all a practical person who had earned nationwide fame for her results as a brilliant riding instructor. What she always demanded from anyone who came to her for specialised tuition was total dedication and no amount of influence would make her change her mind if she decided a rider had no real potential. So in 1968 when Princess Anne drove the five miles from

Windsor Castle to meet Mrs Oliver in her training stables she was under no illusions: she knew that either she would succeed on her own merit or she would have to look elsewhere for an instructor.

It was Anne's good fortune that she not only received enthusiastic approval from Mrs Oliver but also met her at a difficult time in her adolescent life when she urgently needed outside encouragement. At eighteen, she had just left Benenden School and, very much at a loose end, was more than ready for the sort of discipline Mrs Oliver demanded if Elizabeth's daughter was to fulfil her great ambition to make her mark in the world of competitive riding.

At that time, missing the companionship she had known in the sixth form, Anne had very few really close friends and her often moody and difficult manner did not always endear her to some of her very close relatives, and that included even the Queen Mother, noted for her great understanding not only of young children in the Royal Family but of adolescents as well. When Anne was out of sorts she would retreat into her own suite of rooms in Buckingham Palace, where she and Charles lived separately and each had their own 'front door' at opposite ends of a long corridor; there she would stay for long hours on end, refusing to be disturbed.

Elizabeth and Philip knew better than to intrude and wisely left their only daughter to her own devices, knowing that sooner or later she would emerge relaxed and full of beans. Of their four children, Anne was very much the loner of the quartet and from a quite early age had the unusual ability to amuse and entertain herself. Stubborn and impetuous by nature, Anne was a constant source of anxiety to her parents in her growing up years and if they had not worked together in such a concerted way, she might easily have become a real problem child. Anne would probably have been quite a diferent child if she had been brought up in an ordinary family but even then she would have needed very skilful handling to bring out the best in her. When she was in one of her

191

famous tantrums she could make the relatively docile Charles seem a paragon of virtue and there were times when she could drive Elizabeth, despite guire her extraordinary self-control, almost out of her wits.

The one person who could always be relied upon to control this only girl in the family was Philip, who probably understood her early sense of frustration better than anyone else. It had taken him a long time to adjust to his secondary role within the Royal Family, to accept that he would always play second fiddle to his wife, and not surprisingly his natural sympathies went out to the daughter whose drive and energy so much resembled his own. It was undoubtedly Philip's care and understanding that helped to sooth her in the days long before she went to school and when she began to realise that her elder brother occupied a position of importance that she could never even remotely share.

Charles and Anne squabbled a great deal but some of their cat and dog fights were not based on the usual lines of sibling rivalry: Anne was desperate to exert her authority over her brother. The friction between brother and sister did not really ease until the time Anne left school. When she returned home to Buckingham Palace Charles was away and immersed in University life at Trinity College and, with his Investiture as Prince of Wales over, eager to embark upon exciting new projects looming ahead.

It was therefore with a sense of enormous relief that Elizabeth and Philip discovered that in Mrs Oliver Anne had at last found someone who could stretch her enthusiasm to the maximum and the Brookfield stables soon became Anne's favourite haunt, the one place she felt she was accepted in her own right and where her background impressed no one. Early on, however, Mrs Oliver recognised that while the as yet young and untried rider had all the steely determination necessary for anyone intent on a career in competitive riding, there was one real drawback: if she was to succeed it was vital that Anne should put in two or three hours of training every day. Yet in less than a year Anne had to begin carrying out her official engagements; they took her all over the country – flying to Tyneside to launch a ship, opening a Young Farmers' club at Stoneleigh, hostessing a garden party for teachers.

How could Elizabeth's daugher manage to put in sufficient training when so many demands were made upon her? Mrs Oliver was left in no doubt about the answer: Anne was determined that nothing would divert her from riding. She would often leave Buckingham Palace at seven o'clock in the morning, driving her blue Rover 2000 the 50 minute journey to Brookfield Farm where she would put in two hours of training before returning to London to carry out an afternoon engagement.

Sometimes in the summer months she would then hurry back to Buckingham Palace, race upstairs to change into her riding clothes in a matter of minutes, and then drive back again to Brookfield to work hard and talk hard with her instructor, often staying to drink endless cups of coffee until dusk. The pattern was very much the same at weekends only then, while she was staying with Elizabeth and Philip at Windsor Castle, the journey was much shorter and there was more time to spend clearing fences in the large and sprawling paddock and more time to practice the highly skilled art of dressage.

Anne began taking part in competitive trials and people in the knowledgeable world of eventing were beginning to sit up and take notice. While Mrs Oliver and her pupil were delighted, Elizabeth and Philip were both somewhat uneasy about their daughter's future which, often in competition with her Royal engagements, was going to take her all over the country and bring her more and more into the public limelight as her riding career progressed. While happy that all Anne's great energy and interest were being channelled into riding, they knew only too well that Anne did not take kindly to criticism of any sort and when she began coming up against riders who were better qualified than she was, they feared there might be ructions of one kind or another.

They found it almost impossible to make Anne appreciate that no matter how well she rode, no matter how many rosettes or trophies she received, she would never be regarded as an ordinary competitor; wherever she went she would always be Elizabeth's daughter. From that there was no escape. As gently as possible and using all their powers of persuasion, her parents urged Anne to be as careful as possible, to watch her words, to learn to count ten. Several times they put it to her that, all things considered, it might be wiser for her to give up the idea of competitive riding since the long hours of training combined with mounting public duties would probably cause her unnecessary stress and prove to be too much of a strain on her in the end.

Other members of the family expressed their own anxiety but Anne would not be budged, pooh-poohed everyone's fears, boldly went ahead and threw her hat into the show jumping arena. It is just possible that without Mrs Oliver's support she may have succumbed to her parents' sincere desire that she should settle for a less demanding challenge. But Mrs Oliver, untiring in her encouragement, recognised how much her pupil had changed with her early successes and was more than confident when she told Anne that she was now ready to face her first great test and attempt to qualify for the Badminton Three Day Event in April, 1971, generally regarded as one of the toughest equestrian competitions in the world.

Gradually, with Anne's continued progress and success in the riding world, her parents' objections to what they regarded as Anne's perilous and inconvenient hobby had diminished and it was a cheerful Royal party that gathered that spring at Badminton. For years the Royal Family had regarded Badminton as a mini-holiday when they all stayed without fuss or formality at Badminton House, home of the cheeful hunting, shooting and fishing Henry Hugh Arthur Fitzroy Somerset, the Duke of Beaufort, who was not only a close friend of Elizabeth but also her Master of the Horse.

Away from the hunting field he was the nominal ruler of the Royal Mews and the third most important officer in the Royal Household, ranking only after the Lord Chamberlain and the Lord Steward. In any ceremonial involving horses it was his privilege and duty to ride nearest Elizabeth and this he did with pride, always magnificent in a plumed cocked hat and scarlet and gold uniform. That Spring when Anne had the support of the only people who really matter to her – members of her own family – the Beauforts sensed the mood of nervous anticipation as the Royals drove deep into the lush Gloucestershire countryside to watch her ride Doublet, the horse given to her as a present by her mother.

The Beauforts, who always managed an air of easy informality in their vast mansion, never changed their life-style when the Royal Family stayed at Badminton. While Anne ate her breakfasts in the stone-flagged kitchen, which turned out endless gargantuan meals for competitors and stable boys alike, the Royal Family had their meals in a beautiful dining room whose windows were shaded by a glorious cedar tree. The Beaufort dogs and the Royal dogs ambled freely about the gardens with only an occasional growl. Elizabeth and Philip were happy at Anne's newly acquired sense of purpose and obvious sense of well being. Both parents were desperately keeping their fingers crossed that Anne would at least have some success at this long established and famous event which had not only attracted some of the best riders in the country but also the attention of all the top radio and television commentators.

Whether she liked it or not, all eyes would be on Anne, for whom the added element of very real danger sent her adrenalin racing. There were moments when even Elizabeth could not hide her inner tension, aware that the course with its thirty-odd obstacles that included parallel bars, open water, ditches and tree trunks, could topple her daughter just as well as anyone else. Anne had already had several falls, some quite bad. Once she had damaged her little finger and on another occasion ended up with a broken nose at the King Edward VII's Hospital for Officers, the Marylebone hospital often used by the Royal Family.

In many ways this Easter pilgrimage to the Badminton Horse Trials to watch her daughter compete, was an unnerving experience for Elizabeth. She was only too well aware that she alone would have to bear the responsibility if Anne should be seriously hurt – and although Anne was a good rider she was nevertheless known to take risks. It would be said that Elizabeth should, much earlier, have put her foot firmly down and refused to allow Anne to enter competitive riding. But that was not Elizabeth's way. Often against her own instincts she preferred to let not only her own children but also other members of her family make up their own minds about a course of action they wanted to pursue. By nature a worrier and by no means a good sailor herself, she always had qualms when Philip took Charles and Anne out sailing when they were very young.

But always she kept her feelings to herself. 'Enjoy yourselves,' she would say, all the time longing for their safe return. The only time that she is ever known to have forbidden an adventure was when news reached her that Charles was planning to go up in a hot-air balloon. Quietly but firmly and despite all his entreaties, she told him that it was quite out of the question. It was, she said, too dangerous. And that was that. But for her daughter on a warm spring Sunday, the last day of the Three Day Event, there were no problems and she went round the course with only one mistake. She was placed fifth out of forty-eight and there were tears in Alison Oliver's eyes as she told her pupil, 'That really was a splendid performance.'

The outright winner was a jaunty young Army officer, Lieutenant Mark Phillips whose parents, Major and Mrs Peter Phillips, had driven over from their home at Great

Somerford in Wiltshire; they were just as excited about their son's success as Elizabeth and Philip were about Anne's. Their mutual paths never crossed. But Anne, although she did not seem to recognise Mark when she saw him mingling with fellow competitors, had nevertheless met him quite by chance three years earlier when the Queen Mother had invited her granddaughter to accompany her to a post-Olympic party in the Whitbread Cellar in the City of London. Many years later Anne recalled the occasion like this: 'My grandmother took me ... because she thought I, as a beginner at eventing, was very overawed by all these grand people.'

Badminton brought about a great change in Anne who, with her slim and graceful figure, her fair hair and the same peaches and cream complexion as her mother, had already set her sights high – a place in the equestrian team that would represent Britain at the Olympic Games to be held in Munich the following year (1972). But in that pre-Olympic year when a carefully worked-out programme planned by Mrs Oliver was building steadily to a climax, disaster struck. In mid-summer and two months before the final trial for the European Championships, Anne was taken ill at a Buckingham Palace garden party and suddenly rushed once again to the King Edward VII's Hospital, this time for the removal of an ovarian cyst. The Queen's gynaecologist, Sir John Peel, observed that he regarded this as a major operation and that Anne would not only have to cancel her plans to compete at the Wembley Royal International Horse Show but also generally take life more easily for some time to come. He was adamant that she must cut down on her riding.

It was a decidedly depressed Mrs Oliver who made her way to Anne's third-floor hospital room ready to commiserate with the girl she had grown to admire so much for her sheer guts and determination. But when she opened the door instead of seeing a downcast patient she found Anne sitting in a chair and already making plans for a crash get-fit course in order to be ready to ride again as soon as possible. For the next forty days during her convalescence at Balmoral in Scotland Anne carried out all manner of exercises, and walked for miles in order to be fit enough to take her place in the Championships. No one expected her to return to competitive riding so soon after the operation, and although she was in fairly good form she failed a water jump and fell from the saddle.

Nonetheless it was a great summer for Anne and early in September, against stiff opposition, she was invited to compete in the European Championships at Burghley Park in Northamptonshire, home of the Marquess of Exeter, a former Olympic Gold Medallist himself.

Anne's respect for Mrs Oliver was such that the relationship between pupil and instructor could not have been better but there were many people who – through no fault of their own – often got the rough edge of Anne's tongue. She was impatient with people whom she regarded as being either slow or inefficient and if they did not measure up to her own self-imposed standards, then she would say so. Lacking Elizabeth's in-born good manners and Philip's approach which had grown more skilful and subtle over the years, Anne blasted forth in an autocratic manner which did her a great deal of damage.

Her outbursts of temper became well known in the circles she now moved in and appeared all the more dramatic because she was Royal; if she had been a girl from any other family her outbursts would probably have been forgiven. Her misfortune was that she came from a family noted not only for charm but also extraordinary graciousness among its women members. It was sometimes hard to believe that she was the great-granddaughter of Queen Mary, a woman who had been a stickler for perfect manners in the Royal Family all her life. It was equally incredible that she was the granddaughter of the greatest Royal charmer of modern times, the Queen Mother, and the daughter of a sovereign whose serene manner touched all who came into contact with her.

In private almost every member of the Royal Family can lose his or her control at times but Queen Mary, the Queen Mother and Elizabeth all developed such self-control that when and if they felt like blowing their top, no servant or even friend was any the wiser. Not so with Anne. Some members of the Royal Family with far less talent than Anne and lacking her strong personality traits, nevertheless managed to establish a niche for themselves and project an air of both warmth and kindness as they went about their public duties. From the beginning, apart from when she was a little girl and pleased with what was going on about her, Anne never really tried hard enough to create a softer image, so necessary in a family that to a very great extent relied upon charisma to maintain popularity.

Philip changed his style – he had to – as he learned the hard way: his early abrasive manner just did not go down well and of all the services Elizabeth rendered to her husband the greatest was to help him acquire the image of a more understanding and less intolerant man. Charles, who had the great good fortune to inherit some of his grandmother's basic charisma, consciously and deliberately worked hard to project himself in the style of his mother – something which admittedly was not altogether too hard for him, since he was innately a kind and caring person.

For Anne, so very much her father's daughter, it was tantamount to impossible to play any game of pretence, no matter whether she was involved in eventing or public duties. She was blunt, she spoke her mind, she made simple mistakes in handling people which gave the impression that she was indifferent – and therefore sowed the seeds that were to list her in public opinion polls as one of the least popular members of the Royal Family. To those who knew her well and watched her closely it became very apparent that, far from growing up and learning to accept her Royal role, she went to the other extreme and too often open by displayed only resentment.

No one can blame her for never really coming to terms with a job that had never really appealed to her even from her very young days. She had watched first-hand the pressure on her parents, particularly understanding the stress it caused her father who never took kindly to criticism of himself and who was so often irked because even his happy private times, like playing polo, were always in the glare of publicity. She had heard him complain too often for some of his irritation not to rub off to some extent on the daughter who so closely identified herself with him. Would it have been better if she had completely opted out of the Royal scene?

Some people certainly held the view that if she had taken this course she would have become a much happier person at a much earlier age. However, it would have been extremely difficult for Elizabeth and Philip to have permitted this – so many questions would have been asked, not the least concerning her allowance from the Civil List, money provided not, as some people think, to ensure a suitable life-style for members of the Royal Family, but to cover all their working expenses.

But as in all families problems often have a curious way of resolving themselves. Anne, who in her career had collected the titles of Sportswoman of the Year, Teenager of the Year, reached her peak in eventing in her halcyon year, 1971. While everybody was busy talking about her future, what no one had counted on was that she was to meet her match in the shape of a most unexpected person, someone who, socially at any rate, could not be regarded as likely to appeal to Anne since his status in life was far removed from the Royal Family.

Actually, this man with his direct approach and steely blue eyes was just the right person for Anne. An examination of Mark Phillips's basic personality explains a great deal about Anne herself: what Phillips did not know about horses and showjumping was not worth knowing. That, for a start, intrigued Anne and earned him her tremendous respect – and there were not so many people for whom she had real respect. He knew how to get the maximum out of his horses without ever resorting to harsh or tough methods. In itself, that earned her admiration.

Add to that his easy air of command and his self-assurance stemming from his role as a captain in the old and distinguished regiment, the 1st Queen's Dragoons – self-confidence tinged with a certain amount of cockiness – and you had a man who was pretty well tailor-made for Elizabeth's daughter. Another strong point in his favour was his total absorption in his career, which had made him steer clear of any serious entanglements – his life-style was more than satisfactory.

When he went to a dinner-dance during the Horse Trials at Crookham in Hampshire in 1972 he regarded it not so much a pleasure as a duty when he was asked to look after Anne. The notion of dancing attendance on Elizabeth's daugher did not throw him or make him nervous in any way: equally he was not unduly exhilarated, although he accepted that he would be certain to have his leg pulled when he rejoined his regiment at Camberley. Since they had so much in common and had so many mutual friends all drawn from the closely knit world of eventing there was no forced conversation, no long searching-for-words pauses on that first evening together.

Suffering bores was something that Anne constantly had to endure: so often she found, like so many of her relatives, that the most extrovert people, usually men, would either dry up in her presence or, in a desperate attempt to cope with a member of the Royal Family, ask personal questions about her life-style which irritated her beyond measure. Phillips was well aware of Anne's sheer bad luck with her horse Doublet which, because of a damaged tendon, had to be withdrawn from competing and so dashed her hopes of being selected for the British Equestrian Team at the Munich Olympics. She was dogged by various other mishaps – yet another of

201

her horses had problems and she again had to withdraw from a competition.

Anne did not need a shoulder to cry on but certainly the opportunity of discussing and thrashing out some of her problems with a more than sympathetic and understanding professional could not have come at a better time. Anne and Mark came together several times at other events and both deliberately went out of their way to seek the other out. Their friendship was well established long before Mark ever put a foot inside Buckingham Palace or even so much as met Elizabeth and Philip. They swapped telephone numbers and met for lunch or dinner in country restaurants known to Mark and where, curiously enough, Anne was never recognised.

As the months went by and more and more they discovered they enjoyed one another's company, Phillips invited Anne to join him for a weekend with his parents and his sister at Mount House, a pleasant sixteenth-century house standing in some three acres of the sleepy Wiltshire village of Great Somerford. By then, Phillips was on pretty sure ground: the couple had become so close that it seemed quite natural for him to invite Elizabeth's daughter home. From the start, there had never been any stiffness between them and this was almost entirely due to the environment of eventing, with its informality that always broke down any class barriers.

A man or woman was accepted by the showjumping fraternity for their prowess in showjumping and not for anything else. It was fundamental that the individual was a good mixer and this was something that had never been a problem for Anne. She mucked around in old clothes, let fire with bad language when she felt like it and swigged back Coca-Cola from a can as she happily and eagerly listened to stories and the jokes they all swapped. She could laugh infectiously with the rest of them when she found something really funny, just like her mother in private.

Mark's parents knew that their son was seeing more and more of the Queen's daughter but didn't take the affair seriously, at least not until he intimated that he was thinking of inviting her to stay at Mount House. In their wisdom, they kept the news of the friendship very much to themselves, not even imparting a word to relatives or neighbourly county friends. There is no doubt that if they had accidently let a word slip, the publicity would have nipped the romance in the bud before it had really begun to blossom. Mark's parents had no links with Royalty and the prospect of entertaining Princess Anne, even though Mark assured them that there would be no problems at all, was nevertheless a daunting one.

They were not pretentious people but it is not surprising that they were both more than somewhat anxious at the thought of the Queen's daughter spending two nights under their roof in a home which, with all its comfort and mod cons, was by no means grand even when compared with some of the smaller residences on Royal estates. They had to face simple matters like what sort of meals Anne liked: Mark was able to tell them that she was not in the least fussy and a roast and two veg would suit her fine. She always made a joke of the fact that chips were never served at Buckingham Palace because weight-conscious Elizabeth had long ago crossed them off the menu, much to the chagrin of the rest of the family.

However, Mark's father, Major Peter Phillips, an essentially jolly man who was a director of Walls, and his somewhat retiring wife, did observe the correct protocol when Mark finally drove home in his Ford Cortina with Anne sitting in the passenger seat. Major Phillips inclined his head in a bow and Mrs Phillips dropped a curtsey and both of them addressed Anne as 'Ma'am'. The first evening of the visit was relaxed and everyone enjoyed themselves enormously and after an excellent dinner around the family dining table lit by candles, photograph albums were brought out and Anne looked at pictures of Mark as a two-year-old boy sitting astride his first pony, holding a trophy he received at prep school and looking rather lean and lanky after an athletics competition at Marlborough, where he had established himself as a fine all-round athlete. There were photographs of him as a rifleman in the Green Jackets before he won a place at Sandhurst and became an officer cadet.

All this was great fun and Anne found the leg-pulling that went on at Mount House pretty much the same as she was used to at home with her parents and three brothers. Like her own family, Mark's parents had no particular interest in academic life and, just like at home, the Phillips's house was filled with books on country life pursuits and publications like *Farmers' Weekly* etc., which were all well thumbed. The Phillips's obvious pride and absorption in their son's career drew Anne more closely into the Phillips family group, which included Mark's younger sister, Sarah, and many weekends followed at Mount House, where she was never given a second glance as she strolled round the village in a shabby reefer jacket and with a headscarf over her head.

Like Anthony Armstrong-Jones many years before him, Mark Phillips soon became adept at trying to put wily newshounds off the scent and they would find ways and means to meet at the homes of mutual friends. Mark's Commanding Officer finally had to be let into the secret that the couple were in love and several times they spent quiet weekends at his home, once or twice being smuggled in a horse box past reporters.

It was in January 1973 that Elizabeth put her final seal of approval on the affair when she invited Mark to join the Royal Family at Sandringham where they were spending the New Year. It was a slightly nervous young Captain who, in his hacking jacket and grey flannels, turned up in time for tea at the 'big house', just occasionally tending to laugh rather too heartily as he tried to cover up his basic nervousness. Mark had met Anne's parents before and so practised were they in making people feel at ease that he soon merged easily into the family scene and lost his early nervousness.

In the beginning he was very much an object of real curiosity for members of the Royal Family since Anne had never brought any 'serious' boyfriend home for inspection before. Her name had been linked with other men from the world of eventing, men like Olympic gold medallist and showjumper Richard Meade, but none of these friendships had come to anything. It was soon clear to everyone that this was indeed a love match and the more they saw them together, the more Elizabeth and Philip realised that they could almost have been computer dated.

The first clue that this was to be a marriage with a difference and one that would lead to certain traumatic breaks with Royal tradition came after the engagement had been announced and Anne explained that she only wanted a very simple wedding. She had no particular church in mind but what did not appeal to her was all the panoply and pageantry that would be involved if she and Mark were married at Westminster Abbey. There were family discussions and it was not only Elizabeth and Philip who strongly disagreed with Anne's ideas but Charles as well. In the end she had to give in and the great day went off splendidly at the Abbey with Anne in a dramatic, high necked white silk gown and Mark in the scarlet and gold tunic of his regiment, with its blue velvet collar and cuffs and skin-tight trousers.

More than two years were to pass before Anne was able to inform a delighted Elizabeth that in November 1977 she would become a grandmother for the first time. Anne had always given the impression that she was not in a hurry to have a family but for many months she harboured some very real fears that she and Mark might never have a child. This was because the emergency operation to remove an ovarian cyst when she was only twenty had left a legacy of minor gynaecological prob-lems which took a long time to clear up. Her first baby, however, was born in St Mary's Hospital, Paddington, a healthy six and a half pound boy and was christened Peter Mark Andrew by the Archbishop of Canterbury in the Music Room at Buckingham Palace.

It was widely felt that motherhood would not only suit Anne but would also soften her image which, with her continued outspokenness, was getting decidedly blurred at the edges. But nothing of the kind happened. Much as she loved her mother and devoted to her as she was, Anne, soon after she knew she was pregnant, fired off a bombshell that was to upset and shake both Elizabeth and the Royal Family. Anne told Elizabeth that she intended that the grandchild would be brought up in the style of his father – that meant that if the baby was a girl she would be known as plain 'Miss Phillips' and if a boy, as plain 'Master Phillips'. At first Anne's baldly stated proposal was regarded as something of a joke. Elizabeth was aghast and thought that Anne could not possibly be serious. But no amount of pleas or persuasive efforts could make her change her mind.

Normally the procedure would have been for Elizabeth to grant Mark Phillips an earldom. If he had refused this she could have made Anne a Royal Duchess in her own right. In either event all the children of the marriage would have been titled. Mark Phillips, unhappy and distressed both for his wife and his mother-in-law, was hardly able to bring himself to express a positive opinion of his own. He loved his wife and understood her point of view but he was equally able to appreciate and witness at first hand Elizabeth's sadness that her first grandson might grow up without the style of a Royal child.

Anne's argument was that the child would not be Royal since his father was a commoner. Her parents cited the case of Tony Armstrong-Jones who had accepted a hereditary peerage and became Earl of Snowdon so that the children of his marriage to Princess Margaret would have titles. His elder son is David, Viscount Linley and his daughter is Lady Sarah Armstrong-Jones. Anne's first child, Peter Phillips, as fifth in line of succession, was nearer to the Throne than either David or Sarah and it was put to Anne that it would be extremely unkind to Elizabeth for her to continue insisting that Elizabeth's first grandchild should be titleless.

Anne listened to the arguments in favour of a title: it was put to her that the future strength of modern monarchy rested very much in the hands of Charles, herself and her two brothers, Andrew and Edward and their children: for this reason alone, she should acquiesce to Elizabeth's wishes. Until Charles married and had children of his own the direct line of succession was not yet ensured and, at thirty, he was still a bachelor with no serious girl friend in the offing. These issues did not sway Anne who stubbornly went ahead and rejected a title for her son as part of her deliberate policy to free him from the trappings and duties of Royalty in order that, as she claimed, he could lead a completely independent life when he grew up.

Anne is, however, deluding herself since her son can never completely escape his birthright. He is bound, in time, to have to perform various duties, notably as Counsellor of State. These Counsellors have been appointed from the earliest times to operate during the absence of the Sovereign abroad 'to prevent delay or difficulty in the despatch of public business'. When Peter is eighteen he will automatically be appointed a Counsellor, ranking ahead of Princess Margaret because he is more directly in line to the Throne. The children of Elizabeth's three sons, Charles, Andrew and Edward, assuming that all do marry and do have children early in marriage – will still be far too young to take on the duties of Counsellors.

So any statutes or official documents that have to be signed by Peter Phillips in the next decade or so will bear a commoner's signature – for only the second time in British constitutional history. The first commoner to sign such State papers was Oliver Cromwell, Lord Protector of England in the seventeenth century. The desire of Anne, with the quiet acceptance of her husband, to allow Peter Phillips to remain a commoner did the boy no great service: for the rest of his life he will remain 'the

Sovereign's grandson'. A title would have hurt no one and pleased Elizabeth – a mother who gave Anne all the freedom she had ever wanted and asked so little in return.

The battle over, Anne returned to Gatcombe Park in Gloucestershire, surrounded by some of the loveliest countryside in England and with immediate access to the best hunting. Here in this mansion built of Cotswold stone covered with magnolia, winter jasmine and Wistaria which she had only been able to buy with financial help from her mother, she settled down with Mark to farming the estate, hoping to make it a viable and going concern.

The atmosphere at Gatcombe, with its colonial style front, pillared porch and two bow-fronted wings, was relaxed and informal and it was here that Charles frequently spent lazy weekends, getting on with his sister far better than he had ever done in his life. He toyed with the idea of buying a similar sort of house in the area for himself. He finally settled for High Grove ten miles away in the neighbouring village of Tetbury. It would have no mistress, because Charles had then no bride in mind.

11

A Love-Match

THE OBSESSIONAL WORLD interest in Charles's endless stream of girl friends lasted over a period of ten speculation-rife years. The main ingredient that made his love life so extraordinarily fascinating was that most people expected that his would be a real love match – not an arranged marriage. It seemed to the public that when the Heir to the Throne fell in love and was ready to enter a state of Holy Matrimony, his bride could just as easily come from a professional home as from the ranks of the British aristocracy or one of the few remaining minor European Royal houses. The general impression was that once Charles had made up his mind about the choice of a bride, parental blessing was only a formality before the great bells of Westminster Abbey peeled out for the first Princess of Wales since his great-grandfather, Edward VII, had married Princess Alexandra of Denmark in St George's Chapel, Windsor, in 1863.

The truth, however, was not as simple as that. The Queen and Prince Philip were not prepared for their eldest son to marry anyone he fancied – and Charles knew this. Too much was at stake. A future bride for Charles, if life followed its natural course, would one day be Queen: she would one day need in her strong qualities which could not be acquired but must be inherent in her, qualities which were if anything needed far more in the 1980s than at almost any time in modern Royal history. It was not only the continuation of the line of the House of Windsor that was vital but also the quality of charisma, more urgent in this media age than ever before, a charisma which the media could convey to the public.

Charles knew only too well what tremendous pressures would be brought to bear on him if his heart led him in the wrong direction. This had been drilled into him before he left Gordonstoun and long before the time when, at a later stage in life than most young men, he first began escorting elegant girls; they were all girls with the right degree of sophistication and the right sort of family pedigree. He was so conditioned that when he was only nineteen he was already able in his first radio interview, to talk in a most adult fashion with Jack de Manio of the BBC about his thoughts on marriage. The words he used were:

> You have to remember that when you marry in my position, you're going to marry someone who, perhaps, is one day going to be Queen. You've got to choose somebody very carefully, I think, who could fulfil this particular role, and it has got to be somebody pretty unusual. The one advantage about marrying a Princess, for instance, or somebody from a royal family, is that they know what happens.

At this very youthful age Charles had accepted that far from being free to marry anyone he liked, there were certain powerful restrictions which strictly curtailed his choice: he had to marry someone who in the eyes of Elizabeth and Philip would be capable, with him, of taking the monarchy into the twenty-first century.

Not very long after Charles had first expressed his views on marriage in the BBC interview, he returned again to the subject and in so doing again displayed a mature view when he said:

> Marriage is a much more important business than falling

in love. I think one must concentrate on marriage being essentially a question of mutual love and respect for each other. Creating a secure family unit in which to bring up children, to give them a happy, secure upbringing – that's what marriage is all about, creating a home. Essentially you must be good friends and love, I'm sure, will grow out of that friendship.

His philosophy did not change when at a later stage he said, 'I have a particular responsibility to ensure that I make the right decision. The last thing I could possibly entertain is divorce ... I hope I will be as lucky as my parents, who have been so happy.'

Charles was to spend five years with the Services, years in which he always had an elegant escort when he was off duty. It was in March 1971, four months after his twenty-second birthday, that he went to the RAF College, Cranwell, as a Flight Lieutenant and with his natural talent for flying, completed the first-year graduate course in five months. On leave he continued to gravitate towards girls with aristocratic backgrounds, their   parents often having close links with a member of the Royal Family or the Royal Household. He walked with a new air of confidence, seemed very sure of himself and then shortly before the passing-out parade when he received his wings, announced that he wanted to make a parachute jump.

The Queen was appalled and urged her son to forget the whole idea, stressing that it was too dangerous an escapade for an heir to the Throne. Charles sought out and received Philip's support and it was only with great misgivings that the Queen was finally persuaded to allow her son to train at the RAF Parachute Training School near Oxford. The Prince made the jump successfully – after one hair-raising moment when his feet were temporarily caught in the parachute rigging over his head. Many people in Whitehall privately regarded this as both a reckless and foolhardy feat, a feat which nevertheless was to be the start of his build-up as 'Action

Man', an image which was helped, not inconsiderably, by his dashing appearance in uniform.

In September 1971 Prince Charles transferred to the Royal Navy and after a six week course at the Royal Naval College, Dartmouth, joined HMS *Norfolk* as an acting Sub Lieutenant. His cramped living quarters were a seven foot square cabin but he was in his element, even though he had to spend his twenty-third birthday off Sardinia keeping watch in a Force Ten gale. He went on to serve on board other ships, HMS *Gasserton*, a coastal minesweeper, HMS *Minerva* when he was promoted Lieutenant, HMS *Jupiter* as a communications officer and then in September 1974 embarked on a four month helicopter conversion course at the Royal Naval Air Station at Yeovilton. As in his University days, his career was constantly interrupted by official engagements which took him to all corners of the globe: on a State visit to France with his parents, to the Bahamas for Independence celebrations; to New Zealand for the Commonwealth Games; to Nepal for the Coronation of King Birendra and to Canada on a tour of the North West Territories.

At regular intervals the name of yet a new girl friend hit the headlines. When HMS *Jupiter* docked in San Diego Prince Charles met – and clearly liked – Laura Jo Watkins, the blonde and vivacious daughter of a US Admiral. Later that year (1974) she appeared in the Strangers' Gallery of the House of Lords to hear the Prince make his maiden speech and the couple had several secret meetings during her stay in England. Was Britain destined to have an American-born Queen? The United States hoped so. However, the friendship faded and the Prince did not see Laura Jo Watkins again until 1978 when she made a brief appearance at Deauville where he was playing polo.

Charles's naval career ended with a command of his own when in February 1976, and to his great joy, he was given command of the minehunter HMS *Bronington*, one of the smallest ships in the Fleet. Those ten months when he was in command of a complement of four officers and thirty-three ratings he often described as the happiest and most rewarding years at sea. The ship rolled so badly that even the Prince, generally a good sailor, was often sea-sick. His life in the Services finished, as he knew it would, in December 1977 when he had a most unceremonial send off: his crew pushed him on shore in a wheelchair with a lavatory seat slung around his neck, in keeping with the Navy's traditional, if bawdy, sense of humour.

He was twenty-nine and his list of escorts were more intriguing than ever. An examination of some of the girl friends who really mattered to Charles in his twenties explains a good deal about him in those years when he was both able to work extremely hard and play hard as well. Nearly all their names could be found in the pages of Burke's Peerage or Debretts. There was Lady Henrietta Fitzroy, daughter of the Duke of Grafton; Angela Neville, daughter of Lord Rupert Neville, Private Secretary to and friend of Prince Philip; Lady Cecil Kerr, daughter of the Marquess of Lothian; Lady Leonora Grosvenor, daughter of the Duke of Westminster; Lady Camilla Fane, daughter of the Earl of Westmoreland; Lady Victoria Percy and her sister Lady Caroline Percy, both daughters of the Duke of Northumberland, and so on; the total number of girls belonging to the landed gentry numbered more than fifty.

Very occasionally Charles broke away from the pattern but when he did so it was with someone like Caroline Longman, daughter of publisher Mark Longman. Titleless, Caroline nevertheless belonged to the very wealthy closed-circuit group accustomed to entertaining members of the Royal Family and senior members of the Household in their own homes. While the foregoing to some people might suggest that Charles was a snob, nothing could be further from the truth. It was easier for him, as it would have been for anybody in his shoes, to turn to girls who were accustomed to the Royal scene and the protocol that went with it. A girl without any sort of Royal or aristocratic indoctrination would, more than likely, have been like a fish out of water in the circles in which Charles moved, and the result would have been severe embarrassment for both of them. Also, for a man of Charles's disciplined upbringing combined with his still over-sensitive nature, it would have been just as embarrassing for him as it would have been for his parents if he had ever crossed the social barrier and taken home an 'unsuitable' girl.

Both the Queen and Philip were anxious for Charles to marry reasonably early in life and it was their openly expressed hope that he would find a partner when he was somewhere between the ages of twenty-five and twenty-seven, the time when most men in the Royal Family announce their engagement. As time passed and Charles continued to dilly and dally, seemingly flitting easily and carelessly from one girl to the next, the parental desire for him to settle down became more and more urgent. So the wheels were set in motion for him to meet potential brides.

The help of Prince Philip's sister, Princess George of Hanover, and that of other German-in-laws were sought. Had they anyone in mind? Queen Juliana of the Netherlands and her husband, Prince Bernhard, were sounded out. Various names came up, were discussed and dismissed. Too many girls short-listed as 'possible' were Catholic and because of the 1701 Act of Settlement Charles was forbidden to marry a Catholic.

One such girl who appealed to some senior members of the Royal Family was the charming and highly intelligent Princes Marie-Astrid of Luxemburg. However, the fact that she was a Catholic put paid to any serious ideas of trying to arrange a meeting with Prince Charles. Mountbatten never tried to hide the fact that just as he had waited for the Queen and Philip to marry, so he was quietly waiting in the wings for Charles and his granddaughter Amanda to marry, thus, in a second generation, making the name Mountbatten synonymous with the House of Windsor.

It is strange to reflect that but for the resolution, strngth of character and cool judgement of Amanda, today there might well be another Princess of Wales and future Queen. Amanda was the child who had always been so close to Charles and who, born in 1957, was nine years his junior. Mountbatten's favourite and beloved granddaughter grew up in the large rambling family house in Kent. There was not even a butler and in a totally relaxed and informal atmosphere, a crowd of children were encouraged and stimulated into constant and lively discussions over the dinner table. As they grew older, politics tended to dominate the exchanges. Charles often went there and it was probably the only place, except when he was with Mountbatten at Broadlands, where he could drop all formality and become just one of the family.

Charles proposed to Amanda more than once but she always asked for time to 'think it over' because, much as she liked him, Mountbatten's granddaughter felt she could never bring herself to face life as a member of the Royal Family with all its responsibilities and the public life she would have to endure. All her life she had observed the Royal way of life from the inside and it was the thought of giving up personal freedom that swayed her thinking most.

Before his death Lord Mountbatten had taken Amanda with him on a semi-official tour to Africa in a bid to help her overcome her distaste for public life. When they set off from London she was extremely nervous but with her grandfather's guidance and careful encouragement, she made great strides and Mountbatten complimented himself that she was gradually coming out of her shell. Before he was so tragically murdered in Ireland in August 1979 Mountbatten had planned to take Amanda away with him again the following winter, this time to India, and it was arranged that Prince Charles would join them for a time.

As Charles's name continued to be linked with one girl after another, Mountbatten had grown increasingly anxious about his great-nephew's future and became more and more convinced that the only person with whom he could find real happiness was the 'most suitable' Amanda. When a book on his life, *Mountbatten: Eighty Years in Pictures* was published in 1979 he insisted that a special full length photograph of himself and Amanda was included and knowingly hinted to close friends that in future years this would become an 'historic picture'. When Prince Charles told his parents that he had proposed to Amanda, Prince Philip commented to his son that he was glad he was 'keeping it in the family'.

After Mountbatten's death Charles, who experienced an even greater sense of loss than his father, grimly got on with his job and Amanda, still undecided about marriage to Charles, set off on a year-long world tour in order to 'make up her mind once and for all'. With her was a close friend, Diana Sebag Montefiori. However, when Amanda returned to England, Lady Diana Spencer had already captured Charles's heart, and his old childhood friend was one of the first people to wish him well.

From the beginning, there had been strong opposition to the idea of the Charles–Amanda marriage from a Royal quarter resulting from the coolness bordering on antagonism which existed between the Queen Mother and Lord Mountbatten, an antagonism which began in the twenties when it was fuelled by the Queen Mother's disapproval of what she considered to be Lady Mountbatten's over indulgent life-style. In public the Queen Mother and Mountbatten smiled at one another but in private they had very little time for one another.

The Queen Mother was well aware of Mountbatten's long cherished hope that Amanda and Charles would tie the knot. And that was not what she had in mind at all. The Queen Mother's influence on Charles was tremendous and she, just as much as the Queen and Philip, was desperately anxious for Charles, her favourite grandson, to marry. It was significant that her lady-in-waiting and closest friend since childhood years at Glamis was Ruth, Lady Fermoy, a woman with whom she had so much in

216

common and in whom she confided. The two women shared the same friends, enjoyed the same sort of people and had the same brand of wit and sparkling humour.

Significantly, both had tremendous pride in and derived enormous pleasure from their respective grandchildren. The Queen Mother could no more hide the fact that Charles was her favourite grandchild than Lady Fermoy could hide her preference for her youngest granddaughter, Lady Diana Spencer. The Queen Mother had always been noted in the Royal Family for her romantic streak and it was not for nothing that her leg was pulled for her alleged activities as a matchmaker. Certainly nothing pleased her more than to participate secretly in the budding stages of a Royal romance, as she had done with Princess Margaret and Lord Snowdon, and later, with Princess Alexandra and Mr Angus Ogilvy. In both cases she was one of the first, if not the first person, to be let into the secret that they were in love and wanted to marry.

In turn, Lady Fermoy was equally a romantic at heart and her great moment had been in June 1954, when her eighteen-year-old daughter, the Hon. Frances Roche, had married the thirty-year-old Viscount Althorp, heir to Earl Spencer, in Westminster Abbey when almost every member of the Royal Family had been a guest. Althorp knew Elizabeth and Philip at an intimate level: during his engagement he had to leave his fiancée back in England when, as acting Master of the Royal Household, he accompanied the Royal couple on a gruelling six-month tour of the Dominions. Frances Roche was no stranger to the Royal Family either.

Lady Fermoy's four grandchildren, Sarah, Jane, Diana and Charles grew up in what could be called a semi-Royal ambience: their father was a godson of Elizabeth's grandmother, Queen Mary; the Queen Mother was godmother to both Sarah and Jane, and the Queen was godmother to Charles. The Spencer children spent holidays with their grandfather at Althorp (pronounced 'Altrup'), the family seat set in 1,500 magnificent Northamptonshire acres and with its magnificent art collection it had as much, if not more to offer, than some of the Royal homes.

For the rest of the time the Spencers and their family, including Diana, lived at their home, Park House, a comfortable and rambling mansion on the Sandringham estate rented from the Queen. Because of the immediate proximity of the Queen's Norfolk home, Park House could only be leased to someone very close indeed to the Royal Family and the Spencers fitted the bill perfectly. Among those who knew the two grandmothers very well, it was abundantly obvious that if the Queen Mother and Lady Fermoy could have waved a magic wand, their joint wish would have been for one of the Royal children to marry one of the Spencer children.

What made this seem unlikely was that the children of both families had all known each other since they were very young and tended to take their respective neighbours very much for granted, with the Spencers never forgetting their place but never in awe of Royalty. For the two grandmothers an extraordinary moment came when they discovered that the vivacious Sarah, with her auburn hair and outgoing manner, was seeing more and more of Charles and occasionally accompanying him to official evening engagements.

Sarah had not been well and had shown signs of anorexia nervosa, the slimmer's disease, but the trouble, which had also worried her grandmother, Lady Fermoy, gradually disappeared as she went out and about with Charles. She went with him on a skiing holiday to Klosters in 1978 when they were accompanied by the Duke and Duchess of Gloucester. Sarah and Charles continued to meet: she went shooting with the Royal Family at Sandringham and he went to Althorp, the great house which became a permanent home for the Spencer children when their father inherited the title on the death of their grandfather in 1975.

For the Spencers – unlike, say, Major and Mrs Peter Phillips, the parents of Princess Anne's husband Captain

Mark Phillips – the Spencer children's friendship with the Royal children was in no way dramatic and raised no family eyebrows. Sarah went out with Charles, and Diana enjoyed the company of Andrew: it was a perfectly normal and natural part of growing-up in young people from two close families who had known each other all their lives.

What was to prove dramatic was the sudden switch Charles made from Sarah to her sister Diana, a relationship which grew closer and more intense at what was, for Charles, an extraordinary pace. This friendship – for which Lady Fermoy and the Queen Mother had always yearned – was watched intently by both grandmothers and had the clandestine support of both of them. They knew that Charles's interest in Diana was first seriously awakened when he had gone to Althorp to see Sarah and had quickened when he later found Diana at Balmoral – staying there to help her sister Jane (married to Elizabeth's Assistant Private Secretary, Robert Fellowes) with her new baby. It was during the autumn weeks at Balmoral in 1980 that Diana and Charles were able to meet alone – at Birkhall, the Queen Mother's home on the Balmoral estate, without anyone except the immediate Royal Family and Diana's family being any the wiser.

This was one of the most agonising times of their life for Elizabeth, Philip and the Queen Mother, who realised only too well that if Charles was ever to make the perfect match, then this was it. At nineteen Lady Diana presented an identikit picture of precisely the sort of girl they had all longed for Charles to marry, but until Diana's arrival on the scene they had almost lost hope that she would ever turn up. The days when his parents pulled Charles's leg quite unmercifully about his elegant escorts had long since passed: they now showed a certain edginess at this apparently growing indifference to marriage – something which in an ordinary family would have been of little consequence but was of paramount importance to the Royal Family.

For some years Charles had tended to spend

weekends and holidays with married couples who were close friends, and this life-style was not at all to the liking of Lord Mountbatten who was the first relative to marshal all his thoughts on the matter objectively and put them before his nephew. He did not mince his words when he bluntly told Charles that it was time he stopped 'playing the field', even going so far as to liken his nephew's behaviour to the previous Prince of Wales, the late Duke of Windsor. Only Mountbatten could have got away with this withering comment, 'You don't want to end up like your Uncle David, do you?'

Charles still continued to remain close to old girl friends, most of whom had long since married, and there was a decided air of despondency among senior Royals who were beginning to feel that only a miracle would ever break his now all-too-familiar bachelor pattern when, rather than return home alone to his Private Apartments in Buckingham Palace, he would stay at the country homes of people of his own age group who knew and understood him best. Certainly everyone crossed their fingers when Diana Spencer, not in the least in awe of Charles, attracted his attention when she appeared at Balmoral.

It was not only her youth and her air of innocence that appealed to Charles: she was exuberant, enthusiastic and her natural sophistication came from her upbringing and not from experience. Charles soon began to seek her out more often and as the friendship developed the more Elizabeth and Philip prayed that it would not be destroyed by any premature publicity. Their great good fortune was that Diana's own family presented no problem – at least, so far as secrecy was concerned. There was only one delicate issue that had to be faced head on: in 1967 when Diana was only six and at Riddlesworth Hall, a preparatory school near Diss, her mother, Viscountess Althorp, had walked out on her husband 'Johnny' Althorp and her four children. At thirty-one and after thirteen years of marriage she had been sued by her husband for adultery with Peter

Shand-Kydd, heir to a wallpaper business fortune.

The subsequent divorce case had been bitterly contested and ended with Spencer being awarded custody of the four children of the marriage. Shortly afterwards Diana's mother married Shand-Kydd and, turning her back on the world of high society and Court life that she had known throughout the years, went to live at Ardencapel, a white hillside manor house on the remote Island of Seil in Argyllshire – separated from the mainland by what is known as the shortest bridge across the Atlantic, literally three hundred yards long.

Through her mother, Lady Fermoy, Frances Shand-Kydd kept in touch with the Queen Mother but she was no longer seen at great functions, infinitely preferring her relatively quiet life in Scotland where she and her husband owned a great sheep farm: this was big business and was later to embrace rich farming lands in Australia. In Frances Shand-Kydd, Elizabeth and Philip knew they had a staunch ally who was in an even better position than themselves to offer the sort of protection from publicity that was so necessary and vital for Charles and Diana.

Then the Queen and Prince Philip had to consider Diana's father, Earl Spencer, who, in 1976 had married extrovert divorcée Raine, former Countess of Dartmouth and daughter of the headline-making bestselling romantic novelist Barbara Cartland. In 1978 the Earl collapsed in the stable block of Althorp with a massive brain haemorrhage and it was not until two years had passed that 'Johnny' Spencer, although still far from fit, was out of the wood and apart from a slight speech impediment, able to resume a reasonably active life.

Throughout the grave illness Raine Spencer had devoted herself to her husband who rightly claimed later that she had saved his life. It was entirely due to her initiative and efforts that Spencer was given, with remarkable results, a then untried drug as a last resort attempt to combat an infection which had rejected all other treatment.

By the time Charles and Diana were meeting regularly neither the Queen nor Philip had had any personal contact with the second Countess Spencer and knew that Diana, who was very close indeed to her own mother, had very little contact with her stepmother either, and she had never taken Charles to Althorp during their courtship. Should Charles and Diana become engaged, the Queen and Philip were then faced with the thorny problem of divorced in-laws: divorce was no longer an unmentionable word in the Royal Family since with resigned permission from Elizabeth both Princess Margaret and her cousin the Earl of Harewood had experienced the break-up of a marriage. Nevertheless, there was still a stigma attached to divorce for Elizabeth and Philip who set such great store in family unity. What they also did not know was how Earl Spencer and Frances Shand-Kydd would react at the thought of meeting again so many years after their bitter divorce – something that would ultimately be inevitable if the relationship between Charles and Diana continued to intensify.

The thirty-two-year-old bachelor Prince and nineteen-year-old kindergarten teacher's secret meetings were brought to an abrupt end once it was publicly revealed that Diana had been invited by Charles to join him as his personal guest at Princess Margaret's belated fiftieth birthday party – she was fifty in the preceding August – held in November 1980 at the Ritz Hotel, a very special celebration when only members of the Royal Family and their closest friends were present. Somewhere around two o'clock in the morning Diana returned to the comfortable flat in South Kensington bought for her by her father and which she shared with three close girl friends who all paid rent. The next morning Diana woke up to find the flat besieged by London pressmen, their ranks being swelled by ever increasing numbers during the next few days. The public revelation at Margaret's party of Diana's romance with Charles had set the whole world's press agog.

For the next three months Diana Spencer was hounded day and night, her every movement being minutely recorded. With infinite dignity and good humour, she withstood almost impossible pressures without so much as uttering a cross word; that in itself was an incredible achievement. Only a girl with such a close association with the Royal Family, long accustomed to insatiable world curiosity about people she and her family knew well, could have coped in such an assured fashion.

There was another great factor which helped her: her sister Sarah, who subsequently married Neil McCorquodale, had over the years skilfully fended off all questions about her friendship with Charles, a friendship that had been essentially platonic. So from within the ranks of her own family Diana had experience of what it was like to be linked with Charles: following her sister's example she smiled sweetly, said nothing, and kept everyone guessing

Late in January, although no sign of strain was showing, Diana told Charles that she was going to Australia on a short holiday with her mother, Mrs Shand-Kydd, who privately thought it was vital that her youngest daughter should be given a break from the publicity which had made her open smiling face, her hair-do, her casual trendy clothes familiar to almost everyone in the world. Diana's mother, her own privacy constantly disturbed by would-be interviewers who were all brushed off with a brisk, 'No comment', was a tower of strength to her daughter in those days. Well aware that an engagement was in the offing, she was one of the few people who fully understood the nature of the tightrope Diana was treading. A false step, an indiscreet comment by a relative, would have been enough to have caused great trouble for Charles, who deeply resented but nevertheless accepted, the constant prying into his own private life. All the Spencers, true to their tradition as close friends of the Royal Family, presented a united front.

In the end, understandably, Mrs Shand-Kydd's patience snapped and she wrote a strongly worded letter to *The Times*. This was published and in it she said: 'May I ask the editors of Fleet Street whether, in the execution of their jobs, they consider it necessary or fair to harass my daughter daily, from dawn until well after dusk . . .'

Before Diana flew off for three weeks to Australia she had dinner with Charles and it was then that he proposed, giving her, as he said later, 'a chance to think about it – to think it was all going to be too awful'. But Diana had no doubts. It was during their time together with friends in Australia that the great strength of the Spencer mother-and-daughter relationship was fully in evidence; using great skill and expertise, Mrs Shand-Kydd covered their tracks in a brilliant way so that no one ever found them. In peace and quiet her daughter was able to talk and if Mrs Shand-Kydd had had any doubts about Diana's love for Charles, they were utterly dispelled.

At eleven o'clock on the morning of 24 February 1981, before the start of a routine Investiture ceremony in Buckingham Palace, the Lord Chamberlain, Lord Maclean, the senior member of the Royal Household, read the following announcement: 'It is with the greatest pleasure that the Queen and the Duke of Edinburgh announce the betrothal of their beloved son, the Prince of Wales, to the Lady Diana Spencer, daughter of the Earl Spencer and Mrs Shand-Kydd.'

In the happy months which followed, which were to lead up to the great and moving wedding at St Paul's Cathedral on 29 July 1981 with all its pomp, pageantry and brilliant stage-management watched on television by millions of people all over the world, Elizabeth and Philip had good reason to count their blessings: not only was their future daughter-in-law known and liked by every member of the Royal Family but she also, by the very nature of her background, knew and understood their style of life both in public and in private.

One of the immediate problems that faced Elizabeth and Philip and Charles and his fiancée was this: where should Diana spend her time until the great day of the wedding dawned? Everyone was of the same mind: with the Queen Mother in the calm and gracious atmosphere of Clarence House, only a few minutes walk down The Mall from Buckingham Palace. At the time great emphasis was made on the fact that Diana would learn the ropes of her future role as a senior member of the Royal Family from probably the most experienced of them all, Elizabeth's own mother. But this again was another fallacy which sprang up around Diana: since she had been a mere toddler she had grown up accepting close association with Royalty as part and parcel of her way of life.

Not only her parents, her maternal and paternal grandparents but also her forbears going back to the fifteenth century had all been in Royal service, and had been close friends of sovereigns and their families too. In truth Diana needed no instruction in Royal protocol from the Queen Mother. From her father and mother and from her grandmother Lady Fermoy, she knew it all by heart. Added to that, Jane, her eldest sister who knew Charles so well, had married Robert Fellowes who, after some time on the personal staff of Charles, was now an Assistant Private Secretary to Elizabeth.

Relatively few people seemed to grasp at the time the extraordinarily close links that Diana had with the Royal Family. It contributed to Elizabeth and Philip's private astonishment and public delight that as a future Princess of Wales, she was in every respect a dream come true. Diana also had another star quality in Elizabeth's eyes: combined with her historic lineage, equally as blue-blooded as that of Charles, since she traced her ancestry back to Royalty itself in Charles II, she had grown up with a thoroughly modern approach to life, able to look after herself, shopping in supermarkets, riding to the kindergarten on her bicycle, buying clothes off the peg – all small everyday things which make people like Princess Margaret, Princess Anne and even the highly efficient women like the Duchess of Kent, seem stuffy by comparison.

Another outstanding quality was that Diana was obviously an uncomplicated and happy person – again, in striking contrast to the now rather more staid Princess Margaret and the no longer so youthful Princess Anne, who attacked her Royal duties with a determination that showed little delight.

Diana Frances Spencer was also, above all, the sort of tonic the entire British Royal Family badly needed, someone with whom the youth of Britain could identify themselves. She indicated her very strong streak of independence and individuality when she stepped out on her first public engagement with Charles attending a gala at the ancient Goldsmiths' and Silversmiths' Hall in the City of London. There was nothing traditional about her black gown with its plunging neckline combining very real elegance with a dash of daring and worn with the right degree of demureness.

Very soon her strong element of spontaneity and sense of fun came over. When she went to Broadlands, the magnificent home of Lord Mountbatten which now belongs to his grandson, Lord Romsey, and his wife, Diana got mixed up when she was about to plant a tree, the first of thousands she is likely to plant in her life. It was all resolved amid peels of laughter from the Romseys and the vast crowd gathered around.

Five weeks after their engagement had been announced the couple were separated for the first time. Charles had to fly off alone on a gruelling month-long overseas tour which took him to New Zealand, Australia and then to Washington to meet President Reagan. Diana went with him to London Airport and presented a forlorn figure as she watched the aircraft taxi down the runway and disappear into the skies.

Sun blazed down for the Royal Wedding on 29 July 1981, with all the colour and majesty: it all seemed rather endearing when, at the moment of exchanging vows, Diana mixed up the order of her husband's Christian names which instead of being 'Charles Philip Arthur

George' came out in the wrong order as 'Philip Charles Arthur George'. The bridegroom, always word perfect on public occasions, revealed his own nervousness when he missed out the word 'worldly' from the goods which he promised to share with his bride.

Solemnly, the Archbishop, magnificent in his robes of white and gold, declared, 'I pronounce that they be man and wife together'. The register signed, the Prince and Princess of Wales walked down the great centre aisle to the West Door of St Paul's towards the cheering crowds outside. Yet even on this happy and historic day senior members of the Royal Family were only too conscious of how much depended on the stability and success of this marriage.

12

A Family United

IN THE THIRTY years since the Queen succeeded to the Throne at the unexpectedly early age of twenty-five, the Royal Family have had their fair share of personal differences and squabbles. The Queen's own children had outright rows which sometimes ended in punch-ups when they were young. The Queen Mother, who helped Princess Margaret combat a series of depressions which followed the end of one love affair and then the death of a marriage, nevertheless had periods when she lost patience with her younger daughter. Princess Anne and Mark Phillips do not always see eye to eye and when there is a family altercation in this household, it is surprisingly usually Mark Phillips who gets the better of the Princess.

The Queen herself can be cross and even bad tempered when she feels really hard pressed or frustrated. At these times Prince Philip, who has a sixth sense about these relatively rare moments of irritation, knows when to keep out of the way and make himself scarce. Several Royal marriages have had their sticky patches and those of the Queen's sister, Margaret and her cousin, George, Earl of Harewood, have ended in the divorce courts.

But throughout these years which have seen so many dramatic social and economic changes, there have been no danger schisms of any kind and family loyalty to the

Queen is so deep-rooted that it is not out of a sense of duty but out of real love and affection that they surround her as they gather together, often at weekends and for the three major holidays of the year, Balmoral in the summer and Windsor Castle at Christmas and Easter.

As a unit, brothers and sisters, aunts and uncles, parents and grandparents, cousins and in-laws, all still seek out one another's company in preference to finding closer friendships outside the family circle. This is indeed one of the Queen's greatest achievements in that family unity has been sustained and even strengthened during three decades when she was faced with the problem of giving relatives far greater freedom than any previous Royal generation had ever known. On the surface it seemed a relatively easy decision for Elizabeth to make – the decision to send her children away to school: but she knew that each child, once free from the security of Buckingham Palace, would develop on its own and she could not foresee what the outcome would be.

If anything, she was in a more difficult position than any ordinary parent: if any of her children made mistakes or got into trouble, it would become world news. She could no more protect Charles, Anne, Andrew or Edward from outside influences than any other parent. All she could do was keep her fingers crossed and hope for the best, trusting that a stable home background would tell in the end. Her problems as head of the large family were unusual in that she was not only young but in many ways immature when her father, George VI, died at the relatively young age of fifty-six at a time when Elizabeth was still thoroughly enjoying not only the early years of married life in her own home but also the first years of motherhood.

Although Philip did a great deal to break down her innate reserve and shyness, he had not enough time to break down other important personal inhibitions before Elizabeth had to take on her father's job and don the mantle of sovereignty herself, something she had never envisaged until she was at least well into her forties. Much as he sought to help her, Philip, too, felt restless and unsettled when Elizabeth ascended the Throne. This former officer of the Silent Service took his traditions with him and had little sympathy with or understanding of the glare of publicity under which he and Elizabeth must live in future. There were several unhappy incidents involving newspapermen who were not only doing their own job but also, had he appreciated it, doing a big public relations job for him and Elizabeth.

How has the Queen changed over the years? Fundamentally she remains an essentially private person; while so much is known about other members of her family she has guarded her own life so successfully that only a mere handful of very close friends, apart from her relatives, ever see the real woman behind the official smile. This informal Elizabeth has never changed: she is essentially a very jolly woman with an infinite capacity for hard work. She is a firm believer in sensible eating, personal discipline and plenty of outdoor exercise. She likes to surround herself with people who share both her sense of humour – which can be wicked at times – and her energy.

Now heading for her sixtieth birthday, she is superbly fit and healthy and unless she is stricken by some physical disaster she will undoubtedly have much the same stamina when, like her mother, she reaches eighty. The Queen is much less of a worrier than she used to be: for long spells in the 1950s she could be tense both on duty and off duty, excessively troubled about her constant partings from Charles and Anne who were still at the nursery stage. Even when they were in their late 'teens she was still over anxious about them.

Once, a guest whom she had invited to dinner at Buckingham Palace noticed that she slipped out of the room several times, obviously very concerned about something. Only later did she apologise and explain the reason for her several disappearances. It transpired that Princess Anne was riding in horse trials in Germany and

230

the Queen said, 'I hadn't heard from her all day and I really was getting worried. I finally managed to get hold of her and she says she is absolutely fine. Children don't realise how much mothers worry, do they?' Early in her reign the Queen was also much troubled by her political immaturity. Nowadays, whether she is dealing with State affairs or family problems, she can be both firm and positive when the occasion arises. She has a clear grasp of home and foreign affairs and is known to ask pertinent and penetrating questions which keep visiting Ministers very much on their toes.

For long years the nature of the Queen's exchanges with the Prime Minister of the day were never discussed with any other member of the family; from the time of her accession, it was accepted by Prince Philip that unlike his famous predecessor, Prince Albert, the Prince Consort, he did not want to enter his wife's world of State affairs. With Prince Charles the situation was entirely different since he is to be the future King of England. When, therefore, he was eighteen, following the pattern established by her father, she began initiating him into the complexities of her job as monarch. The Queen was a remarkable and gifted teacher. She did not overtax Charles but gradually led him through the labyrinth of monarchial procedures so that long before he reached his mid-twenties, her son was already sufficiently equipped to take over the responsibilities of State should that be necessary.

There is little doubt that the Margaret-Townsend affair would never have reached the state of high drama it did, if it had happened today and not in the mid-1950s. This was one of the unhappiest periods in Elizabeth's life when, longing as she did to help her sister find real happiness, without realising it she unwittingly allowed the matter to get completely out of hand. The whole business was allowed to drag on far too long: the public grew impatient and the *Daily Mirror*, then the paper with the biggest circulation in the world, expressed what a great many people were feeling in a headline that read:

'Come on Margaret! Make up your Mind!'

In her own marriage, one that has not been without its occasional ups and downs, Elizabeth has found a near perfect partner in Philip. When they spend weekends in the country with friends, it is noticeable the way she will suddenly pause in the middle of a conversation and look around her saying, 'Where's Philip got to?' This does not mean she is adopting a possessive attitude: on the contrary she still urges him if it is necessary to fly the globe without her, supporting one of his many world-wide causes.

The marriage has matured with the years in a fascinating way: when members of the Royal Household are anxious to resolve a non-State matter – it may be something quite trifling like an alteration or renovation in a Royal Apartment in one of the Royal homes – they will often first sound out Philip and get his reactions. They know that Elizabeth and her husband are now so alike that very often, even though neither of them have consulted each other before, their views on most things tend to be almost identical.

Philip, however, still maintains his streak of independence and has a number of friends who rarely enter Elizabeth's orbit, basically because they are drawn from the worlds of science, high technology or industry – which tend to leave Elizabeth bored if they are discussed for hours on end. On these issues Philip really comes into his own at special dinner parties he gives at Buckingham Palace for about twelve people and which Elizabeth never attends. They are held four times a year and before the death of Lord Mountbatten in 1979 the guest list was always drawn up by what Philip called the 'home team' – himself, Lord Mountbatten, Lord Brabourne (Mountbatten's son-in-law) and Lord Rupert Neville, Philip's Private Secretary and close friend. The object of these dinners is for one specific subject to be discussed and industry has got together in this way for what have turned out to be extraordinarily frank and honest exchanges. Charles was enlisted into the 'home team' when he was quite young – it was at these working dinners and in a most relaxed and easy atmosphere, that he met MPs drawn from all sides of the House of Commons, members of the House of Lords, Trades Union officials and leading figures in the CBI (Confederation of British Industries).

Elizabeth and Philip have proved themselves to be good parents, and certain difficult relationships they experienced when their children were going through difficult adolescent years have now been completely ironed out. There was a time when Charles, hesitant and seemingly unable to assert himself, came in for some pretty blunt criticism from his father; Andrew, in his turn, knew as a teenager what it meant to be packed off to bed for what his father considered to be bad behaviour. If Elizabeth and Philip have any criticisms to level against themselves as parents it is probably that they were often too soft with Andrew and left it too long before urging Charles to go ahead and buy an establishment of his own.

It was not until he was thirty-one, a year before he began to regard Lady Diana in a serious light, that their eldest son finally decided to leave the parental home and live at High Grove, the Georgian mansion set in the heart of the Cotswolds. Charles had long since wanted to make such a break-away but Elizabeth, always very money-conscious and hesitant about anything she regarded as inordinate expenditure, felt that her son's suite in Buckingham Palace, with its three big rooms and long corridor on a first floor and his secretariat on the ground floor, was adequate. Charles had his privacy in his own apartments on one side of the Buckingham Palace quadrangle, just as his parents had theirs on the opposite side.

It was as they grew older and Anne married that Charles and his sister forgot their old childhood feuds and became close friends. Charles found the Phillips's home, Gatcombe Park in Gloucestershire, relaxed and informal: it was Anne who first suggested to her brother that he should consider looking for a house somewhere in the same area and it was to the satisfaction of both of them when High Grove, which was only ten miles from Gatcombe Park, came up for sale. What Charles really enjoyed at the Phillips's home was that while, like so many Royal homes, it had elegant rooms with charming pieces of period furniture, it was nevertheless basically comfortable and in no way regal.

It is a popular fallacy that Royal homes are more or less swamped by liveried flunkeys: in fact footmen are a rarity except at the Royal Palaces and Clarence House. There were certainly none at Gatcombe Park. Anne and Mark were both efficient cooks and Charles could help himself to a snack from the 'fridge or sit down to a quick meal in the kitchen, with young Peter Phillips, his nephew, free to come and go as he pleased.

It is this sort of informal atmosphere that Elizabeth has always preferred herself although she has never been able to take it to the same extreme as her daughter. Nevertheless, in those parts of her official homes which are private and never seen by outsiders, they are always both cosy and lived-in, something she never experienced until she married Philip. At that time she had only a vague and rudimentary notion of cooking, but when she succeeded to the Throne and returned to Buckingham Palace, they planned an up-to-date kitchen which they could use themselves free of servants. Elizabeth's culinary skills developed apace and Prime Minister Harold Wilson was able to recall an excellent meal she prepared for him at Balmoral, the main item being savoury pancakes. When the meal was over, the Queen and women guests shared the washing up. It is this off-duty Elizabeth that is so impressive; now a mature woman in the prime of life who is so often seen in majestic settings she is at the same time able to relax in relatively simple ways.

As she has grown older so she has acquired a greater capacity for self-containment. In the old days it was the habit of many monarchs to surround themselves with courtiers to provide a constant supply of small talk and amusement in off-duty hours – not so Elizabeth. She can thoroughly enjoy a good gossip as well as anyone else but what she does need at some point in every day is time to be left quite alone.

In London she can find her odd quiet hour of escape wandering in the gardens of Buckingham Palace, always with a scurry of dogs at her heels. At Balmoral or Sandringham it is much the same, walking long distances free from any sort of chatter or disturbance and wearing her familiar attire: an old mac, if the weather is poor, worn over a tweed skirt and a twin set, a pair of well-used wellies and a scarf over her head.

It is curious how Elizabeth's approach to clothes, very much like the Queen Mother and her grandmother Queen Mary before her, has never changed radically over the years. She has moved with the times but has never followed high fashion, preferring to stick to the sort of classical dresses and coats in which she feels most comfortable.

Within the ranks of the Royal Family she has come in for some criticism because they feel that she has for too long been accustomed to uncritically accepting advice about the clothes she wears from Mrs 'Bobo' Macdonald, her lifelong friend and dresser. 'Bobo' has usually had the last say in what Elizabeth wore all her life, from babyhood to maturity, and Elizabeth never broke the habit of turning to Bobo even when she became sovereign. This is not surprising since the dresser, who first nursed Elizabeth when she was only six weeks old, travelled the globe with her mistress on foreign tours and was responsible for all the Royal clothes. Even today Elizabeth's relationship with Bobo is unique: to Bobo she has always been 'Lillibet' and so she will always remain.

Three decades have gone by since television recorded the moment when, with infinite poise and dignity, the Queen sat in the great carved Coronation Chair as the magnificent St Edward's Crown was placed upon her head to the time-honoured cry, 'Vivat! Vivat! Vivat!'

Over the years the Queen has gradually adapted herself to the new medium, first in black and white and then in colour. Having urged the televising of her Coronation in 1953, her second positive and dramatic move and one which tested her nerves to the utmost occurred in 1957 when she agreed that her Christmas broadcast should be televised for the first time.

That was in the pre-video-tape era when television recordings were so poor that the Queen had no alternative but to make a live broadcast in the afternoon of Christmas Day. This meant that try as she might, she could not relax over Christmas lunch, always casting an eye down at her watch and waiting for the hands to point to three o'clock (GMT) when she had to go before the cameras. When the programme was over she would bury her head in her hands in relief before turning to Philip and asking him, 'Was I all right?'

Unlike Prince Charles, Elizabeth has never enjoyed appearing on the small screen and so it was all the more laudable in 1969 when, encouraged by Prince Philip, she finally gave the go-ahead for a film to be made about her family. It was called simply *Royal Family* and was shown all over the world, giving an unprecedented peep into the lives of the Royals.

One person who could not be persuaded to join in the film was the Queen Mother who, despite the fact that she has carried out far more public duties than any other member of the Royal Family, remains as nervous as a kitten at the thought of any sort of interview, whether before a camera or a microphone. Many times it has been put to her that, for the sake of posterity, she should give a television interview about her own life, a life which has spanned so many epoch-making and dramatic Royal years.

Several times she has almost given in, and then, shaking her head, has said, 'I'm very sorry to disappoint everyone but I simply cannot bring myself to do this.' No matter how much she is at ease in public anywhere in the world, she is simply too nervous to face close-ups. This is a tragedy for historians since when she was Queen she herself initiated what were then considered bold steps to bring Royalty out of the Palace to the people. She closely identified herself and her husband with the bombed East End during the Second World War, she was a pioneer of walkabouts and did a great deal to identify monarchy with ordinary family life. Between 1937 and 1952 she had already established a strong sense of family unity which her daughter was able to take over when she succeeded to the Throne.

Thirty years ago when Elizabeth's mother first faced the years of widowhood, there were grave doubts both among members of her family and close friends about her future: there was very real concern and anxiety that she would never really overcome the loss of her husband. It was widely felt that she would probably buy herself a house in Scotland and settle for 'retirement'.

In the beginning she was loathe to leave Buckingham Palace with all its memories of the life she had shared there with George VI, and for many long weeks she showed no sign of giving up the suite they had always used. She saw few friends and gave no indication about her plans for the future. It was three months before she began to take any interest in Clarence House, which was to be her new home, and then to the delight and surprise of both Elizabeth and Philip, the Queen Mother calmly announced that, far from giving up and going into retirement, she was already actively working on plans for immediate future engagements, her first intention being to fill what she felt was a Royal gap in the foreign field, a worthwhile trip that she felt she could make on her own.

In the event, she went to Southern Rhodesia, an eminently successful visit which did much for Britain and Royalty. For the rest of her life she immersed herself in two major roles: Royal engagements which not only gave her great pleasure and satisfaction but also eased the load on Philip and Elizabeth; and the role which brought her the greatest happiness of all – that of grandmother. The door of Clarence House was always open to the children from Buckingham Palace, Charles, Anne, Andrew and Edward, to their cousins from Kensington Palace, David and Sarah, the children of Princess Margaret and Lord Snowdon. The six children all grew up knowing that whenever some problem arose which they could not bring themselves to talk about to their parents, they could always reveal all to their grandmother.

Stored away in the Queen Mother's memory are precious secrets of Royal childhoods. Her influence for the good over this sextet cannot be over-emphasised. More objective than their own parents, she was able to relieve many of their young doubts as they each uneasily began to realise they were 'different' to other children. By far the greatest beneficiary was her eldest grandchild Charles who in adulthood has never ceased to pay tribute to her kindness, patience and infinite understanding.

Charles represents many things to his grandmother but most of all he has become the son she never had herself. Their relationship began when she took him into her own home and looked after him when Elizabeth and Philip went away on their many long tours abroad. Their mutual affection and love for one another grew with the years. She was never an 'interfering' person: when Charles was gloomy or upset – as he often was at school – she never bothered Elizabeth or Philip with their son's troubles. Instead it was by personal example and encouragement that she helped him understand more clearly the complexity of his position.

Charles was enthralled by his grandmother's intimate stories and it was she, more than anyone else, who enabled him to come to terms with his role and was directly responsible for moulding him into the dedicated man he is today.

The Queen Mother's influence over Anne was considerable but not until she was out of her 'teens and moving into more mature years did grandmother and granddaughter begin to see eye-to-eye. Anne's strong streak of individualism and basic competitive nature did not endear her to the Queen Mother. Always at the back of the Queen Mother's mind was the traumatic period of the 1930s when her brother-in-law, David, later Duke of Windsor, gave up his crown for the woman he loved, and in Anne she probably recognised certain strong traits which she feared, wrongly as it happened, might one day lead her into troubled waters.

One of the few people for whom the Queen Mother could never find a kind word to say was her sister-in-law, the Duchess of Windsor: yet when, quite alone and in a state of great sorrow and distress, the Duchess came to London for her husband's funeral on what was to be her last and final visit, it was the Queen Mother who was the first person within the Royal Family to stretch out a warm and comforting hand.

The Windsors' personal physician, Dr Arthur Antenucci, who had flown over from New York for the funeral and stayed at Buckingham Palace, well knew of the coldness that existed between the two women and was as deeply touched as the Duchess by the Queen Mother's kindness. After the service at St George's Chapel and later the private burial at Frogmore, in the grounds of Windsor Castle, Elizabeth gave a lunch at Buckingham Palace for members of the Royal Family.

It was the first time in her life that the Duchess of Windsor had ever been with all the members of her late husband's family and Dr Antenucci, sitting next to Elizabeth and opposite his patient, was anxious: the Duchess looked pale and nervous and seemed to be staring into space. He watched, intrigued, as the Queen Mother gradually managed to engage the Duchess in conversation and, when the meal was over, he found them drinking coffee together in a small ante room, sitting knee to knee, bent over and talking earnestly to each other.

When Dr Antenucci recalled the occasion some years later, he told me, 'The Queen Mother was graciousness personified. It was a great tragedy that so soon after the Duchess had returned to her Paris home in the Bois de Boulogne, she was taken seriously ill and never recovered normal health: the two ladies who late in life found they had so much in common, were destined never to meet again.' With the birth of Anne's two children, Peter and Zara Phillips, the Queen Mother, already a grandmother, became a great-grandmother and so the tradition of her famous tea parties for young children began with yet another generation at Clarence House and Birkhall.

For Elizabeth and Philip, now grandparents, Anne's method of bringing up her children is a far cry from the nursery and schoolroom of Buckingham Palace, both now closed until another Sovereign with young children lives there. That Elizabeth derives great joy from her first grandchildren is unquestioned, but that Peter and Zara will grow up without titles or Royal responsibilities is something she has been forced to accept – but with deep regret. This was one of the hardest family decisions with which she had to come to terms – but Elizabeth has never flinched from change.

There are members of the Royal Family who may never see the Coronation of Prince Charles. For many years there have been carefully hedged bets that when Elizabeth gets older, perhaps in her mid-sixties or early seventies, she will consider abdicating in favour of her son and heir. The frequent argument put forward is that Elizabeth will never subject Charles to the frustrating ordeal suffered by his great-great-grandfather King Edward VII. The unfortunate Edward waited in fretful idleness until he was fifty-nine, and already a grandfather, before the death of his mother, Queen Victoria, at eighty-two, brought him at last to the Throne.

Charles's position, however, cannot be compared with that of his great-great-grandfather. He has not been kept 'waiting in the wings' and nor does his mother bar him from State papers. He is privy to most of her major decisions and this has been the case since he first went to

University at the age of nineteen. Now maried and satisfactorily 'settled down', Charles takes on a vast number of Royal duties which will increase rather than diminish as his parents get older. It is his belief that there is no urgent necessity for him to take over the central role which would, in fact, restrict many of his important globe-spanning activities and confine him more closely to the executive business of monarchy which, quite apart from anything else, has no overwhelming appeal for him.

Elizabeth is proud to point out that she has already seen seven Prime Ministers come and go and once tellingly quoted Gladstone saying of Queen Victoria: 'Parliaments and Ministers pass, but she abides in life long duty and she is to them as the oak in the forest is to the annual harvest in the field.' Elizabeth believes in the continuity of monarchy and those people who know her well believe that, given good health, she will not waver in seeing her job through to the end – whenever that might be.

Another important factor surrounding the issue of abdication is the presence of Philip who, now passed sixty, has no personal interest in 'retirement' in any shape or form. The word 'retirement' is an anathema to Philip: you might as well try to turn a modern nuclear submarine into a pleasure boat as to try and make him slow down. This then, is the man who more than anyone else, would sway Elizabeth's thinking if she ever seriously considered abdication as a way of moving with the times.

So far as the future is concerned, Elizabeth's hopes rest on the Prince and Princess of Wales and their family. For her other relations their roles in the next decade are now clearer. Andrew, who certainly caused her more anxiety during his growing-up days than any of her other children, is carefully being kept on course as a career officer in the Royal Navy, his private life no longer hitting the headlines. His teenage 'Randy Andy' image not only appalled but upset his mother. His practical jokes and general horse-play, which became a by-word in the seventies, have faded. Just what sort of a dressing down Andrew was given by his parents at the time is not known, but from the day he moved to the RAF Station at Leeming in 1978 and began his training as a helicopter pilot, he has kept as low a profile as possible. But he really won his spurs and proved his courage and manhood in the battle for the Falkland Islands.

Others, like Princess Margaret, are moving smoothly into their middle years and still have positive roles to play within the family group. As a private individual Princess Margaret, shrewd, highly intelligent and artistic, still has much to offer the younger generation. Unlikely ever to marry again, she has made her mistakes and paid for them dearly in ill health and emotional turmoil, all of which have left their permanent scars. Her search for happiness in her middle years which found its outlet for a time in the person of Roddy Llewellyn, a man much younger than herself and content to dance attendance on her, is over: now in Margaret a more stable, more worthwhile and far less demanding personality has emerged.

There are many things the Queen would have done differently if she could start her reign again – she would probably have been tougher, more decisive and as a result, less tolerant. Surrounded as she is by a strongly united family, the Queen is not the sort of person ever to rest on her laurels. It is the future that gives the Queen the greatest reason for concern as we move nearer towards the twenty-first century and possibly a Golden Jubilee in 2002.

13

A View of the Future

HER YEARS ON the Throne have been a personal triumph for the Queen. She has proved herself to be a warm, caring and forward-looking person with the right degree of reserve necessary to preserve the mystique of monarchy. She has shown real courage, unafraid to make personal appearances on tours in terrorist-threatened parts of the world; insisted upon going ahead with walkabouts despite possible violence in the streets; revealed nerves of steel when shots were fired as she rode down The Mall at the Trooping of the Colour in June 1981. (These turned out to be blanks fired by a seventeen-year-old youth who was tried for treason and sent to prison for five years.)

Her statesman-like qualities have been praised in private not only by the eight Prime Ministers who have served under her – from Sir Winston Churchill to Mrs Margaret Thatcher – but also by men and women in seats of power in Western and Third World Countries. Just what influence she has exercised behind the scenes in national and international spheres will probably never be fully known until after her death when biographers with access to Royal diaries and official archives write the definitive story of her life.

Yet by far her greatest and most outstanding achievement is the way in which she has moulded the Royal

Family into the closely knit unit it is today and which reached a new zenith of popularity when Prince Charles married Lady Diana Spencer in St Paul's Cathedral on 29 July 1981, a spectacle that held the whole world spellbound. Under her leadership, the British monarchy has been one of the few real success stories in British twentieth-century history; amidst economic and political turmoil, the dissolution of the Empire, and social struggles, it has stood out as a monument of stability. During the Queen's reign nearly all political institutions have come under criticism – Local Government, the Civil Service, the electoral system, Parliament and even Cabinets and the Crown.

Yet the monarchy alone has emerged unscathed and unbelievably popular the world over. Those who have attacked it have seen their attacks rebound in their faces. The time in the midfifties (1957) when a young peer, Lord Antrincham, thought it fit to criticise the monarchy and the Queen's advisers in particular, is now all but forgotten, as are the comments attributed to Malcolm Muggeridge, ex-Editor of *Punch* and one-time TV pundit who caused an uproar when, in an analysis of British Royalty in the *Saturday Evening Post*, he wrote of 'the Royal soap opera ... a sort of substitute or ersatz religion'. Muggeridge protested that he was quoted out of context. Nowadays such pockets of republicanism that do exist in Britain are so insignificant that they are of no consequence and even constant quibbling over the years about Royal costs and expenses voiced by Willie Hamilton, Labour MP for Fife Central, have had no lasting impact.

It would seem, therefore, that the Queen has every reason to rest on her laurels. She has watched her family produce some remarkable personalities with whom the public can easily identify – people like her husband, Prince Philip, a man of great integrity and enormous talent; he, when a poll was taken in 1968 was revealed as the public's number one choice to lead the country as President if Britain ever became a republic. She has watched the Queen Mother, still making public appearances at the age of eighty-one, reach such a peak of popularity that when she reached four score years, the nation downed tools to celebrate her special birthday.

Together with her husband, Prince Philip and Heir, Prince Charles, the Queen has brought a new and important dimension into modern Royalty. In their joint and individual world tours the trio have each been directly responsible for paving the way for Britain to clinch new and vital trade deals, and on the diplomatic front their achievements have been equally remarkable. No high-ranking politician or diplomat is under any illusion about their often unheralded value to this country: it is invaluable.

The Queen has given personal freedom to members of her family in a way that no Royal generation has ever known before and she has brought up her own four children, Prince Charles, Princess Anne, Prince Andrew and Prince Edward, to be far better equipped to cope with life outside the hothouse atmosphere of Buckingham Palace than she was herself at their age.

Although her second son, Andrew, as the son of a reigning sovereign has a pre-destined role to become an active working member of the Royal Family, he has nevertheless been allowed to choose his own career as a helicopter pilot in the Royal Navy and lead his own private life. His whole future does not lie in an endless round of launching ships, laying foundation stones and making speeches about subjects that do not interest him at all. He will combine a professional working life with his Royal working life.

Then there is the Queen's youngest child, Prince Edward, who when University days are over, will probably be the first Royal Prince to take a full-time job in the world of industry or modern technology; his Royal appearances, if he so chooses, will be minimal.

The Queen still has many years of active life ahead of her, years in which if life follows its natural course, she will continue to work hard and accept each new challenge as it comes along. She recognises, however, that no matter how hard she continues to work, no matter how great and unfaltering her sense of dedication, the future of the British monarchy can only remain in her hands for at the most the next two decades. After that, the destiny of the House of Windsor will come to rest in the hands of Prince Charles and his young wife, the Princess of Wales – and therein lies the Queen's greatest task. To leave nothing undone to see that her successor is capable in every respect of stepping into her shoes.

In her reign, the Queen has seen the whole pattern of British society turned upside down – and has coped with the problems arising from it, leaving the Royal Family secure in the affections of the public. How will Prince Charles and the Princess of Wales cope when their turn arrives? As a team, will they be able to take dramatic new changes in their stride and still keep the common touch while nevertheless retaining the magic aura of Royalty? These are the lines upon which the Queen thinks today.

The marriage of Charles and Diana Spencer came at just the right time – when the House of Windsor needed a new injection of youth and someone with real magic. And magic is what the arrival of the young Princess of Wales provided. By Royal standards, thirty-two was relatively old for an Heir to the Throne to marry and as she looks ahead today, the Queen is preparing for an acute shortage of Royalty for at least the next twenty-five years.

Charles and Diana's son, Prince William, will not be ready for active Royal duty until after the year 2000. By then the Queen will be seventy-four, the Duke of Edinburgh seventy-nine and Princess Margaret seventy. For a long time, therefore, there will be a serious shortage of men and women of the right age and with the necessary experience to carry out Royal duties. What will happen? There will, inevitably, be fewer Royal faces about and the workload imposed on the Prince and Princess of Wales will be very great. The shortage of Royals will not even begin to diminish until Prince

Andrew and Prince Edward marry and have children of their own – children who will cousins to each other and styled His or Her Royal Highness.

However, just as she faced and overcame seemingly insoluble problems when she succeeded to the Throne in 1952, the Queen remains a permanent optimist about the future. She accepts that while every occupant of the Throne has a slightly different way of conducting matters to that of his or her predecessor, the Prince of Wales and his wife share her total sense of service and devotion to duty. In a future in which many old institutions, could be in peril, the British system of monarchy stands a far better chance than most of survival in a changing world.

Epilogue

Prince William of Wales

No one in their right senses would ever have predicted that the greatest agent for change within the ranks of the present British Royal Family would prove to be a stripling of a twenty-year-old girl with no great claim either to ultra-sophistication or to intellectual pretension. Yet within a year of her marriage to Prince Charles, the former Lady Diana Spencer had firmly established an incredible rapport with all sections of society and all generations in the country. This slip of a girl had the magic which brought tears of happiness into the eyes of old men in wheelchairs, just as she created exuberance among coloured immigrant teenagers as they shinned up lamp-posts to cheer their first glimpse of her approach on a walkabout. What was equally remarkable was that the Princess of Wales, who can trace her ancestry back to the later Royal Stuarts* – something her husband cannot do – somehow managed to achieve an almost classless image despite the blue-blooded background of the aristocratic family into which she was born. In all the hoo-ha

---

*Diana descends four times over from Charles II and once from James II. She thus has six lines of descent from Mary, Queen of Scots. Curiously enough, Prince Charles himself descends from neither of the later Royal Stuarts, and so the Princess of Wales brings back their blood into the Royal Family.

248

which attended the news of Charles's selection of the girl who was to be his bride, singularly little attention was paid to the fact that Althorp, the vast sixteenth-century Spencer family seat in Northhamptonshire, was larger than most of the Royal residences. Instead, far more attention was paid to the comparatively short period when the Princess shared a flat in London's Old Brompton Road with three girl friends. There, although the flat had been bought for her by her wealthy father, Earl Spencer, she enjoyed a life-style well distanced from the world of liveried footmen, chauffeurs and butlers that she had known since childhood. Her brief years in London's bustling and cosmopolitan Royal Borough of Kensington, free from constant parental supervision, gave the Princess of Wales the sort of background with which so many people could identify: she had shopped in supermarkets, bought clothes off the peg, queued for cinema seats, cycled to her part-time job as a kindergarten teacher – all ordinary everday experiences which the public could share with Diana, but which had always been denied the Queen's children, and most of all, Prince Charles.

There was another powerful factor which contributed to the Princess's extraordinary appeal and that was her innate spontaneity, a rare quality that has so often eluded members of the Royal Family brought up, as they always have been, never, by so much as a look or a glance, to reveal their emotions in public. For those senior members of the Family who carry the heaviest burdens a stiff upper lip, no matter what may be going on in their private lives, is a pre-requisite that has been ingrained into them. When the Queen Mother knew that her late husband, George VI, was a dying man, she betrayed nothing of her anxiety to the public; and similarly, at times of real personal anxiety, the Queen maintains a fixed and almost enigmatic smile that only those very close to her can recognise as masking some degree of inner disquiet. The Princess of Wales was not brought up to this sort of self-containment; in addition, the Princess's basic make-up was such that she could not help wearing her heart on her sleeve.

When she was unhappy, as she was when Prince Charles had to leave her behind in London while he carried out a six-week world tour only two months before their marriage, she was quite unable to hide her true feelings. As she watched his plane take off and disappear into the clouds above London Airport, her lips quivered and tears welled in her eyes, tears which she made no attempt to brush aside. As the months went by, in a hundred and one small and endearing ways she openly registered her love for Charles, a man who had previously always guarded his private emotions most jealously: she held his hand, put her arm around his shoulders, and when she looked at the Queen's eldest son, no one could doubt her love for him. This easy naturalness on the part of the Princess had an immediate impact upon Charles, who, with something of the charm of a schoolboy, came out of his emotional shell and responded in an equally demonstrative manner. All the world loves a lover, and when the lover was a young girl whose bloom and innocence were always manifestly obvious, affection for her grew and seemed to know no bounds.

Scheldules on Royal engagements are planned with military precision and when members of the Royal Family are on the job they know by heart the exact amount of time they can spend on each pause, whether they may be visiting troops or shaking hands with factory officials. This split-second timing is the key to the success of Royal duties, but such meticulously planned schedules were not only new to the Princess but not at all in keeping with her spontaneous nature. Time and again on public engagements, even on her first great walk-abouts when she and Charles carried out a tremendously successful three-day tour of the Principality of Wales, she was so entranced by the opportunities offered her by her new role that, often to the astonishment of highly disciplined Royal Household officials, she would

250

suddenly dart off and become speedily immersed in happy and earnest conversations with whoever happened to be at hand in the crowds. More often than not, and this was possibly a product of her training at the Young England Kindergarten school, she made a bee-line for young mothers with babies in their arms, or young housewives with toddlers by their side, with everyone laughing, everyone smiling and the Princess blissfully happy. Royal schedules began to run twenty and twenty-five minutes late, the Princess gaily oblivious of the passing of precious Royal minutes and responding with charm to the cries of 'Di!' 'Diana!' and 'Come and talk to us, Di!' that echoed from all sides.

The Royal honeymoon was not quite over when the Princess provided the first of many indications that she did not intend to be wrapped in any sort of protective Royal cocoon. She flew to London – not on an aircraft of the Queen's Flight but on a scheduled British Airways flight – supposedly to inspect her vast array of wedding presents still on public display in St James's Palace. In fact her real destination was 96 Harley Street, the consulting rooms of the Queen's eminent surgeon-gynaecologist, Mr George Pinker, who, at that time, was unable to give immediate confirmation that the Princess's suspicions that she might already be pregnant were correct.

It was a telling sign of the freedom she had already established for herself within the Royal Family, that she managed to find time to get behind the wheel of her Mini and look up her former flat-mates before returning to Balmoral twenty-four hours later. All this was at the end of September 1981. It was not until the morning of Guy Fawkes Day, 5 November 1981, that the official announcement came, couched in traditional Palace terms, revealing to the world that the Princess was expecting a baby.

What was to follow the announcement was not just a Princess quietly awaiting the birth of a future sovereign but a complete revolution in the style of Royal pregnan-

251

cies – a revolution brought about not only by this young girl but also by the obvious support and encouragement of a husband conscious of and intent upon the inevitable approach of a total change in the Royal scene. The manner in which the former Lady Diana Spencer coped with her pregnancy added yet a further dimension to a romance that had, from the very beginning, all the ingredients of a modern fairy tale.

In the recent past all Royal mothers-to-be kept out of the public eye as their pregnancies advanced, and even the Queen, as late as 1960 when her youngest child, Prince Edward, was on the way, chose to spend much of her time behind the walls of Royal homes accepting only invitations from relatives or very close and intimate friends. While Princess Anne has dropped many bricks in her Royal career, it is to her that the credit must go for being the first person to bring about some change in the style of Royal pregnancy. When the whim took her, she occasionally ventured out as a spectator at local horse trials wearing the inevitable denim cap and bulky sweater; she, however, never presented a soft or gentle image and only had curt words to offer any photographer who came within her pregnant orbit.

Totally uninfluenced by Royal precedents and determined to 'do her own thing', the Princess continued to add to her already glowing lustre by carrying her future child with grace, charm and the utmost dignity. It was almost as though at some unconscious level she wanted everyone to share in the joy of her pregnancy and it was hardly surprising, therefore, that the public reacted in a warm, caring and loving fashion. The first clue that the Princess was feeling out of sorts and bedevilled by early morning sickness came from Prince Charles, who confessed that his wife was feeling 'very queasy', adding somewhat mournfully that he hoped it 'wouldn't last long'. It didn't. By Christmas, hatless and wearing a warm overcoat, the Princess braved bitterly cold weather and turned up for Holy Communion in Gloucester Cathedral. Wherever she went the Royal mother-to-be blazed a new open-style Royal trail, never hesitating to answer questions about her state of health saying that she felt 'marvellous', 'wonderful', and 'tremendously excited'. Occasionally and sometimes with a knowing wink, she would make a friendly joke at the expense of her husband: once, when she was asked how she felt, she replied, 'I'm fine thank you very much . . .' and then, adding in a whisper and pointing in the direction of Prince Charles, 'You ought to ask him about all the baby books he is reading!' The world saw a new and blissfully happy Prince Charles who, in turn, had his own moments of fun: when his wife was quietly shaking hands as she moved down a line of waiting dignitaries, he suddenly dodged away from his official place at her side and joined the waiting line. When the surprised Pricess reached Prince Charles and stretched out her hand, he said, 'I think we've met before, Ma'am!'

It was not only her infectious happiness and ease of manner that endeared the Princess to everyone. Unlike some of her predecessors who married into the Royal Family and were not in the least enthusiastic about taking on Royal duties – men like Lord Snowdon and Captain Mark Phillips – the Princess of Wales was captivated by Royal work, but was also convinced that she could still maintain personal freedom of movement. She went on shopping expeditions with her mother, Mrs Peter Shand-Kydd, and had regular lunches with former flat-mates in their old favourite haunts, such as the first-floor restaurant of the Harvey Nichols store. She insisted on driving herself, accepting with good grace the inevitable presence of a detective. These simple activities might, on the surface, appear to have little significance and yet, taken in the context of long-established and hitherto unquestioned traditions of the House of Windsor, they take on an entirely new and important perspective. Despite, or perhaps because of, her youth the Princess was not prepared to give up all the independence she had enjoyed during her few years in her Kensington flat. To be fair to the Queen and Prince

Charles, no attempt was ever made to clip her fledgling Royal wings. On the Pcontrary, this very clear streak of stubbornness was actively encouraged, although there were some real doubts in Royal Household quarters as to whether in terms of Royal Precedents she would be able to get away with her unconventional behaviour. Questions were certainly posed in that hallowed sanctuary, the private dining-room in Buckingham Palace used only by very senior members of the Royal secretariats. Chief among them was the concern about her movements as a private individual: would she be recognised as the Princess of Wales – and then what? As it transpired, the Princess was only very occasionally noticed and people who did spot her, generously and understandingly kept their distance and their eyes averted. Only a week or so before the birth of her first baby, the Princess spent a quiet hour making last-minute purchases in the first-floor baby-wear department of Harrods, once again doing her shopping without any interruptions. She proved beyond doubt that it was possible for her to combine a Royal life-style with a much more informal approach that was vital for her personal well-being.

There was another achievement, barely noticed at the time, to be chalked up at the end of the year; that was the manner in which members of the Royal Family reacted to the arrival of a super-star who plunged into their closely knit circle almost like a meteor from outer space. In what is and always has been a very rank-conscious group, their quiet aceptance of the Princess was more than admirable since even those in lofty positions are sometimes subject to ordinary human weaknesses of envy and jealousy.

One of the great strengths of the House of Windsor in the twentieth century has been the way in which it has adapted to change within the family – often very dramatic change indeed. One has only to go back to the trauma of the abdication in 1936, a brief period of time in historical terms, to find evidence of this: only weeks after the uncrowned Edward VIII had set sail across the

English Channel heading for voluntary exile as Duke of Windsor in France, his nervous and ill-equipped younger brother, George VI, not only firmly grasped the reigns of State in both hands but also provided Britain with a godsend – a happy family unit in Buckingham Palace. All this was achieved without fuss and almost overnight.

The arrival of the Princess of Wales, whilst it did not involve constitutional issues of any kind, could nevertheless have been the cause of emotional tantrums among the more temperamental members of the family, as their own personal popularity was eroded by their new young in-law. As it transpired, the Princess managed to steer a careful and tactful course and members of her new family accepted her presence among them and her fantastic popularity in a most commendable fashion. Even Princess Margaret, at fifty-two one of the most protocol-conscious members of the family, commented: 'Well, at least Diana has taken some of the flak off me!' So often the target for barbed and often very unfair criticism, the Queen's sister was only too relieved to discover that far less attention was being paid to her social comings-and-goings, and that speculation as to whether she might remarry for the second time had completely disappeared.

Apart from her husband, the one person in the Royal Family to whom the Princess undoubtedly owed the greatest debt during her first year of marriage was to the Queen herself. She, more than anyone else, fully understood the unique position in which her daughter-in-law found herself and well in advance recognised the vast range of new pressures that would face the Princess. Members of the Royal Family take the many facets of Royal duties in their stride, but the Queen was well aware that they could prove highly stressful for an inexperienced twenty-year-old with the eyes of the world upon her. What the Queen feared most of all was that Diana, so willing, so eager, so happy, would find herself mentally exhausted and unable to maintain the pace she had set herself. The exact nature of the advice given by the Queen to Diana during her first year of marriage will probably never be known, but one fact emerges quite clearly: the Queen was a tower of strength to her young daughter-in-law and the way in which the older woman stretched out her maternal wings to protect the younger one, was nothing short of magnificent. It was first to Charles and then to the Queen that the Princess of Wales automatically turned when it came to making some of her early major decisions. The search for a suitable nanny became very much a family affair, with the Princess making it abundantly clear that she wanted a nanny who was not tied too strictly to rules and regulations, and above all was not the type to want to rule the roost in the nursery. Her preference was for someone less orthodox, with a more modern and flexible general attitude towards bringing up children. Finally, it was through Princess Margaret that Diana was put in touch with 39-year-old Barbara Barnes, who had no formal nursery-training but had a great deal of experience with two of Margaret's closest friends, the Hon. Colin Tennant and his wife, Lady Anne Tennant. Barbara, the daughter of a retired forestry worker, was nanny to the three Tennant children and the entire Tennant family was devoted to her. She was just the sort of person the Princess of Wales wanted as nanny for her own baby.

There was yet one more Royal tradition to break. As dawn was breaking on the morning of Monday, 21 June 1982, Prince Charles climbed behind the wheel of his car to drive his wife the short distance from Kensington Palace to the Lindo Maternity Wing of St Mary's Hospital, Paddington. It was in keeping with the Princess of Wales' image, as a member of the Royal Family whose experiences are not so far removed from those of people throughout the nation, that she gave birth to her child outside Palace walls.

Prince Charles, in his shirt-sleeves, was at his wife's side throughout the birth of their first baby. Sixteen hours after Prince Charles drove with his wife from Kensington Palace to the Hospital, Prince William Arthur Philip Louis of Wales, second in direct line of succession to the Throne, came into the world.

He was blue-eyed, fair-haired and 'crying lustily', weighed in at 7 lb 1½oz.   The time was 9.03pm.

And at that moment on Monday, 21 June 1982, a new chapter in the history of the British Royal Family began.

Index

Ascot 11, 18

Albert, Prince Consort 40, 91, 101, 231

Alexandra, Princess 24, 70, 136–7; and 'Thatched Cottage' 137; meets Angus Ogilvy 138; courtship 139; engagement announced 140

Alice, Princess (*née* Battenberg) 17, 20, 24, 128, 132, 159–61

Anderson, Mabel 50, 166, 168

Andrew, Prince 15, 52; birth 55, 81, 161; relationship with mother 55–6; temperament 83, 84, 85, 167; relationship with Charles 84; at school 83–5; as an actor 85; the artist 88; girlfriends 107–8; his need to be in the spotlight 136, 163; problems with 168; friendship with Diana 219; new 'low profile' 242; his future 245; in the Falklands 242

Anne, Princess 9, 45, 109–17; birth 50; and Mrs Lightbody 51; as a child 52–3; relationship with Charles 54–5, 110, 192, 233; affinity with father 71, 112, 192, 199; education 75, 79, 81; relationship with mother 52, 71; friendships at school 79–80; strength of character 80, 109, 192, 199; love for horses 80–2, 111, 113, 115, 116, 190; relationship with grandmother 106; admiration for Margaret 109,

110, 116–17; difficult temperament 109, 191, 198, 252; as a sportswoman, 110, 112, 113; ambitions 111; dress sense 112; at public engagements 114–15; with Alison Oliver 190–1, 192; dedication to a riding career 193; early competitions 193–5, 196; illness 197; early relationship with Mark Phillips 202–3; engagement and marriage 205; children 205–6

Armstrong-Jones, Lady Frances 20

Armstrong-Jones, Ronald 121, 124, 125, 126

Armstrong-Jones, Lady Sarah 12, 20, 125, 169

Art of the Possible (Butler) 187

Ashmore, Admiral Sir Peter, Master of the Household 13

Babington-Smith, Susan 75, 117

Balmoral Castle 13, 49, 86–108, 117; considered private property 90–1; building the new castle 91; as a Royal sanctuary 90–2, 99–100; modernisation of 92–3; life at 96–102; picnics at 97; Ghillies' Ball 104

Barrogill Castle 65

Beaufort, Henry Somerset, Duke of 195

Beck, Peter 75

Benenden 79–81, 109, 111

Birkhall 86, 95, 103, 139

Bloodhound 110

Brabourne, Lady Patricia 72
Britannia 89, 158, 171
Buckingham Palace 10, 11, 37, 49
Butler, Lord 'Rab', 173–80

Callaghan, James 93
Canada, tours of 31, 32
Cavendish, Lady Elizabeth 118
Charles II, King 10
Charles, Prince *see* Wales, Charles,
  Prince of
Charteris, Colonel Martin 35
Cheam 74–6
Churchill, Sir Winston 35, 43, 93
Clarence House 36, 50, 51
Clarke, E.B. 79
Coronation of Elizabeth II 45–8;
  Prince Charles at 45–6; the
  spectacle of 46–7; Princess
  Margaret at 47; state procession 47
Constantine, Crown Prince, of
  Greece 138
Cruz, Lucia Santa 186

Daily Mirror 64
Daily Telegraph 59
Diana *see* Wales, Diana, Princess of
Dimbleby, Richard 44
Douglas-Home, Sir Alec 93

Eden, Anthony 93
Edward VII, King 43, 92, 185, 209, 240
Edward VIII, King 41, 61, 66, 146,
  254–5
Edward, Prince 12, 52, 167; birth 55,
  81, 163; relationship with mother
  55–6; temperament 83, 85;
  academically ambitious 85;
  Andrew's influence on 108, 168;
  'unspoiled' 169; his future 245
Egerton, Lady Alice 28
Elizabeth II, Queen
  Family's fealty towards 18, 102,
  164; Christmas broadcast 24, 236;
  Malta, her love of 27–31; social life
  before Coronation 27–31;
  marriage, early days 27–31, 49,
  105; and George VI's illness 31;
  Canada, tour of 31, 32; learns of
  father's death 34–5; and her
father's funeral 43–5; Churchill's
  concern for 44; Coronation 45–8;
  honeymoon 49, 105; workday
  routine 58–9; at Balmoral 90–108;
  and George V 91; relationship with
  her PMs 93–4; at 'The Glassault',
  Balmoral 95; and the 'Second
  Eleven' 127, 136; the unifier of the
  Family 229
  personal matters: tastes in food 10,
  22, 23, 203, 230; meticulous nature
  14, 38, 95, 97; as a mother 27, 52, 53,
  54, 55, 56, 69, 72, 78, 81, 83, 84, 94,
  112–13, 163–70, 185, 196, 229, 233;
  temperament 34–5, 38, 39, 42–3,
  159, 249; thrifty nature 39; Philip's
  influence on 39, 54, 82, 229;
  capacity for work 39, 230; relaxation
  149–52; remarkable memory 153;
  self-reliance 42, 234; dress sense 57,
  58, 97, 235; relationship with
  Margaret 61–2, 63–8, 154; affinity
  with Charles 71, 78; pets 94, 96, 149;
  health 96, 98, 162; strong marriage
  151–3; hopes for a large family 162;
  concern for Charles 171–2, 174–5,
  178, 185; problems with Anne 191–
  2; and Diana 253, 255–6
Elizabeth the Queen Mother 9–10,
  17, 18; love of helicopters 21;
  accomplished pianist 25; during
  husband's illness 31, 36, 37, 249;
  and Clarence House 36–7; approach
  as Consort 41–2; as a grandmother
  54; reaction to the 'Townsend
  Affair' 65; relationship with Anne
  and Charles 86, 87, 182, 217, 238;
  robust health 98; at Birkhall 103;
  and Snowdon 120–1; on Kent's
  marriage 142; on Mountbatten 217;
  fear of interviews 236–7; influence
  on Family 238

Face of London (Gloucester) 135
Fermoy, Ruth, Lady 216–19
Fisher, Geoffrey, Archbishop of
  Canterbury 43, 45, 46

Garnett, Thomas 176
George III, King 10, 19

George V, King 17–18, 22, 43, 56, 91, 136
George VI, King 19, 27, 101, 125, 160; illness 31, 32, 33, 249; death 34, 229; personal style 37–9, 255; tendency to equivocate 39; funeral of 43; and Balmoral 92; and Elizabeth's engagement 104
Ghillies' Ball 104
Gibbs, Kensington 83, 170
Gloucester, Birgitte, Duchess of 17, 20, 132; marriage 129–30; public engagements 132–3; charitable work 133; children 133
Gloucester, Richard, Duke of 15, 20, 50; 'reluctant Royal duke' 127–8, 135; childhood 136; marriage 129–30; death of brother William 131; friendship with Charles 132, 135; the architect 132; the photographer 134, 135
Gloucester, Prince William of 50, 128, 185–6; diplomatic career 130; love of flying 130; problems of 'being Royal' 130–1; death 131, 136
Gordonstoun 76–9, 83, 85, 108, 171, 173, 176, 185

Hamilton, Caroline 75, 117
Harrods 13
Hatton-Hall, Cherie 81
Heath, Edward 93
Heatherdown 82
Hicks, Lady Pamela 72–3
Hill House, Knightsbridge 71
Hobhouse, Hermione 135
Holt, Harold 179

Jones, Hywel 181–2

Kempe, John 93
Kent, Edward, 2nd Duke of 138, 141; limited finances 141–2; first meets Katherine 142; playboy image 142; marriage 142; the linguist 143; in Ulster 143; character 143–4
Kent, Katherine, Duchess of 141; importance of privacy 141; miscarriage 141; lack of private income 141; meets Edward 142;

marriage 142; influence on husband 142–3; children 141, 164
Kent, Prince Michael of 18; marriage 144, 145, 146; the socialite 144–5; interest in dangerous sports 144–5
Kent, Princess Michael of marriage 144, 145, 146; strength of character 145; children 146; dedication to position 146; dress sense 147; Mountbatten's affection for 146

Lacey, Robert 158
Lawrence, A.K. 117
Lawrence, Sir Thomas 17
Legge-Bourke, Victoria 79
Lichfield, Lord Patrick 134
Lightbody, Helen 45, 50, 51, 52, 53, 167
Linley, David Armstrong-Jones Viscount 15, 125, 170

MacDonald, Margaret 'Bobo' 57–8, 235
Mackenzie, Dugal 78
Maclean, Lord, Lord Chamberlain 87
Macmillan, Harold 93
Malta 27–31
Margaret, Princess, Countess of Snowdon
the photographer 15; the Family entertainer 25, 102, 242; reaction to father's death 31, 37, 62; her independent spirit 33; and Peter Townsend 47, 61–8; relationship with Anne 116–17; difficult temperament 61, 118; spoilt by father 61; as a horsewoman 81; engagement to Snowdon 105; as a model for Anne 109, 110; early courtship 120–1; engagement announcement 123; her need to be in the spotlight 136; good with children 164–5; divorce 186; mellowing of 242, 255
Marina, Princess, Duchess of Kent 138, 139, 142
Mary, Queen 36
Maskell, Dan 113
Millward, Edward 184
Mountbatten, Amanda 215–16

Mountbatten of Burma, Admiral of the Fleet Lord Louis Mountbatten, Earl 15–16, 53–4, 143, 153–4; affinity with Philip 39; support of Philip 40–1, 73, 157; relationship with Charles 72–4, 78; and Kent 145–7; unique relationship with the Sovereign 154–6; meticulous nature 158; fears for Charles' future 220

Norfolk, Bernard Marmaduke Fizalan-Howard, 16th Duke of 43, 45

Ogilvy, Hon. Angus 136–7; limited income 137; education 137; career 138; meets Alexandra 138; courtship 139; reservations about marriage 139; proposal 139; refuses peerage 140; illnesses 140; children 140–1, 171
Ogilvy, James 12, 140, 169
Ogilvy, Marina 140
Old Man of Lochnagar, The 95
Oliver, Alison 190–1, 192
On Public View (Gloucester) 135
Order of the Garter Ceremony 11
Oxford and Cambridge (Gloucester) 135

Philip, Prince, Duke of Edinburgh the artist 15, 88; interest in technology 21, 151, 177, 232; in Malta 27–31; Commander of Magpie 28; influence on Elizabeth 39; bluntness 39–40; early days as Consort 39, 40, 41, 59, 230; flair for detail 49; organising ability 50; as a father 53, 81; as a speech-writer 59; pragmatist 59–60; antagonism towards Townsend 63–4, 65; relationship with Margaret 63; affinity with Anne 71, 112, 192; relationship with Charles 71, 77, 107, 174, 177; temperament 81–2, 150; Elizabeth's influence on 81–2, 199; engagement to Elizabeth 104–5; strength of marriage 150, 232; preference for evening functions 151; the 'workaholic' 152;

remarkable memory 152–3; dissatisfactions with public life 158; and Princes Alice 161; and Andrew 168; the over-critical parent 180; lack of interest in retirement 241
Phillips, Lt Mark 9, 196–7; master horseman 201; early relationship with Anne 201–2; as an all-round athlete 204; engagement and marriage 205; children 205–6
Phillips, Peter 206–7, 240
Phillips, Zara 240

Queen's Housekeeper 10, 11

Ramsey, Michael, Archbishop of Canterbury 175
Richmond, Kirsty 108
Ringer, The 29
Royal Family
  at Christmas 9–26; passion for horse-riding 22, 80–2, 111, 113, 115, 116, 190; and sport 24; dislike of Buckingham Palace 37; and nannies 50; need for stability 61; at Eton 76–7; and amateur dramatics 85; as artists 88; travel preparations for 87–8; and servants 92, 100–1, 134; the health of 98; respecters of privacy 134; and the Act of Settlement 144; birthday parties 165; Royal children 162–72; Family solidarity 228–9
Royal Lodge of Windsor 19, 104, 139

St Edward's Crown 43, 46
St James's Palace 87
Sandringham House 12, 18, 22, 26, 36, 49, 57, 90, 99, 108, 142, 180
Shand-Kydd, Frances 221, 222, 223–4
Simpson, Wallis 185
Sitwell, Osbert 22
Smith, Sybil 81
Snowdon, Anthony Armstrong-Jones, Earl of 134; first Royal portraits 117; first meets Margaret 118; and the Rotherhithe hideaway 119; engagement announced 123; temperament 123; children 125–6,

170; as a father 170; divorce 186; organisational flair 188
Spencer, Earl 221–2, 249
Strickland, Mabel 30
Sunday Times 125

Thatcher, Margaret 93–4
Time and Chance (Townsend) 100
Times, The 59, 100, 224
Times of Malta, The 30
Townsend, Peter, Group Captain 47, 61–6, 100, 116, 118

Victoria, Queen 10, 16, 21, 41, 58, 90

Wales, Charles, Prince of 14, 19, 45, 48; at the Coronation 45–6; birth 50; affinity with mother 52, 53, 71, 171, 199; relationship with Anne 54–5, 110, 233; modern upbringing 56, 69; problems at school 69, 70, 71, 74–9, 107, 171–2, 176; reliance on Mountbatten 72–4; as a sportsman 77; relationship with father 71, 77, 125, 174, 177; and dangerous sports 84, 196, 211; adolescent problems 86, 107, 185–6; the artist 88; and Balmoral 94; and food 96; engagement to Diana 105, 224; 'common touch' 114; friendship with Gloucester 132, 135; at Trinity College, Cambridge 173–89; support from Lord Butler 173–80; shyness 174, 185; interest in Australia 176; and Aberystwyth University 184; and the opposite sex 185, 186, 209, 212; the Investiture 187–9; pressures to find a bride 210, 214; in the Services 211–12; and Sarah Spencer 218–19; interest in Diana 219; marriage 224, 225, 227; mother's guidance 231; Diana's

influence on 250, 253
Wales, Diana, Princess of 15, 19, 21, 96; background 217–18, 248; friendship with Andrew 219; courted by Charles 219; characteristics 220, 226, 249, 250–1; reactions to publicity 223; mother's support 224; announcement of engagement 224; familiarity with 'the Royal way of life' 225; marriage 227; extraordinary appeal 248, 249–50; pregnancy 251–3; captivated by Royal duties 253; independence 253–4; acceptance of by Royal Family 254–5; debt to the Queen 255–6; and choice of nanny 256; birth of first child 256–7
Wallace, Billy 33, 66
Werher, Lady Zia 138
William I, the Conqueror, King 9
William IV, King 49
William, Prince of Wales 256–7
Wilson, Sir Charles 175
Wilson, Sir Harold 92, 153, 175
Windsor, Alexander, Earl of Ulster 20, 133
Windsor, Lady Davina 20, 133
Windsor, Lord Frederick 18, 146
Windsor, Lady Helen 12, 141
Windsor, Lady Rose 20, 133
Windsor Castle 11; the Round Tower 9; strong rooms 10; Sovereign's Entrance 11, 15; improvements to 11–12, 38, 59–60; the Private Apartments 12; Queen's Tower 12; Great Corridor 12; Christmas Ball 16–17; Waterloo Chamber 16; St George's Hall 16; craftsmen of 17; St George's Chapel 21, 22–3; pantomimes at 25
Windsor Great Park 11, 26, 63
Woods, Dr Robert 175
Worsley, Sir William 141

263